A HIGH PRICE FOR FREEDOM

A HIGH PRICE FOR FREEDOM

Raising Hidden Voices from the African American Past

∻ ∻ ∻ ∻

CLYDE W. FORD

AMISTAD
An Imprint of HarperCollins*Publishers*

 For information, address HarperCollins Publishers, 195 Broadway, New York, NY 10007. In Europe, HarperCollins Publishers, Macken House, 39/40 Mayor Street Upper, Dublin 1, D01 C9W8, Ireland.

HarperCollins books may be purchased for educational, business, or sales promotional use. For information, please email the Special Markets Department at SPsales@harpercollins.com.

harpercollins.com

FIRST EDITION

Designed by Jason Kayser

Library of Congress Cataloging-in-Publication Data has been applied for.

ISBN 978-0-06-330981-4

PRINTED IN THE UNITED STATES OF AMERICA

25 26 27 28 29 LBC 5 4 3 2 1

This book is dedicated to my nephew Nasir in the hope that the world he grows up in will reconcile with the truths of the African American past in order to create a better future for all humankind.

CONTENTS

INTRODUCTION

JIMMIE LEE JACKSON LAY FIGHTING FOR HIS LIFE IN THE Good Samaritan Hospital in Selma, Alabama, the only hospital in the city that would treat Black patients in February 1965. Jackson, who'd just been shot by a white Alabama state trooper, had been in Marion, Alabama, to pick up his mother and grandfather, marching in support of voting rights. He pulled Catholic nun and nurse Barbara Lum closer before whispering, "Sister, don't you think this is a high price to pay for freedom?" A few days later, Jimmie Lee Jackson died.

While his death was the principal reason behind Bloody Sunday, Turnaround Tuesday, and the final Selma-to-Montgomery march, most people do not even know his story, let alone his name. For when people think of Selma, they think not of Jimmie Lee Jackson but perhaps of John Lewis, and certainly of the iconic images of Martin and Coretta King, arm in arm, leading a long line of marchers over the Edmund Pettus Bridge. King and Lewis were towering figures in the Selma campaign of the Black Freedom Struggle, but it is in the lesser well-known story of Jimmie Lee Jackson that we are treated to a deeper understanding of Selma and its meaning in the continuing struggle for freedom and equality in America. As one observer said, "The Selma-to-Montgomery march actually started here in Marion," the city where Jimmie Lee Jackson was shot.

This book represents an attempt to surface the voices of those buried in the past; to tell the stories of critical moments in the Black Freedom Struggle from the ground up rather than the top down; to honor the many who paid this high price for freedom.

Each essay in *A High Price for Freedom* focuses on an issue, an event, or an aspect of the Black Freedom Struggle, examining it from the point of view of the people who were there, especially those who are not well-known.

History is at its best when new perspectives and findings challenge old ideas about the past, even overturning common wisdom. Benjamin Banneker's grandmother was a white English milkmaid, transported to colonial America for spilling a pail of milk, right? Perhaps not. My essay on Banneker and his grandmother Molly Welsh offers some alternative ways of thinking about this significant figure from the African American past. The song "Follow the Drinking Gourd" contains a coded message with navigation aids for enslaved men and women escaping to freedom, right? Not so fast. The song may not have been an encoded message about escaping to freedom but instead may have had an even deeper encoded message with holdovers from African traditions among the enslaved. Think you know everything about Juneteenth? Felix Haywood, who was actually there in Galveston, Texas, at the time of the first Juneteenth, then years later interviewed at ninety-two years old, tells a completely different story than the one many have come to believe. Writing *A High Price for Freedom* challenged much of what I thought I knew about Black history, and I hope it will challenge readers as well.

In some ways, this book is a continuation of my last, *Of Blood and Sweat: Black Lives and the Making of White Power and Wealth*. In fact, this was originally conceived of as volume two. That earlier work took a more standard historical approach to unfolding a deeper story of the African American experience, beginning in Africa in the fifteenth century and ending ten or twenty years after the American Civil War. When I was settling down to write *A High Price for Freedom*, it became clear that such a sequential presentation of Black history starting in the post–Civil War period would not work. There are far too many threads in the fabric of that history from the turn of the twentieth century to the present day. Therefore, *A High Price for Freedom* takes a slightly different approach. The essays in this book are put together in a roughly historical sequence, but each essay itself may reach back into the past or forward to present times. What I have attempted to do is take the historical figure or idea the essay is about and use that figure or idea as a gateway to other relevant ideas and people. The image I had while writing each essay was of a fireworks display, where a single explosion high in the air gives rise to other explosions, which, in turn, give rise to further explosions as the fireworks tumble to the earth. These self-contained essays span a range of nearly three hundred years, yet they stand alone and need not be read in sequential order. Taken together, it's my hope that they paint a picture of the importance of examining the historical record with an open mind and allowing unheard individuals to speak for themselves when records of what they did or said or saw can be found or, at least, inferred.

What I found most surprising about *A High Price for Freedom* was a common thread woven through so many of these essays, a thread I had not even considered before I began to write. From the recorded dreams of Benjamin Banneker, to the writings of enslaved Muslims, to the music of gospels, spirituals, R & B, and hip-hop, to the discussions between Mahatma Gandhi and the Thurmans, right down to the speeches of Martin Luther King Jr., what comes through time and again is the survival of African sacred wisdom in the experience of African Americans. Sometimes unconsciously, nearly always unwittingly. A survival observable not just theoretically but literally as a symbol appearing in dreams, written in manuscripts, embodied in dance rhythms and drumming, or played out in the music we listen to today. But I will leave it to the reader to discover, as I did, this sacred African wisdom and these symbolic forms through the following pages.

I intentionally use the term "Black Freedom Struggle" more often than other terms like the "African American experience" or the "Civil Rights Movement." In particular, I have never understood the use of "Civil Rights Movement," for example, in describing an effort to achieve the full rights of liberty and equality enshrined in the American Constitution. Black men and women fought for and died for—and they are still fighting for and dying for—the right to vote, the right to assemble, and the right to equal justice. Would we dare call the American Revolution or the Civil War a "movement"? Of course not. Then why call the long history of Black Americans seeking these rights a "movement," when in every aspect it really was, and is, a struggle?

I am aware this approach breaks with the ranks of those who feel the "scientific method" should be applied to the study of history and that personal opinions of the historian should be left out. But I also feel that too many Americans know so little about history and fail to see its relevance precisely because it is presented in an overly academic and sanitized way. I'd like to believe it is possible to reverse this disdain for the past by making the past relevant to the present and the future.

With this aim in mind, I have resisted modernizing word spellings and usage from how they appear in original sources. In seventeenth- and eighteenth-century America, writers frequently spelled words as they heard them. Add to this, English in those times still showed influences from Old English, German, Latin, and other languages: *f*, for instance, was often used in place of *s*; *v* occasionally used in place of *u* and vice versa; *y* sometimes found where we might expect an *i*; *e* tacked onto words in a seemingly random fashion.

Similarly, when using the narratives of enslaved men and women from the Library of Congress Slave Narrative Collection, I quote the words of individuals as they were written, full of "dats" and "dems" and "deys." Recorded near the ends of their lives during the Great Depression by out-of-work white writers given jobs under the New Deal, these narratives are a rich source of material from Black men and women alive during some of the times covered in these essays. Works Progress Administration (WPA) writers were instructed to scour the South for older Black men and women who grew up during slavery. Only a few had the newfangled massive portable recording devices wired to heavy batteries weighing down the trunks of their cars. Most had only pen and paper, or a typewriter with which they tried to capture the vernacular these ex-slaves spoke. In some instances, the transcriptions are very difficult to read because they are laden with the paternalism and racism of the white writers.

Many consider this use of English revealing of the uneducated and ignorant state of the formerly enslaved—a view I wholeheartedly reject. It's actually amusing to contrast the strange English used by white men and women in historical documents with the equally strange English used by the formerly enslaved. They are not the same. Yet in bending English, both help me feel closer to the individuals behind the words.

Another holdover from the past is how chapter notes have been used. Either placed at the bottoms of pages, as footnotes, or collected in a separate reference section at the end of a book, as endnotes, these references are essential aids in documenting sources. Yet they also bump readers from the flow of the story. In an essay, the story's flow is critical. So, instead of documenting my sources with numbers that might interrupt readers, I've collected all my notes and references for each essay and placed them online at www.ahighpriceforfreedom.com/references. If a reader is interested, they can consult them there.

The pages of a book offer a limited canvas on which to paint the marvelous stories that I have incorporated into this book. So, I've also moved to the online site additional details, further information, and related images for the reader.

Moreover, placing notes and references online allows for a novel interactive, multimedia experience. No longer do readers have to imagine a painting from my description. They can see it. No longer do they have to wonder how a piece of music or drumming sounds. They can hear it. No longer does someone have to wish they better understood where an event actually took place. They can fly to that location. All thanks to modern-day internet technology. So, in this separate collection of notes and references, I've also placed images, playlists, and links to click for flying to locations using 3-D models of the Earth.

As a student of history, I am constantly searching for better ways to bring others to the wonders and insights of the past, just as I am constantly searching to unearth the hidden treasures that the past might hold. These are the tasks I've set before myself in writing the essays contained in *A High Price for Freedom*. As such, I fully accept responsibility for any oversights contained in this book.

If I have any regret upon completing this work, it is that a few hundred pages is not enough to tell all the stories that could be told. Too many stories I found compelling and informative had to be left out. Space did not allow for the inclusion of important stories related to the history of other groups helping to shape the

African American experience—groups like Native Americans, Europeans other than enslavers, or the poor whites in America. I also could not include all the stories of Black women that should be told, due to their erasure from so much of the historical record. Still, I'm comforted in knowing that what has been omitted from this book holds out the possibility of more books to come from those of us working and writing in this field.

Clyde W. Ford
March 2024
Bellingham, Washington

CHAPTER 1

FROM THE WOMB OF STRUGGLE

TWO YEARS AFTER NATIVE AMERICAN PRINCESS POCAHONTAS died, her English husband, Sir John Rolfe, recorded a ship entering a small cove at the mouth of the James River.

Rowed ashore from the *White Lion* that August 20, 1619, was a woman and her partner, perhaps already her husband. They were known only as "Isabell, Negro" and "Antoney, Negro" in a subsequent colonial muster. Their African names lost to the tides. Captain William Tucker purchased them to work on his plantation. Together, Isabell and Antoney had a child, William, around the time of that colonial muster. The first child of African descent born in the American colonies. Although no records exist of Isabell giving birth to any other children, symbolically millions came through her womb. These sons and daughters of Africa began not only a steady decline into the dark night of slavery but an equally steady struggle forward toward the light of freedom.

In 1630, less than a decade after Isabell gave birth to William, another Black woman, whose name has been lost to the annals of time, gave birth to a daughter named Elizabeth from her union with an Englishman, Thomas Key. The recorded evidence of Elizabeth Key's birth in 1630 makes clear that her mother was one of the first Africans sold into bondage in Virginia. In 1656, Elizabeth Key, then a single mother, stood before the Virginia General Assembly, the Supreme Court of the colony, pleading her case for release from her indentures and the freedom of her young son, John.

Executors of the estate of John Mottrom, defendants in this case, held that she and her son could be sold as property. The stakes in this case could not have been higher. How the court decided, and how colonial legislators and the public responded, would shape the contours of enslavement in America and the treatment of people of African descent for the three hundred years that followed.

Through her lawyer, and lover, William Greenstead (Greensted, Grinstead, or Grimstead—the spelling varies in the records), Elizabeth Key presented these facts at the Northumberland County Court: Prior to his death, Thomas Key entered into a signed agreement with prominent Northumberland County colonist Humphrey Higginson that Elizabeth would be transferred as a servant to his care for a period of nine years, at which point she would be freed. The agreement further stipulated that Higginson would provide for Elizabeth's needs during her nine years with him and that, should he travel back to England to live, he would pay for her passage and carry Elizabeth with him as well. Finally, Higginson agreed he would not sell, barter, or transfer Elizabeth to anyone else.

But Thomas Key died in 1636, and Elizabeth Key was transferred to the custody of Humphrey Higginson based on the signed agreement. Higginson did move back to England—only he did not take Elizabeth with him. Through a sale or some other unrecorded series of events, Elizabeth passed into the possession of Colonel John Mottrom, a Northumberland County justice of the peace. At the end of her nine years of service, Mottrom refused to release her. Instead, he attempted to keep her under his control and authority for life through an indefinite indenture.

Then Mottrom died in 1655, and the executors of his estate noted the inventory included "Elizabeth the Negro woman & her sonne." They considered her and her son property, which they intended to sell. Sometime prior to Mottrom's death, Elizabeth Key became romantically involved with William Greenstead, also under indentures to Mottrom but whom Mottrom apparently used for legal representation. Together, Elizabeth Key and William Greenstead had two children; one of them, John, survived.

The Northumberland County Court first heard the case, and Elizabeth argued she could not be held in perpetual bondage for three reasons: (1) She was the daughter of a free Englishman, whose status she therefore inherited; (2) she was a baptized and practicing Christian who could therefore not be held in perpetual servitude for religious reasons; and (3) she had already been held longer than the nine years agreed to between Thomas Key and Humphrey Higginson.

After a two-day trial, a jury ruled in her favor, but Mottrom's estate won on appeal. Elizabeth Key, however, refused to give in and further appealed to the colonial court of last standing, the Virginia General Assembly, which, recognizing the significance of the matters being contested—religion and the status of mixed-race offspring—agreed to hear her appeal.

While anxious masters awaited, the Virginia General Assembly issued its findings on July 21, 1656: (1) Elizabeth Key was, in fact, the daughter of Englishman Thomas Key, and according to prevailing English law, which stated the status of the offspring followed the status of the father, Elizabeth Key was free; (2) Elizabeth Key was, in fact, a baptized Christian and therefore could not be held in perpetual servitude; and (3) Elizabeth Key had already been held in servitude longer than she should have. The Virginia General Assembly reverted the case back to the original Northumberland County Court, which declared Elizabeth and her son, John, free and ordered the Mottrom estate to pay certain expenses.

Elizabeth Key's legal strategy was brilliant. But from where did this idea of challenging bondage based on parentage and religion come?

Perhaps your assumption was similar to mine when I first read of this case many years ago. I said to myself then, *Thank god, she had a good lawyer.*

If your answer in any way focused on William Greenstead, Elizabeth's lover and lawyer, then you, like me, would have become ensnared in that unconscious trap that erases Black women from history, in part, by assuming they have little agency of their own.

Chances are that Elizabeth Key, not her lover-lawyer, devised her own cunning legal strategy on the basis of observing "court-days"—essentially, colonial American holidays when the public was invited inside county courthouses to witness legal proceedings. Even servants and the enslaved had time off from work for "court-days."

Greenstead, on the other hand, lacked formal legal education and was a member of no bar in either colonial America or England. He apparently represented his master, John Mottrom, before colonial courts and, therefore, may have received some rudimentary legal training on the job.

When Elizabeth Key and Sojourner Truth and Kamala Harris are held up as powerful and exceptional Black women—and indeed they are—what we are really saying is that Black women with power are exceptions to the rule. When in fact, Black women with power are the rule, not the exception.

But let's go back to July 21, 1656, that extremely good day for Elizabeth Key, which sent shock waves through British colonial America by exposing glaring loopholes in the legal architecture of slavery. The consequences were monumental, for this was no small matter. One concerned sixteen hundred years of religious belief that underpinned all of colonial Christian society; the other related to five hundred years of English common law, upon which the American legal system had been erected.

The legal principles underlying the case were somewhat

abstract, as court cases often demonstrate. At issue were two Latin phrases used to determine whether a person was enslaved or free—*partus sequitur patrem* ("that which is brought forth follows the father") and *partus sequitur ventrem* ("that which is brought forth from the womb follows the womb"). In one instance, a person was enslaved or free based on whether their father was enslaved or free. In the other, a person was enslaved or free based on whether their mother was enslaved or free. English common law at the time of the Key decision held that a person's status followed that of their father, and the colonial justices ruled on that basis.

American slavery would not have taken hold had a "follows the father" rule been allowed to stay in effect. Enslavers regularly raped, and had children by their female slaves and servants, and free Black men regularly had children with women who were enslaved. Under a "follows the father" rule, children of such unions would be free, leading to the steady growth of a free Black population. Planters and merchants in colonial America, ever more dependent on the labor of the enslaved, could not allow that to happen.

In 1662, the Virginia General Assembly put an end to "follows the father" with a law titled "Negro womens children to serve according to the condition of the mother." Maryland followed suit in 1671 with a similar law.

But reversing English common law from *partus sequitur patrem* to *partus sequitur ventrem* still left the religious loophole wide open. Maryland struck first, passing a law that stated people of African descent were obliged to serve their masters *durante vita.*

Yet again, another Latin phrase, this one meaning "service for lifetime."

But it wasn't enough for slave owners who wanted a specific exemption for religion. So, in 1671, Maryland legislators took another bite at the apple with "An Act for the Encourageing the Importacon of Negros and Slaues into this Province":

> That where any Negro or Negroes Slave or Slaues being in Servitude or bondage is are or shall become Christian or Christians and hath or have Received or shall att any time Receive the Holy Sacrament of Babtizme before or after his her or their Importacon into this Prouince the same is not nor shall or ought the same be denyed adjudged Construed or taken to be or to amount vnto a manumicon or freeing Inlarging or discharging any such Negroe or Negroes Slaue or Slaues or any his or their Issue or Issues from his her their or any of their Servitude or Servitudes Bondage or bondages . . . becoming Christian or Christians or Receiveing the Sacrament of Babtizme Every such Negroe and Negroes slaue and slaues and all and every the Issue and Issues of every such Negroe and Negroes Slaue and Slaues Is are and be and shall att all tymes hereafter be adjudged Reputed deemed and taken to be and Remayne in Servitude and Bondage . . .

And the religious loophole first exposed by Elizabeth Key was permanently sealed! One by one, colony by colony, laws were enacted to close the "Elizabeth Key" religious loophole. The

Virginia General Assembly, which in 1656 had ruled in Elizabeth's favor concerning her status as a Christian, enacted a law in 1682 entitled "An act declaring that baptisme of slaves doth no exempt them from bondage."

The significance of Elizabeth Key cannot be understated. In her successful fight for her freedom and that of her son, she exposed two gaping holes in the legal underpinnings of American slavery, which forced American jurisprudence to break from its English heritage and American Christianity to break from its religious dictates. The laws of bondage and freedom in America were first enacted on the bodies of Black women. And they still are. Black women, many poor, have been most beset by the US Supreme Court overturning *Roe v. Wade*. No longer guaranteed the right to abortions, the bodies of Black women continue to be battlegrounds for reproductive rights, as they were in Elizabeth Key's day—battlegrounds where powerful white men feel they have an inalienable right to rule.

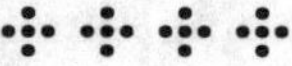

While Elizabeth Key fought for her freedom in court, other Black women fought for theirs on the streets, in plantation fields, and aboard slave ships. The evidence, unsurprisingly, is not direct. Historical records too often hide the roles Black women played by simply excluding any mention of them. The underlying assumption, tinged with both racism and sexism, is simply that Black women lacked the intelligence, determination, and power to mount effective resistance and revolt against their enslavement. While we know this is not true, this assumption begs the question: How do you get at the truth of Black women's significant roles in the earliest days of the Black struggle for freedom in America?

Perhaps the best way is to start at the beginning of our journey to the Americas. It is a fact, though not a widely known one, that Black women tipped the balance in favor of revolts aboard slave ships. The more Black women aboard a ship, the more likely that ship was to have a revolt.

The Trans-Atlantic Slave Trade Database (TASD), first published as a CD-ROM in 1999 by David Eltis, Stephen Behrendt, and David Richardson, encompasses extensive data on more than thirty-six thousand slave trade voyages between the years 1514 and 1866. When David Richardson looked to the TASD in order to explain why Africans on more than one in ten ships revolted, he seemed surprised by his findings. Richardson's analysis of TASD data showed that "ships trading south of Upper Guinea that had revolts carried proportionately more women than normal among their captives." More women, more revolts. What gives?

Captive African women aboard slave ships were treated differently than captive African men. Generally speaking, women remained unshackled, even when slave ships lay at anchor, taking on more human cargo. Underway, enslaved women were housed apart from adult males, placed close to officers' quarters for entertainment and sexual gratification by the crew. But that also meant African women were closer to the caches of weapons, keys to chains and shackles, and information vital to a revolt. Did they use the access unwittingly granted to them? Yes, they did!

Richard Brooke wrote in 1853 of the September 2, 1797 revolt on the slaver *Thomas* out of Liverpool. *Thomas* was headed to Barbados with a cargo of 375 captive Africans taken from the Angola–Congo coast.

> [W]hilst all hands were occupied at breakfast, two or three of the female slaves having discovered that the armourer had incautiously left the arms chest open, got into the after-hatchway, and conveyed all the arms which they could find through the bulkheads to the male slaves, about two hundred of whom immediately ran up the forescuttles, and put to death all of the crew who came their way. For a little while some of the crew, with their captain at their head, fought desperately with the few arms which we usually kept in the cabins, but were eventually overpowered, and the vessel remained in the hands of the slaves.

It's a fascinating tale. The captive Africans spared some of the crew to steer the boat back to Africa, but the crew steered her instead to Long Island, then to Providence, Rhode Island. Eventually, she encountered the HMS *Thames*, which recaptured the *Thomas*. Although the fate of the Africans aboard remains unclear, presumably all involved in the revolt were executed once back in Britain. Of course, the point here is that Black women played a crucial role as initiators of the revolt.

The Trade Committee of the Royal African Company (RAC) heard a similar report of a revolt aboard a slave ship more than seventy years earlier involving an African woman. On May 2, 1791, the committee held a meeting that considered the report of Royal Navy Surgeon John Atkins. The RAC was one of the world's first limited liability companies, and it oversaw Britain's Crown-supported venture into the slave trade. The RAC bought captive Africans along what was then called the Guinea Coast of Africa and sold them primarily in the Americas. In February 1721, Atkins had sailed from the south coast of England, along the English Channel, with the HMS *Swallow* and *Weymouth* on a voyage to Africa, Brazil, and the West Indies, in patrol and pursuit of pirates hampering the trade of the RAC. Throughout that voyage, he had reported on the activities of RAC ships and personnel in capturing and transporting Africans.

In late May 1721, Atkins and his naval escort met the slaver *Robert*, under the command of a Captain Harding, out of Bristol. Harding told the story of an African called Captain Tomba by the British, a captured leader, perhaps a military commander, whom Atkins had encountered earlier in his voyage, when Tomba was jailed and shackled. Although now Tomba was apparently aboard the *Robert*, ready to be sold.

> *Tomba*, about a Week before, had combined with three or four of the ftouteft of his Country-men to kill the Ship's Company, and attempt their Efcapes, while they had a Shore to fly to, and had near effected it by means of a Woman-Slave, who being more at large, was to

watch the proper Opportunity. She brought him word one night that there were no more than five white Men upon Deck, and them afseep, bring him a Hammer at the fame time (all the Weapons that fhe could find) to execute the Treachery. He encouraged the Accomplices what he could, with the Profpect of Liberty, but could now at the Push, engage only one more and the Woman to follow him upon Deck. The three Sailors fleeping on the Fore-caftle, two of which he prefently difpatched, with fingle Strokes upon the Temples; the other rouzing with the Noife, his Companions feized; *Tomba* coming foon to the Affiftance, and murdering him in the fame manner. Going after to finifh the work, they found very luckily for the reft of the Company, that thefe other two of the Watch were with the Confufion already made wake, and upon their Guard, and their Defence foon awaked the Mafter underneath them, who running up and finding his Men contend for their Lives, took a Hand-fpike, the firft thing he met with in the Surprize, and redoubling his Strokes home upon *Tomba*, laid him at length flay upon the Deck, fecuring them all in Irons.

The Reader may be curious to know their Punifhment: Why, Captain Harding weighing the Stoutnefs and Worth of the two Slaves, did, as in other Countries they do by Rogues of Dignity, whip and fcarify them only; while three others, Abettors, but not Actors, nor of Strength for it, he fentenced to cruel Deaths; making them firft eat the Heart and Liver of one of them killed. The Woman he

> hoifted up by the Thumbs, whipp'd, and flafhed her with Knives, before the other Slaves till fhe died.

Once again, it is the unnamed, nearly invisible Black woman whose role in this ship revolt is important because of her insights, actions, and timing. Not surprisingly, she received perhaps the most gruesome, tortured death sentence of all. In 1735, after returning to Britain, Atkins published his reports in a book titled *A Voyage to Guinea, Brafil, and the Weft-Indies; In His Majefty's Ships, the Swallow and Weymouth.*

Historian Rebecca Hall, who's played a leading role in uncovering the stories of Black women in slave revolts such as those aboard the *Thomas* and *Robert*, writes of a similar incident occurring on July 13, 1729, aboard the slaver *L'Annibal*, explained by a lone white survivor:

> A flock of our negresses burst into the main bedroom and punched M. Bart, sublieutenant of the ship. Being suddenly awakened, he believed that it was the negres who had come to murder him. He jumped out of his window into the sea [and then climbed back on deck]. This tumult caused great alarm. We ran to arms and fired several rifle shots. Seeing that they were trying to come on the deck in a crowd, and believing it was the negres, the gunfire had alarmed the entire port.

In this report "negres" means the male captives, and "negresses" means female captives. So, the first assumption of the survivor, notes Hall, was that only men would mount such an attack. Not all slavers manifested this level of denial over the agency of Black women. "For your safety as well as mine," wrote Samuel Waldo, owner of a slave ship, in 1734 to his captain, Samuel Rhodes, "you'll have the needful guard over your Slaves, and put not too much Confidence in the Women nor Children lest they happen to be Instrumental to your being surprised which may be fatall."

Ship's physician John Bell, aboard the Rhode Island slaver the *Thames*, wrote on December 15, 1776, of a revolt and forty-minute battle that had occurred.

> We had 160 Slaves on board and were that day lett out of the Deck Chains in order to wash. About 2 o'clock they began by siesing upon the Boatswain but he soon got disengaged . . . after receiving a wound in the Breast and one under his chin . . . They Continued to threw Staves, billets of wood etc., and in endeavoring to get down the Barricade, or over it for upward of 40 Minutes, when finding they could not effect it, all the Fantee and most of the Accra men Slaves jumped overboard. It was thought that the slaves intended to get abaft of the ship but the current was so strong they could not reach the vessel. When all was settled we found 32 Men and boys with 2 women a mising, the best Slaves we had.

Bell suggested that the female captives had not joined in the attack because it had occurred so suddenly. Had they been involved, the doctor wrote, "Your property here at this time would have been but small." What is clear, however, is that too often Black women have been erased from the historical record. To correct that erasure is no simple matter, for the very assumptions of those recording historical events, and those who write of them afterward, are biased to treat or render Black women as invisible, passive figures rather than principal agents of action and change. The true stories of Black women and their courageous engagement in a struggle for freedom may only be surfaced by looking more deeply into what is not said rather than what is—by investigating the silence rather than accepting the common wisdom.

Yet another way that American slavery countered the threat posed by Black women and rendered them invisible and seemingly ineffective was to promote the caricature of the big-bosomed, do-ragged, all-welcoming but also nonthreatening "Mammy" or "Aunt Jemima." White Americans fell for these false stereotypes of Black women in part because they served to calm the fears they also harbored of a sleeping giant lurking just beneath the surface, should Black people wake up fully to the injustices they suffered and take action. Those deeper fears then projected back onto Black people in the form of other hypersexualized stereotypes—the "predator" Black man waiting to rape white women, and the exotic "temptress" Black woman waiting to seduce white men.

But let's not delude ourselves that these racist tropes of Black women are a thing of the past. In the 2024 American presidential campaign, for instance, such racist, sexist memes were constantly flung at Kamala Harris—"Joe and the Hoe gotta go," or "She slept her way to the top."

When the tortured consciousness of white Americans that was necessary for enslavement met face-to-face with Black women (and men) who did not fit their racist tropes, the answer, of course, was simple: Erase them. Erase them at the end of a rope hanging from a tree. Erase them from the annals of history for the actions they undertook. For if they are erased and therefore invisible, they need not be feared.

But this cloak of invisibility thrown over Black women actually worked both ways.

Ellen Craft possessed a light-enough complexion that she could pass for white. But instead of passing for a white woman on December 21, 1848, Craft put on men's clothes, wrapped her face to feign an injury, and passed for a white man. Craft boarded a Philadelphia-bound train in Macon, Georgia, with her husband, William, posing as her personal slave, taking what the couple later described as "a desperate leap for liberty." He rode in the "negro car"; she in first class. From train to steamboat to train, the couple dined with a steamboat captain after narrowly escaping detection by the boat's purser, who suspected their ruse. Ellen and William made it to Philadelphia and then on to Boston, where William worked as a cabinetmaker and Ellen as a seamstress. But in 1850, slave hunters arrived in Boston, looking to return the pair. The Crafts fled again, this time by ship to England, where they raised a family and wrote a book about their great escape. After the Civil War, in 1870, the Crafts finally returned to Georgia, setting up a school for newly freed Black men and women.

What was it that early white Americans feared about Black women? Could it be that the power and strength of Black women in Africa during the height of their enslavement in America required them to be rendered invisible? Africa has long been the repository of white European fears, the mythologized underbelly of a collective white consciousness and imagination afraid of facing the inconvenient truths that bondage and oppression represent, the inconvenient truths also of masculinity and femininity. So when European men encountered powerful Black women in Africa, they came face-to-face with their deepest fears around race and sexuality.

European soldiers called the women warriors of the West African kingdom of Dahomey (today Benin) Amazons, in reference to Greek mythology. They called themselves *Ahosi* (king's wives) or *Mino* (our mothers). If this all-female military force represented the sum of fears for European men, in many ways it was of their own doing, for the *Ahosi* emerged in part as a female fighting force at a time when the kingdom's male population was in decline from frequent, deadly warfare with neighboring kingdoms in support of the European slave trade.

Ahosi training was intense. These women practiced survival skills, often storming thorn-laden defenses in mock attacks and actually executing prisoners to instill indifference to pain and death. They perfected their skills with rifles, bows and arrows, clubs, knives, and swords. One European observer noted that in a speech, the chief of the *Ahosi* said, "As the blacksmith takes an iron bar and by fire changes its fashion, so have we changed our nature. We are no longer women, we are men." Much like how celibate nuns are already married spiritually to Jesus, *Ahosi* women reportedly were considered married to the king and therefore celibate as well. Some reports claim they voluntarily underwent female genital mutilation to excise their clitorises, that way reducing their sexual appetites, which could then be directed toward combat—perhaps an allusion to the Amazons of Greek mythology, who amputated one breast.

All of the reports about the *Ahosi* coming from outside, mainly white European observers cannot be taken simply at face value. But certainly in war, especially against French forces in the later 1800s, the *Ahosi* proved a formidable fighting force, though never achieving battlefield victory from being outgunned by more modern European weaponry. French legionnaires did not underestimate them in hand-to-hand combat and believed that they "handled admirably," though the legionnaires were dismayed that the *Ahosi* fired their rifles from the hip rather than from the shoulder.

The "Amazons of Dahomey" have found their way into popular culture through Hollywood films like *Black Panther*, where the Dora Milaje, an elite all-female group who served as the special forces for Wakanda, were modeled after them; or *The Woman King*, a film in which Viola Davis plays the character of Nanisca, a real-life *Ahosi* found dead on the battlefield in the First Franco-Dahomean War of 1890.

While these women were fierce, it's also important to remember that they were fighting for the kingdom of Dahomey to retain its central position in the transatlantic slave trade. From the African villages and kingdoms that the *Ahosi* vanquished came the captives whom they sold to willing and waiting Europeans. The *Ahosi* were not fighting for the freedom of their sisters across the sea; instead, they were fighting for the right to the trade, which kept those sisters enslaved. Still, the importance of the *Ahosi* is not which side of the slave trade they were on but that they represented Black women of power, who consciously and conspicuously occupied a place outside the norms of femininity defined by a male-dominated European and American white society. The *Ahosi* were not alone in occupying this place. Queen Nzinga, a Ndongo leader, headed a similar all-female fighting force against the Portuguese in Angola in the seventeenth century. If there is an American equivalent of the "Amazons of Dahomey," the *Ahosi*, it would surely be the Black women of the post–Civil War American West.

Black cowgirls? Surely you are joking. Yet many colorful characters are found among the Black women of the West—women who refused to be silenced, or hidden, or rendered invisible. Their names alone are suggestive of their tales: Mary "Stagecoach Mary" Fields. Bridget "Biddy" Mason. Clara "Aunt Clara" Brown. Johanna "Chona" July. Henrietta "Aunt Rittie" Williams Foster. Nellie "No Excuses" Brown. Their stories are engaging and exciting, some even having found their way into Hollywood films. But focusing on one of the lesser-known characters, Cathay Williams, shows once again how Black women were, and still are, made invisible in the historical record.

Cathay Williams was born near Independence, Missouri, to a free Black father and enslaved mother in 1844 (some historical records say 1842), which, according to the law of *partus sequitur ventrem*, legally made her a slave. On June 15, 1861, Union forces captured Jefferson City, Missouri, and Williams became a "camp follower" (a civilian who follows an army from place to place, providing services to soldiers that the army does not provide), working as a cook, a launderer, and a nurse.

Williams claimed service with the Union Army at major campaigns, mostly in the West—the Battle of Pea Ridge, the Red River Campaign, the Siege of Vicksburg, and Sherman's March to the Sea. Though no surviving documentation specifically supports or refutes these claims, a soldier named Finis Cathay did enlist in 1862 and participated in these same campaigns. *Finis* means "conclusion" in Latin and Cathay Williams may have used this pseudonym as her first name because she had come to a conclusion this was the only way to serve, since women were not allowed in the Union Army.

When the Civil War ended, Williams was twenty-two, and army life was all she had known. So she determined to enlist in the US Regular Army. Again, the problem of her gender arose. On November 15, 1866, Cathay Williams voluntarily rendered herself invisible a second time. She donned men's clothes and enlisted under the name of William Cathay. She passed a cursory medical exam and was assigned to the 38th US Infantry Regiment, one of six regiments making up the famed Buffalo Soldiers.

Now, the principal role of the Buffalo Soldiers was fighting in the postbellum Indian Wars—in other words, killing Native Americans who were, in turn, fighting for their rights to their ancestral lands. Even the term "Buffalo Soldiers" came from Native Americans calling Black soldiers that because they had curly, kinky hair and dark skins, like a bison.

Several years ago, I had a meeting with the chief of a Native American tribe just south of where I live to discuss the technology that might be used to reduce the numbers of missing and murdered Indigenous women (MMIW). When he walked into the room, he immediately turned to me and, with a measure of disdain, said, "You know your people, the Buffalo Soldiers, killed ours?"

I leaned over and whispered, "And, you know, your people tracked down my people and returned us to slavery."

The chief immediately grew silent, and our discussion turned to MMIW.

Of course, there is also the possibility that Cathay Williams was a lesbian, which would only have made her invisibility doubly painful. Today the US Army claims her as the first enlisted female soldier. Though in 1893, near the end of her life, it was the army that delivered the final blow rendering this Black woman invisible. While serving in the army, Cathay Williams contracted smallpox, forcing her to leave the army early, but still with an honorable discharge. Ultimately she moved to Trinidad, Colorado. Her deteriorating health from the consequences of smallpox placed her in a hospital, where she remained for some time before leaving penniless. Williams applied for a disability pension based on her military service, such pensions having been given to other women who served. But the army denied her request, claiming that serving under the disguise of a man rendered her service illegal and her pension claim null and void. Cathay Williams died not long after that.

Around the time of Cathay Williams's death, at the end of the nineteenth century, Black women began stepping into a new world of possibilities, despite the growing Jim Crow laws of the American South. In business and politics and voting rights and women's rights, Black women were flexing their muscles and also encountering racism that attempted to hold them in check. In literature and music and the arts, Black women like Bessie Smith, Ma Rainey, and Zora Neale Hurston were demonstrating the power to create. In international affairs, Sue Bailey Thurman accompanied her husband, Howard Thurman, on his trip to meet Mahatma Gandhi in the 1930s. Gandhi acknowledged and complimented her on the contributions she made to their conversations about nonviolent resistance and the Black Freedom Struggle in America. In the 1940s and early 1950s, Black women like Pauli Murray—though perhaps it would be better to say "a Black trans person like Pauli Murray"—contributed immeasurably to the early legal victories of the nascent civil rights phase of the Black Freedom Struggle. Many know the role of women like Rosa Parks, and perhaps Fannie Lou Hamer, during that civil rights phase, but there were hundreds, if not thousands, of more Black women without whom that struggle would not have borne the fruit it did. These women did not sit at the table of the Southern Christian Leadership Conference, headed by Martin Luther King Jr. But their actions and sacrifices moved the Black Freedom Struggle forward, and more of their stories need to be uncovered and told.

Toward the end of the 1960s, a more radical element of the Black Freedom Struggle grew, as the Southern Christian Leadership Conference (SCLC) gave way to groups like the Student Nonviolent Coordinating Committee (SNCC), the Black Panthers, and the Young Lords—new groups in which Black women did have more seats at the table, though their contributions still remained invisible and unrecorded.

More recently, with the rise of Black Lives Matter, founded by three women, came a refreshingly new opportunity for female voices to be heard at the highest levels of leadership in the Black Freedom Struggle.

Black women were made invisible in American society in large measure because of fear of their power. Yet tracing how stories of Black women have been consistently erased and hidden in the historical record also suggests ways in which those stories can be recovered and told. The hidden voices of Black women must be raised and heard if the full account of African American, and American, history is to be known.

CHAPTER 2

THE LEGEND OF MOLLY WELSH, THE STORY OF BENJAMIN BANNEKER

A TEENAGER IN 1683, MOLLY WELSH NEVER DREAMED THAT a pail of milk would place her in front of an English court, facing a death sentence. Once a dairymaid and now accused by the lord of the manor of stealing milk. She stood in the defendant's dock, hauled before a judge, scared. Molly ran her hand along the top edge of the highly glossed wooden dock. She tapped her finger repeatedly on its inside panel. She shifted her stance from one foot to the other, then back, anticipating the judge's appearance.

A tall, gaunt man, under a wig of white hair, with a powdered face, ceremoniously strode into the small courtroom. He stared straight ahead at Molly. Then lowered his eyes to a sheet of vellum.

"Molly Welsh," he intoned. "You have hereby been accused of theft of milk, then tried and convicted by this court of that same crime, for which a sentence of death by hanging is justified."

Molly stood expressionless.

"But I see you have also 'called for the book,'" the judge said.

The judge waved a bailiff forward, pointed to Molly. "Hand it to her," he demanded, "opened to the correct page."

Molly held the book in trembling hands.

"Read," the judge demanded, "the underlined passage aloud so the whole court might hear."

"Miserere mei, Deus, secundum misericordiam tuam," she said.

The judge raised his hand, interrupting her. "Stop," he said.

He chuckled low. A smirk crossed his face. He whispered, "At least we know you have an excellent memory." Suddenly, he thumped the podium with a flat hand, then thundered, "Now translate what you have just read into English!"

Molly bowed her head slightly. "Yes, m'lord," she said. "The verse is Psalm 51 in the King James Version of the Bible, Psalm 50 in the Latin Vulgate translation."

The judge's head snapped back. "Its meaning?" he insisted.

"Yes, m'lord. 'O God, have mercy upon me, according to thine heartfelt mercifulness.'"

The judge stammered, "A rare . . . rare accomplishment for your sex . . . ahem." He cleared his throat, brushed down his robe.

"Women acquired the benefit of clergy, 'calling for the book,' as you have requested, in 1624, so long as their crime, if it was a theft of goods, was valued at less than ten shillings. Your theft of less than ten shillings' worth of milk, Molly Welsh, qualifies you to seek the Crown's mercy. Discussions are underway now in Parliament about a new transportation act regulating the transportation of convicted criminals who plead the benefit of clergy, as you have, to the British colonies of North America. Since there is no law passed to this effect, this court retains considerable leeway in administering a sentence. But the outlines of this new law are well-known. So, by the powers granted to this court, Molly Welsh, and seeing how you have claimed being a Catholic, I commute your death sentence to seven years of indentured service in the colony of our Lord Calvert, in Maryland, with penalty of death should you return to England before working off your seven years of service."

Molly's hand flew to her mouth.

"Do you understand, dear girl?" the judge asked.

Molly curtsied from behind the dock. "Yes, m'lord, I understand. Thank you, m'lord." Though in her mind she repeated several times, *I shall never see English soil again. 'Tis a punishment as good as death.*

Seas tossed around the small ship she sailed on. On board, sailors tossed her around as well. Her body and soul felt bedraggled upon her arrival in a large bay where men loaded barrels on a few other ships. She walked down the gangway to a small boat that would row her to shore. When she stepped off onto solid ground, the first time in two months, a man broke away from discussions with the captain. He stepped forward and swept her off with him, told her he had a tobacco farm along a river with a strange name.

"Pataso?" Molly asked.

"Patapsco," the man said.

She felt the weight and the work of each of the seven years passing, callousing her hands, wrinkling her skin. As best as she could figure, she was in her mid-twenties when she got her "freedom dues"—a barrel of grain, a change of clothes, a small plot of land, and a few tools.

Something, she thought. *Something*.

Now, as Molly held her grandson, Benjamin, in her arms, she rocked back and forth inside the small log house she'd helped to build. She looked out a window over the fields of broad green leaves waving in the gentle breeze as far as her eyes could see.

My land, she thought. *My land*.

The land had been good to her; so had life. As good as a servant's life could be. She'd worked the land hard, mostly by herself, with a few hired workmen to help her get the barrels of tobacco down to the river and onto the small boats that transported them to larger ships waiting in the bay. Yes, she'd worked the land hard and saved her money, and when she needed more land to raise more tobacco to make more money, she bought that land. Only then she needed more hands to work that land.

"Miss Welsh," she remembered a neighbor telling her. "Why, you gotta git some slaves, ma'am. Some slaves."

She bought two.

One didn't work for her very long before he died. And the other didn't work for her very long before . . . Well, she tickled Benjamin's stomach. The baby cooed.

"You have your granddaddy's eyes," she said. "You have Bannaka's eyes."

And Molly recalled to herself, *He said he'd been a prince in Africa before he'd been captured. He knew things about the stars, about counting, about a funny-sounding language he spoke in. He died too young, too soon. He left me to raise our family.*

Benjamin Banneker's life is then woven in an intricate historical, social, and cultural tapestry: He went on to build clocks as a mechanic, publish almanacs as a mathematician, search the heavens as an astronomer, lay out the streets of Washington, DC, as a surveyor, and correspond with Thomas Jefferson as an early social justice advocate. Still, there is more. He had a drinking problem. He did not like women. He kept largely to himself. And recently, scholars have begun to purport that he was gay.

The legend of Molly Welsh is the origin story of Benjamin Banneker, passed along as oral history supposedly gathered from Banneker family members and close Maryland friends. Little source documentation has survived. The Molly Welsh story sounds like the script of a period-piece Hollywood romance movie, written to bring viewers to tears. Yet it's a story that so many people, Black and white, take unquestioningly as historical truth. But beyond popular belief, beyond how much people adore this version of the Benjamin Banneker story, particularly that of his grandmother Molly Welsh, how much of it is actually true? How does one go about separating Benjamin Banneker the man from Benjamin Banneker the myth? And why are both the man and the myth important?

One of the first elements of this tale that comes to mind is the multiple storylines. There's the storyline of the white milkmaid Molly Welsh, persevering against all odds: the English Crown and court and indentured servitude in the English colonies. There's her storybook interracial marriage to a Black man in early America, one she purchased as a slave, then fell in love with—a love story as repugnant to many then as it still is now. Of course, there's Benjamin Banneker himself—learned, accomplished, the correspondent of a president—and finally, there's the possibility of his being gay.

Originally, the Benjamin Banneker story was a darling of abolitionists for obvious reasons—learned Black man achieves much and beats the odds to success. "Who knows how many Bannekers are being enslaved? Set them all free," the abolitionists put forth. But the story of Benjamin Banneker changes in the post–Civil War era as other constituencies latch on to it. Molly Welsh is a woman seen persevering against the patriarchy in Europe and in America. Her marriage to a formerly enslaved man places their union in the spotlight of nineteenth- and twentieth-century calls to end miscegenation and set integration as a goal. Benjamin Banneker's accomplishments emerge alongside the growth of pride in the achievement of Black Americans and the role they played in the founding of this country. While Banneker being gay, a more recent addition to his story, spotlights the role of queer people in Black history and the history of the United States.

A woman against the patriarchy. An interracial marriage. A Black man who accomplishes much in a white world. A closeted gay Black man. These make at least four major themes that emerge from the Benjamin Banneker story and at least as many constituencies with a stake in how the story is fashioned and told: women's rights, racial equity, Black consciousness, and LGBTQ+ pride.

Myths are not falsehoods. They are stories erected on pillars of truth in order to provide a framework for comprehending larger issues or sets of beliefs. The Benjamin Banneker story is all the more fascinating because through it, one can see this interplay between the pillars of truth and the stories erected upon those pillars.

Over the years, depending upon who is telling the tale, Molly Welsh has been described as Black, white, and mixed race. She has been presented as coming from Africa, England, Ireland, and Scotland. Her status has been portrayed as free, enslaved, and even a slave owner. She has been reported as Benjamin Banneker's grandmother but also as his one-time owner.

So who, then, was Molly Welsh, where did she come from, and what was her relationship to Benjamin Banneker? We will probably never know the ultimate truth, but here are some things we do know:

On the day Benjamin Banneker was buried, his home in Oella, Maryland, along the Patapsco River, ten miles west of Baltimore, suspiciously burned to the ground, destroying all documents inside. In his surviving papers, Banneker never once referred to his grandmother, and in his now-famous 1791 letter to Thomas Jefferson, Banneker said, "Sir, I freely and cheerfully acknowledge, that I am of the African race, and in that color which is natural to them of the deepeft dye." In one copy of the letter, there is a footnote in which Banneker further attests that his father was brought to America as an African slave. This has been taken by some authors and scholars as evidence that Banneker had no ancestry other than African. The thinking goes, if he did have a white grandmother, why wouldn't he have mentioned that fact? One possibility is because Benjamin Banneker understood Thomas Jefferson's racism all too well.

In *Notes on the State of Virginia*, Jefferson put forth a notion that has continued down through the present day: that Blacks are inherently inferior to whites. "I advance it therefore as a fufpicion only, that the blacks, whether originally a diftinct race, or made diftinct by time and circumftances, are inferior to the whites in the endowments both of body and mind."

So, writing to Jefferson as both a Quaker and an abolitionist, Banneker may not have wanted to afford Jefferson the luxury of suspecting that his intellectual prowess was due to his white ancestry. If so, Banneker would have been justified in his thinking, because in his later letters, Jefferson disparages Banneker and passes off his intellectual achievements to the assistance Banneker received from George Ellicott, a neighbor from whom Banneker apparently learned spherical geometry. In one of these letters, Jefferson writes to his friend Joel Barlow on October 8, 1809, regarding a letter Jefferson received from the French priest and French revolutionary leader Abbé Henri Jean-Baptiste Grégoire. Grégoire was also an ardent abolitionist, one who'd published a book on the literary accomplishments of Blacks. Jefferson tells Barlow that Grégoire

> wrote to me also on the doubts I had expressed five or six & twenty years ago, in the Notes on Virginia, as to

> the grade of understanding of the negroes, & he sent me his book on the literature of the negroes. his credulity has made him gather up every story he could find of men of colour (without distinguishing whether black, or of **what degree of mixture**) however slight the mention, or light the authority on which they are quoted. the whole do not amount in point of evidence, to what we know ourselves of Banneker. we know he had spherical trigonometry enough to make almanacs, but not without the suspicion of aid from Ellicot, who was his neighbor & friend, & never mifsed an opportunity of puffing him. I have a long letter from Banneker which shews him to have had a mind of very common stature indeed. [Emphasis added.]

In 1792, at the request of Baltimore publishers William Goddard and James Angell, founder, statesman, and signatory to the US Constitution from Maryland James McHenry wrote an introduction to Benjamin Banneker's 1792 almanac, in which he notes that "Benjamin Banneker, a free Negro, has calculated an Almanack, for the ensuing year, 1792 . . . This Man is about fifty-nine years of age; he was born in *Baltimore County*; his father was an *African*, and his mother the offspring of *African* parents." (Italics from original.)

Lawyer, inventor, and author John H. B. Latrobe prepared a short tract, "Memoir of Benjamin Banneker," for the Maryland Historical Society in 1845. Latrobe, too, noted Banneker's African origins and the need to affirm that his intelligence was not due to any white ancestry.

> Benjamin Banneker was born in Baltimore County, near the village of Ellicotts Mills, in the year 1732. [N.B. He was actually born on November 9, 1731.] His father was a native African, and his mother the childe of natives of Africa; so that to no admixture of the blood of the white man was he indebted for his peculiar and extraordinary abilities. His father was a slave when he married; but his wife, who was a free woman and possessed of great energy and industry, very soon afterward purchased his freedom.

All of this presents reasonably strong evidence that Benjamin Banneker possessed no white ancestors. So from where does the story of Molly Welsh as Banneker's grandmother come? Molly Welsh first enters the tale more than thirty years after Benjamin Banneker's death, through writings by historian, author, and women's rights advocate Martha Ellicott Tyson. Tyson was born Martha Ellicott, the daughter of George and Elizabeth Ellicott, Quakers who lived among a community of Friends in Ellicott's Mill, Maryland. Benjamin Banneker, certainly with Quaker leanings, lived a mile away from the Ellicott home and visited there often, as he was befriended and tutored by Martha's father, George.

In 1836, Tyson began conducting a series of interviews with Banneker's family and friends and preparing the surviving papers of Banneker that her family held, which resulted in two books. In the shorter first book, *A Sketch of the Life of Benjamin Banneker*, meant to be notes for a presentation to the Maryland Historical Society, Tyson begins,

In preparing an account of an humble individual, it is rarely deemed necessary to furnish a long line of ancestry. The first member of the family of the subject of our notice, of whom we shall speak, is his maternal grand-mother, Molly Welsh, a native of England, who came to Maryland, (at that time an English Colony,) with a ship load of other emigrants, and, to defray the expenses of her voyage, was sold to a master with whom she served an apprenticeship of seven years.

After her term of service had expired, she bought a small farm, (land having then merely a nominal value,) and purchased as laborers, two negro slaves, from a slave ship, which lay in the Chesapeake Bay. They both proved to be valuable servants. One of them, said to have been the son of a king in Africa, a man of industry, integrity, fine disposition and dignified manners, she liberated from slavery and afterwards married. His name was Bannaker, which she adopted as her sir-name, and was afterwards called, Molly Banneker.

In an extended version of the Tyson manuscript, *Banneker, the Afric-American Astronomer*, compiled posthumously by her daughter, Anne Tyson Kirk, and published in 1884 by the Quaker publishing house Friends' Book Association, Kirk presents Tyson by writing,

The first that is known of the name of Banneker is that it was borne by an African prince. He was the son of the

> king of his country, who, being captured and brought to America as a slave, was purchased by Molly Welsh, an English woman owning a small farm near the Patapsco River, about twelve miles from its mouth.

This Molly Welsh, who was a person of exceedingly fair complexion and moderate mental powers, had been an involuntary immigrant to America:

> When a servant on a cattle-farm in her native land, where milking formed a part of her duty, she was accused of stealing a bucket of milk which a cow had kicked over. For this supposed offence, she was, by the stern laws of her country, sentenced to transportation, escaping a heavier penalty from the fact that she could read. On her arrival here she was, as was the custom, sold, to defray the expenses of the voyage, for a term of seven years, and purchased by a tobacco planter on Patapsco River.

Martha Ellicott Tyson's early and historic advocacy for women's rights should be celebrated—she was, significantly, a cofounder of Swarthmore College—but this advocacy also should not be overlooked in her crafting of the Benjamin Banneker story. That is not to say that Tyson fabricated the Molly Welsh backstory, for additional evidence suggests she did not. But Tyson brought it to light, and it provides an additional fascinating element to an already engaging account.

If Molly Welsh were, indeed, a felon in seventeenth-century

England sentenced to transportation to Maryland for the offense of stealing—or spilling, as some accounts contend—a pail of milk, records of her crime and sentence might very well exist.

Most who have searched for Molly Welsh in Europe agree she would have been tried and convicted sometime between 1682 and 1692. By the time of her trial, at least two dozen crimes in the English penal codes had been deemed worthy of a death sentence: murder, for sure, but also theft. As draconian as it sounds today, Molly Welsh, once convicted, could have been sentenced to death for stealing or spilling a pail of milk. It is also historically accurate and completely verifiable that Molly could have been given a more lenient sentence by "pleading the benefit of clergy" and proving she could read and interpret the Bible.

The problem with this story is there apparently exists no record of a Molly Welsh being convicted of theft anywhere in England and then sentenced to transportation to Maryland in the years between 1682 and 1692, or at any point within ten years on either side of that window.

Old Bailey is the common name for the Central Criminal Court of England and Wales, which was once attached to Newgate Prison, a gap in the Roman Wall surrounding the City of London on Bailey Street. Old Bailey contains fairly comprehensive records for criminal trials—crimes, pleas, verdicts, and punishments—from 1674 to 1913, nearly 250 years, and those records have been transferred to a searchable database accessible from an online site.

Searching the two hundred thousand entries in Old Bailey for the name Molly Welsh in the thirty-five-year time period between 1675 and 1710 yields nothing. Nor does searching for such names as Molly Welch, Molly Walsh, Molly Wells, Molly Walls, Molly Wallace, or Molly Willis. "Molly" is a diminutive of "Mary," sometimes used in a similar fashion with women named Margaret or Martha. But even when using these alternate names and spellings, Old Bailey yields only a few results, which are for crimes either unrelated to milk or out of range from the time period in which the grandmother of Benjamin Banneker could have been on trial in England. In fact, Old Bailey contains no record of milk theft by anyone prior to Elizabeth Wallbank, who was convicted of shoplifting in September 1716 for stealing from a sheriff a mug that happened to be full of milk. The milk spilled as Wallbank fled, leaving an easy trail to follow.

Of course, there are many possibilities for this inability to find Molly Welsh in Old Bailey. Court data, and hence the online database, might be incomplete. In a coming update to Old Bailey, new data may be added that includes Molly Welsh. There are also instances in Old Bailey when one finds a person sentenced without being able to find them convicted of a crime. Molly could have been tried in a venue other than Old Bailey, perhaps somewhere in Ireland or Scotland. If she were a criminal, she may also have wanted to hide that fact from her family. One Mary Marshal was convicted of grand larceny on October 17, 1681, then sentenced to transportation out of England, though Old Bailey gives no destination. Her trial, if there was one, could have taken place in a remote corner of England and not in London, so records of Molly Welsh may yet be discovered in a parish or a courtroom somewhere.

But I do not believe it likely that a person with the surname Welsh, or any of its variations, and given name Molly, or any of its variations, who was convicted of the theft of milk ever existed in England, Scotland, or Ireland in the seventeenth century. Instead, I believe it much more likely that "Welsh" became the last name of our matriarch after she came to the American colonies and after she married a man with the last name of Welsh.

"Rule, Britannia!," that stirring patriotic anthem sung by millions of British citizens, contains the following refrain, hollered amid clenched, pumping fists: "Rule, Britannia! Rule the waves: / Britons never, never, never will be slaves." There's a historical irony in this verse, lost by most who sing it—an irony at the center of the Molly Welsh story. In the British colonies of North America, Britons working as indentured servants were treated as de facto slaves from the seventeenth century to the early part of the nineteenth century.

The auction block; the plantation pass system; the fugitive laws; the overseer; the house servant; the Uncle Tom; the forced separation of husbands, wives, and children; the sexual exploitation of servant women; the whipping post; the chains; and the branding irons—all of these brutal mechanisms were tried out and perfected first on white men and white women. A theory of internalized white racism even developed, using traditional Sambo and minstrel tropes to characterize white servants who were said to be good-natured and faithful but biologically inferior to their masters and subject to laziness, immorality, and crime.

White indentured servitude was not some beneficent employment program for Europeans seeking to immigrate to America. White servitude was a colonial-era dress rehearsal for Black slavery. A "historic proving ground," wrote Lerone Bennett Jr., for the monumental and consequential system to succeed it.

On May 20, 1731, William Cumming Esq. petitioned the Maryland Provincial Court on behalf of his client Mary Beneca of Baltimore County. Mary, whose last name was, in all likelihood, a misspelling of "Banneker" by a clerk of the court, stated through Cumming that she "was born of a White Woman, a Servant of John Newman of the County aforesaid whom your Petitioner Did Serve until she attained to the Age of thirty-on Years." Thus, Mary Beneca (or Banneker) attested through Cumming that her mother and then she had both been servants to John Newman. While it is strange that both mother and daughter were servants to the same master but at different times, stranger still is that Mary Beneca was actually petitioning the court to release three of her "Mollatto" children from being bound in service to William Rogers for the crime of childbirth out of wedlock, of which she was acquitted. By the time of this petition, Mary Beneca was no longer married to a man named Beneca (Banneker), whose last name her children bore (in all likelihood he had died), but was instead married to a formerly enslaved man from Guinea named Robert, who, absent of a surname of his own, took "Banneker" as his last name.

Benjamin, born on November 9, 1731, was a child of Robert and Mary Banneker. Mary apparently sent Benjamin to her mother to raise, not as a relative but as a servant, bound to John Welsh, whom Mary's mother had since married, in Prince

George's County. Mary's mother, also named Mary, was the white matriarch of the family, and it is in this marriage that the name Mary (Molly) Welsh first appears in source documents. John Welsh owned slaves. Molly Welsh was free. Her daughter, Mary, was also free. Maryland laws stipulated that the status of the child followed that of the mother, which meant that Benjamin was free, too. But Molly made a rather strange will in 1752 in Prince George's County, Maryland, in which she manumitted her grandson, "Negro Benjn," as though she had enslaved him, and then on December 3, 1773, Molly put her hand to an even stranger deed, releasing her rights to Benjamin to her daughter, Mary.

Pretty easy to see how anyone digging into the Banneker family's genealogy and history might come away confused, thinking Molly Welsh was a slave owner rather than Benjamin's white grandmother. So why not stick with the story that Molly Welsh was a persecuted English milkmaid who married one of her slaves? It certainly makes for an easier telling. First, because it is, in all likelihood, the least accurate version of the backstory to Benjamin Banneker, and because there are better, perhaps even more important ways to contemplate the machinations of the Banneker clan.

One lens through which to view the story of Molly Welsh yields a much finer appreciation of the nuances of enslavement in colonial America. My own research suggests that a woman called Molly, probably born Mary somewhere in England, was actually a Quaker. Furthermore, she *was* prosecuted in England—not for spilling a pail of milk, but instead for her religious beliefs. As much as the harsh consequences for theft can be documented in seventeenth-century England, so, too, can the persecution of Quakers.

The dates for the beginning of Quakerism are certainly consistent with the dates for the Molly Welsh legend. Quakerism started as an offshoot of Protestantism during and after the English Civil Wars of the middle seventeenth century, which were fought over the balance of power between the monarchy and the civilian population and the balance of power between the church and the state. During these wars, an English king, Charles I, was imprisoned and executed. A commoner, Oliver Cromwell, was named the head of state and then later overthrown. The Anglican Church of England was replaced by a Presbyterian state church, then later restored. And a number of disillusioned, dissenting religious groups emerged, among them the Society of Friends, or Quakers.

Quakers proposed their version of free religious thought in England in the seventeenth century, and it was immediately met with fierce opposition and persecution. The Quaker Act of 1662 stipulated that all English subjects swear loyalty to the Crown—such loyalty oaths Quakers were opposed to—and stipulated three levels of punishment for violation of the act: (1) First-time offenders were to receive a sentence of either five pounds (over eight hundred US dollars in 2024) or three months' imprisonment with hard labor; (2) second-time offenders were to receive a sentence of either ten pounds or six months of hard labor; and (3) third-time offenders were to be **transported from England to a colony abroad**. This act was followed in 1664 by the Conventicle

Act, which forbade religious assemblies of more than five people outside of the state-designated Church of England.

Now, another aspect of Quakerism that ran afoul of the laws and customs of seventeenth-century England was the role of women. Margaret Fell, considered the mother of Quakerism, petitioned Parliament on behalf of seven thousand women in 1659. Fell also authored the 1666 pamphlet *Womens Speaking Justified*, which argued for the equality of women and the departure from traditional male and female roles. In this nexus between women and Quakerism in seventeenth-century England lies the possibility of another interpretation of the origin of the milkmaid-who-spilled-milk tale associated with the heroine of the Benjamin Banneker story.

"No use crying over spilt milk" is a phrase attested to by some researchers as an ancient Hebrew proverb related both to the actual instance of milk being spilled on the ground and being therefore unrecoverable, and to releasing oneself from lamenting or mourning past acts—such as Saul's sparing of the Amalekites—that cannot be undone, either. While the phrase may have originated in Hebrew, it returns to English at least as early as the seventeenth century through two collections of proverbs, one published by James Howell (1659) and another by John Ray (1678). Unlike most Christians, Jews, and Muslims, who would have identified with Samuel, Quakers, as devout pacifists, would have identified with Saul. So, whomever Molly actually was, she, like most Quakers of that time, would most likely have been familiar with that phrase.

In Molly's case, the "spilt milk" may have been a metaphor

for her acceptance of Quakerism, her noncompliance with the Quaker Act of 1662 and the Conventicle Act of 1664, and thus the punishment she received of transportation from England to the American colonies. Documentation exists that shows other English Quakers were arrested, prosecuted, and sentenced this way.

Regardless of whether there ever was a pail of spilled milk that caused a young woman in seventeenth-century England to be sentenced to transportation and servitude in Maryland, we know for certain that many Quakers emigrated from England at this time—some by choice, others by force of law. William Penn, granted land in the present-day states of Pennsylvania and Delaware by King Charles II, outfitted a fleet of twenty-three ships that sailed from England between the years of 1682 and 1686. Many ships found the Delaware River, which led them into Philadelphia. Some, like the *Submission*, did not.

In the later part of 1682, damaged and blown off course by a storm, the *Submission* limped toward the North American coast, finding not the Delaware River but the Chesapeake Bay and the Choptank River, leading to Choptank, Maryland. The Quakers disembarked there, some continuing by land north to Pennsylvania, and others, like Richard Ratcliffe, staying to establish themselves as prominent Quakers in Maryland.

From this point on, the story of the Maryland Quakers merges with that of the Banneker clan. Richard Ratcliffe from the *Submission* went on to become well-known in the Maryland Quaker community, marrying Mary Caterne on May 13, 1691, in front of witnesses that included Jon Newman, who was possibly one and the same with the John Newman for whom Mary Beneca

(Banneker) and her mother, our Molly, worked as servants. In 1728, Quaker Richard Gist, a Baltimore County justice and commissioner, put down security for the payment of court fees for Mary Beneca in her successful defense against charges of giving birth out of wedlock. In the court filing by William Cumming, Mary Beneca was reported living in the house of George Rogers, and after her acquittal on charges of a baseborn child (out of wedlock), the court remanded the three children she had with a man whose last name was Lett to servitude under William Rogers. The Rogers (or Rodgers) family of Maryland is peppered with individuals who are shown in various source documents as being Quaker. The Welsh family, into which Mary Beneca's mother, also Mary and most likely the real Molly Welsh, married is a large family split between southern Pennsylvania and Maryland not only with Quaker members but with at least one John Welsh, who was disinherited for marrying a Quaker woman. Add to this the existence of a principal, though early, site known as the Patapsco Meeting, mentioned first in 1703. "Meetings" are where Quakers gather in prayer and communion. "Patapsco" is the name of the river along which the Bannekers had a tobacco farm.

None of this evidence is conclusive, but taken as a whole, it is suggestive. Maryland Quakers might still yield more secrets about Molly Welsh. One possibility is that she was a Quaker in England, persecuted but not wealthy enough to pay for her own transportation to America, and thus came as an indentured servant to an already established planter who was a Quaker, perhaps John Newman. Another possibility is that Molly came from England as a non-Quaker indentured servant and underwent conversion ("convincement") while working at a Quaker-owned plantation. A third possibility is that Molly was a Quaker already in the American colonies, who migrated internally to Maryland from Pennsylvania, North Carolina, Virginia, or some other colony, following many other early Quakers who made similar journeys in search of a place to freely practice their beliefs. Still a fourth possibility is that Molly immigrated to Maryland from Barbados or Jamaica, where, in the early parts of the seventeenth century, more than ten thousand Quakers lived and ran slave-based plantations. The number of Quakers in the West Indies dwindled steadily throughout the seventeenth century as most started to flee, either from Quakerism or from their plantations, in part over the issue of slavery.

Furthermore, the complicated and convoluted relationship between Quakers and slavery may well explain aspects of the complicated and convoluted relationships in the Banneker family. Early in the history of America, Quakers enslaved Black people—in some instances by the hundreds. Yet Quakers professed a belief that all souls, Black and white, were equal. Early slave-owning Quakers received advice from their leaders for the humane, rather than harsh, treatment of those they enslaved. Antislavery advocates among early Quakers were not tolerated well. By the middle of the eighteenth century, that started to change as reformers within the religion began to openly condemn slavery and the slave trade, claiming slavery ruined the moral character of those who engaged in it. By the time of the American Revolutionary War, most Quaker meetings disowned members who refused to manumit their slaves. By the nineteenth century, many American Quakers were deeply involved in abolitionist movements seeking to end slavery completely.

The timing of this shift from Quakers as enslavers to Quakers as abolitionists varied widely. By the end of the seventeenth century, some Quakers in Maryland were calling for an end to enslavement and for the extension of religious and secular education to all people, regardless of color. Benjamin Banneker, for example, may have attended a Quaker school paid for by his grandmother, and he certainly received tutelage in science and mathematics from George Ellicott, a lifelong Quaker. But Molly (or Mary), Benjamin Banneker's grandmother, may also have benefitted from Quaker beliefs.

The pronouncement for "humane treatment" extended not only to the enslaved but to indentured servants as well. If Molly was a Quaker or if she worked under a Quaker master, there's every possibility that her experience as an indentured servant was vastly different from others' experiences. Since honoring secular contracts is a core part of Quaker beliefs, she probably would not have had to fight for her release when the time of her indentures ended, as many servants needed to do. Since indentured servant contracts in Maryland at that time called for the provision of "freedom dues"—clothes, grain, seed, and land—at the end of service, there's a fair chance she received them, too. And when it came time for her to purchase slaves, there's every likelihood she passed these Quaker beliefs on in the way she treated those she enslaved, thus making the freeing and marrying of one of the men she enslaved not out of line with the Quaker beliefs she either possessed or found herself surrounded by.

∴ ∴ ∴ ∴

A few remaining elements of the Benjamin Banneker story still need the attention given to Molly Welsh: His accomplishments. His exchange of letters with Thomas Jefferson. The question of his sexual orientation. And, finally, an exploration of his dreams.

Many date the start of the civil rights phase of the Black Freedom Struggle as December 1, 1955, when Rosa Parks chose not to relinquish her seat on a Montgomery, Alabama, public bus. Others would step back farther, to the May 17, 1954, US Supreme Court ruling in *Brown v. Board of Education*. Still others would point to the end of World War II and the homecoming of Black soldiers, too often welcomed not with thanks for their defense of democracy but with the oppression of Jim Crow. Some would want to go back even farther, to the militancy of the "New Negro" and the Harlem Renaissance growing out of returning World War I Black soldiers. But I trace the start of the civil rights phase of the Black Freedom Struggle to August 19, 1791, when Benjamin Banneker authored a letter to then–Secretary of State Thomas Jefferson.

Maryland, Baltimore County, Auguft 19, 1791

Sir,

I am fully fenfible of the greatnefs of that freedom which I take with you on the prefent occafion; a liberty which feemed to me fcarcely allowable, when I reflected on that distinguished, and dignifyed ftation in which you stand; and the almoft general prejudice and prepoffeffion which is fo prevailent in the world againft thofe of my complexion.

I fuppose it is a truth too well attefted to you, to need a proof here, that we are a race of Beings who have long laboured under the abufe and cenfure of the world, that we have long been looked upon with an eye of contempt, and that we have long been confidered rather as brutifh than human, and fcarcely capable of mental endowments.

Sir I hope I may fafely admit, in confequence of that report which hath reached me, that you are a man far lefs inflexible in fentiments of this nature, than many others, that you are meafurably friendly and well difpofed toward us, and that you are willing and ready to Lend your aid and affiftance to our relief from thofe many diftreffes and numerous calamities to which we are reduced.

Now Sir, if this is founded in truth, I apprehend you will readily embrace every opportunity to eradicate that train of abfurd and falfe ideas and oppinions which fo generally prevails with respect to us, and that your fentiments are concurrent with mine, which are that one univerfal Father hath given being to us all, and that he hath not only made us all of one flefh, but that he hath alfo without partiality afforded us all the fame fenfations, and endued us all with the fame faculties, and that however variable we may be in fociety or religion, however diverfifyed in fituation or colour, we are all of the fame Family, and ftand in the fame relation to him.

Sir, if thefe are fentiments of which you are fully perfuaded, I hope you cannot but acknowledge, that it is the indifpenfible duty of thofe who maintain for themfelves the rights of human nature, and who profeff the obligations of Chriftianity, to extend their power and influence to the relief of every part of the human race, from what-

ever burthen or oppreffion they may unjuftly labour under, and this I apprehend a full conviction of the truth and obligation of thefe principles fhould lead all to.

Sir, I have long been convinced, that if your love for your felves, and for thofe inefteemable laws which preferved to you the rights of human nature, was founded on fincerity, you could not but be folicitous, that every individual of whatsoever rank or diftinction, might with you equally enjoy the bleffings thereof, neither could you reft fatifyed, fhort of the moft active effusion of your exertions, in order to their promotion from any ftate of degradation, to which the unjuftifyable cruelty and barbarifm of men may have reduced them.

Sir I freely and Chearfully acknowledge, that I am of the African race, and in that colour which is natural to them of the deefest dye; and it is under a fenfe of the moft profound gratitude to the Supreme Ruler of the Univerfe, that I now confefs to you, that I am not under that ftate of tyrannical thraldom, and inhuman captivity, to which too many of my brethren are doomed; but that I have abundantly fasted of the fruition of thofe bleffings which proceed from that free and unequalled liberty with which you are favoured; and which I hope you will willingly allow you have mercifully received from the immediate hand of that Being, from whom proceedeth every good and perfect gift.

Sir, fuffer me to recall to your mind that time in which the Arms and tyranny of the Britifh Crown were exerted with every powerful effort in order to reduce you to a ftate of fervitude, look back I intreat you on the variety of dangers to which you were expofed, reflect on that time in which every human aid appeared unavailable, and in which even hope and fortitude wore the afpect of inability to the

Conflict, and you cannot but be led to a ferious and grateful fenfe of your miraculous and providential prefervation; you cannot but acknowledge, that the prefent freedom and tranquility which you enjoy you have mercifully received, and that it is the peculiar bleffing of Heaven.

This Sir, was a time in which you clearly faw into the injustice of a ftate of flavery, and in which you had juft apprehensions of the horrors of its condition, it was now Sir, that your abhorrence thereof was fo excited, that you publickly held forth this true and invaluable doctrine, which is worthy to be recorded and remember'd in all fucceeding ages. "We hold thefe truths to be felf evident, that all men are created equal; that they are endowed by their Creator with certain unalienable rights, that among thefe are life, liberty, and the pursuit of happynefs."

Here Sir, was a time in which your tender feelings for yourfelves had engaged you thus to declare, you were then impreffed with proper ideas of the great valuation of liberty, and the free poffeffion of thofe bleffings to which you were entitled by nature; but Sir how pitiable is it to reflect, that altho you were fo fully convinced of the benevolence of the Father of mankind, and of his equal and impartial diftribution of thofe rights and privileges which he had conferred upon them, that you fhould at the fame time counteract his mercies, in detaining by fraud and violence fo numerous a part of my brethren under groaning captivity and cruel oppreffion, that you fhould at the fame time be found guilty of that most criminal act, which you profeffedly detefted in others, with refpect to yourfelves.

Sir, I fuppose that your knowledge of the fituation of my brethren is too extensive to need a recital here; neither fhall I presume to prefcribe methods by which they may be relieved; otherwife than by recommending to you and all others, to wean yourfelves from thefe narrow prejudices which you have imbibed with refpect to them, and as Job proposed to his friends "Put your fouls in their fouls ftead," thus fhall your hearts be enlarged with kindnefs and benevolence toward them, and thus fhall you need neither the direction of myfelf or others in what manner to proceed herein.

And now, Sir, altho my fympathy and affection for my brethren hath caufed my enlargement thus far, I ardently hope that your candour and generofity will plead with you in my behalf, when I make known to you, that it was not originally my defign; but that having taken up my pen in order to direct to you as a prefent, a copy of an Almanack which I have calculated for the fucceeding year, I was unexpectedly and unavoidably led thereto.

This calculation, Sir, is the production of my arduous ftudy in this my advanced ftage of life; for having long had unbounded defires to become acquainted with the fecrets of nature, I have had to gratify my curiofity herein thro my own affiduous application to Aftronomical Study, in which I need not to recount to you the many difficulties and difadvantages which I have had to encounter.

And altho I had almoft declined to make my calculation for the enfuing year, in confequence of that time which I had allotted therefor being taking up at the Federal Territory by the requeft of Mr. Andrew Ellicott, yet finding myfelf under feveral engagements to Printers of this ftate to whom I had communicated my defign, on my return to my place of residence, I induftriously apply'd myfelf thereto, which I hope I have accomplifhed with correctnefs and accuracy, a copy of which I have taken the liberty to direct to you, and which I humbly request you will favourably receive, and altho you may have the opportunity of perusing it after its publication, yet I chofe to fend it to you in manufcript previous thereto, that thereby you might not only have an earlier infpection, but that you might alfo view it in my own hand writing.

And now Sir, I fhall conclude, and fubscribe myfelf with the most profound refpect,

Your moft obedient humble fervant,
Benjamin Banneker

Philadelphia Aug. 30. 1791.

Sir

I thank you sincerely for your letter of the 19th. instant and for the Almanac it contained. no body wishes more than I do to see such proofs as you exhibit, that nature has given to our black brethren, talents equal to those of the other colours of men, and that the appearance of a want of them is owing merely to the degraded condition of their existence both in Africa & America. I can add with truth that no body wishes more ardently to see a good system commenced for raising the condition both of their body & mind to what it ought to be, as fast as the imbecillity of their present existence, and other circumstances which cannot be neglected, will admit.

I have taken the liberty of sending your almanac to Monsieur de Condorcet, Secretary of the Academy of sciences at Paris, and member of the Philanthropic society because I considered it as a document to which your whole colour had a right for their justification against the doubts which have been entertained of them. I am with great esteem, Sir Your most obedt. humble servt.,

Th: Jefferson

Mr. Benjamin Banneker
Near Ellicott's, lower mills. Baltimore county

Reading Banneker's letter to Jefferson, reproduced here in its entirety and original spelling, reminds me of traveling to far northern Minnesota, to Lake Itasca, then farther up one of the small streams that feed the lake to an inauspicious spot where water bubbles from the ground—water that feeds the stream that feeds the lake that feeds a mighty nearly 2,400-mile-long Mississippi River. Banneker's letter is also the headwaters of a mighty river—the Black Freedom Struggle and its demand for civil rights, racial equality, and social justice.

Banneker's letter turns on a simple proposition: The rights enshrined in the founding documents of America need to be extended to all American citizens, regardless of color. This simple proposition lies at the core of a mighty river that flows in a winding but inexorable way on its course toward the freedom and expanse of the sea. A river that slowed down with Jefferson's tepid response to Banneker and the long nights of enslavement that followed. A river whose speed quickened with the dawning of an American Civil War and the promises of freedom. Quickened ever further through the words of Frederick Douglass, only to slow down once again when those promises were broken and the harsh realities of Reconstruction, Jim Crow, and lynching set in. And still the river flowed. Past Booker T. Washington and W. E. B. Du Bois it flowed. Past Ida B. Wells and Zora Neale Hurston it flowed. Past Howard Thurman and Pauli Murray it flowed. Past Rosa Parks and Medgar Evers it flowed. Past Emmett Till and James Chaney and Andrew Goodman and Michael Schwerner it flowed. Past Jimmie Lee Jackson and James Reeb and Viola Liuzzo it flowed. Past Bayard Rustin and Martin Luther King Jr. and Malcolm X it flowed. And that river also flowed past Breonna Taylor and Ahmaud Arbery and George Floyd. That mighty river carrying the Black struggle for freedom in America, set off in the gentle headwaters of a letter from Benjamin Banneker to Thomas Jefferson in 1791, continues to flow to this day.

There should be no question that Benjamin Banneker was a learned man of science, mathematics, and engineering. It was reported by many that he designed a wooden clock from a pocket watch he owned by scaling up the gears of the watch. Foreign visitors to the United States in the late 1700s and early 1800s traveled to Banneker's home to view it. The clock apparently worked from its design in the 1750s until a fire burned down Banneker's Patapsco River home on the day of his internment. But some have suggested, without any evidence, that the bell of the clock tower in London, affectionately known as Big Ben, was actually named after Benjamin Banneker, when in all likelihood it was really named after Sir Benjamin "Big Ben" Hall, the politician and engineer who oversaw the bell's installation. In fact, little credit is given to Benjamin Banneker for his less glamorous scientific findings, such as being a naturalist and one of the first, if not the first, to observe, describe, and predict the seventeen-year cycle of the cicada.

From 1792 to 1797, Benjamin Banneker published a yearly almanac, which included, interspersed between his ephemerides (tables to show the times of various celestial events like the sunrise, sunset, moonrise, and moon phase), weather predictions, notes to farmers on planting, poems, and prose that often spoke to issues of racial equality. The almanacs were popular and commercially successful. Leafing through Banneker's lone surviving astronomical journal, one is impressed by the depth of spherical geometry he mastered to produce these detailed calculations. Yet when detailed comparisons are made to other contemporary almanacs, Banneker's calculations have been shown to be off, sometimes by a few minutes and at other times by more than a day. They were still close enough to make his almanacs practically useful, and his lack of accuracy may also have been due to his lack of the resources needed to obtain the mathematical tables that other almanac makers had access to. This does not diminish in the least what Banneker achieved through these volumes and his love of mathematics and astronomy, but it also does not warrant the extravagant claims that some have made regarding his mathematical and astronomical prowess.

Exhibiting next to no scientific understanding, some modern-day authors claim that Banneker investigated relativity two hundred years before Einstein did. Spherical geometry does not come anywhere close to the theories of general and special relativity that Einstein put forth at the turn of the twentieth century. In fact, spherical geometry is based on Newtonian physics, which general and special relativity eclipsed. Others have claimed that Banneker's interest in astronomy—and in particular Sirius, one of the brightest stars in the constellation Canis Major—led him to posit that Sirius was, in fact, a binary star—i.e., two stars moving around each other—before English astronomer John Goodricke did so in 1782. Hermann Vogel would finally prove Goodricke right in 1890, but adherents to the Banneker story claim that Banneker made that assertion before Goodricke, based on knowledge passed along from his grandfather to his grandmother and then finally to him.

This assertion about Sirius came into the Banneker story with the 2002 publication of *Benjamin Banneker: Surveyor, Astronomer, Publisher, Patriot* by author Charles Cerami. He claimed, with what I consider to be questionable evidence, that Benjamin Banneker's grandfather was of Dogon heritage, causing Benjamin to pick up this astronomical knowledge as it was passed along in oral tradition by his grandmother Molly to him.

That the Dogon people of Mali actually claimed Sirius to be a "double star" comes, in turn, from books by the French anthropologist Marcel Griaule, who spent years studying the Dogon, in the 1940s. Subsequent, more modern visits by other anthropologists to the Dogon turned up no evidence of the astronomical knowledge that Griaule claimed the Dogon had. The suggestion has been made that Griaule received the answers he got from Ogotemmeli, the Dogon elder, by the manner in which he insisted on the questions—an outcome described as "investigator basis." Regardless, for a student of history it is a leap too far to suggest, without convincing evidence, that Banneker believed that Sirius was a "double star" and that therefore his grandfather must have come from the Dogon. Other researchers have placed Banneker's ancestry among the Wolof, the Yoruba, and recently the Vai of Liberia, based on everything from the mathematics he used to solve puzzles to the existence of a town in modern-day Liberia named Banaka.

As an engineer and surveyor, Benjamin Banneker is often credited with laying out the plan for the streets and buildings of Washington, DC, after Secretary of State Thomas Jefferson recommended him to President George Washington. This story is actually an inflation of a request made by Jefferson to his friend and surveyor Major Andrew Ellicott, a cousin of Banneker's friend George Ellicott, to lay out the boundaries of the new federal district. In early 1791, Andrew Ellicott hired Banneker to work on a survey team that was to merely place boundary markers (stones) every mile along the ten-by-ten-mile square area that would become Washington, DC, created from land ceded to the federal government by Virginia and Maryland. Banneker worked on Ellicott's team for only three months before returning to his home to tend to his tobacco crop and further calculate the ephemerides for his 1792 almanac.

Perhaps one of the most interesting and recent additions to the Banneker story concerns his sexual orientation. Many LGBTQ+ historians claim Banneker as a gay learned Black man in the tradition of Langston Hughes and Bayard Rustin.

Cerami, in his biography of Banneker, tells the story, also without any specific documentation, that Benjamin Banneker fell in love in 1759 with an enslaved woman named Anola, whom he met at a market near Elkridge Landing, Maryland. She so captivated Banneker that he went to her enslaver and asked to purchase her so that he might wed her and set her free. Upon hearing Banneker's request, Anola's enslaver replied vociferously and furiously, "No!" Banneker's broken heart drove him deeper into his intellectual pursuits of mathematics, science, astronomy, and engineering. But then, apparently based on no factual evidence, Cerami speculates about Banneker being unable to "come out of the closet," perhaps attempting a homosexual relationship but then being rebuffed. Cerami then offers another proposition: that Benjamin Banneker was of "low sex drive" and therefore asexual at a time when there were no words for that sexual identity. I find Cerami's assertions unsatisfying and untenable.

Heterosexual? Homosexual? Bisexual? Asexual? Benjamin Banneker lived nearly three hundred years ago, at a time when sexuality, regardless of orientation, was repressed, even among the more progressive Quaker community that surrounded him. Any attempts to claim we know definitively Benjamen Banneker's sexual orientation represents a disservice to him and to LGBTQ+ communities who might otherwise claim him. Applying twenty-first-century standards and analyses of sexual orientation to a person from the eighteenth century, for whom there is little supporting evidence, has to be considered a fool's errand.

However, one area where we are offered a window into the inner workings of Benjamin Banneker's mind comes from his lone surviving astronomical journal, in which he wrote not only of his scientific insights but also of his dreams. One dream in particular captures a universal mythic theme of African origin that people from all over that continent carried with them through their long night's ordeal of capture, transport, and enslavement—a mythic theme represented by a mythic symbol still very much rooted in African American and American popular culture to this day. Banneker writes:

December 5, 1791

On the night of the fifth of December 1791, Being a deep Sleep, I dreamed that I was in a public Company, one of them demanded of me the limits of Rasannah Crandolph's Soul had to display itself in, after it departed from her Body and taken its flight. In answer I desired that he show me the place of Beginning "thinking it like making a Survey of the Land." He replied I cannot inform you but there is a man about three days journey from Hence that is able to satisfy your demand, I forthwith went to the man and requested of him to inform me place of beginning of the limits that Rasannah Crandolph's soul had to display itself in, after the Seperation from her Body; who gave me answer, the Vernal Equinox, When I returned I found the Company together and I was able to Solve their Doubts by giving them the following answer Quincunx.

Dreams are private myths; myths, public dreams. Accepting, excepting, that Rasannah Crandolph was most likely a person (Rosannah, Roseanna, Rosana) whom Banneker actually knew and who may have died, his dream is presented in the three principal stages of a universal myth: departure, initiation, and return. It is demanded of him to discover the limits of a human soul—the mythic challenge of departure or call to adventure. He then accepts this challenge and embarks on a quest to where a man informs him of the answer he seeks—the moment of initiation, given here through the wise man of the way. And finally, he brings back a boon, in the form of an answer first held in doubt or incomplete, until he delivers a fuller answer of his own: quincunx.

An able astronomer and mathematician such as Banneker would have known the quincunx (pronounced "kwin-kunks") as the angle that is five-twelfths of a circle (150 degrees) or a geometrical pattern in which five points are arranged as a cross such that four are at the ends of each crossarm (often invisible) and one lies in the center: ⁙ . In European history, a quincunx was a Roman coin whose value was five (*quinque*) twelfths (*uncia*) of the standard Roman coin called an *as* or *assarius*. But the symbol also has a history in tile design known as Cosmati, which came to Europe through Sicily, from North Africa and Islam. It is thought that through Islam, the quincunx found its way across the Sahara with the ancient conquering Muslim raids into West Africa, there to become an elemental feature in West African pattern design and art, particularly in the Senegambia region, among the Wolof people. Researchers, investigators, and interpreters of Banneker's written dream have stopped here upon the quincunx reaching West Africa, suggesting for this reason that Banneker's father or grandfather was Wolof. Certainly this is a fascinating connection.

But had these investigators traveled three thousand miles farther south to the Angola–Congo region, from where enslaved Africans had been taken since the 1400s, they would have uncovered an even more significant, more pervasive truth of this symbol.

In the Angola–Congo region the quincunx was known as the *yowa* or *dikenga* millennia before the arrival of Europeans. The principal cosmology of this region is compacted into this symbol: the world of the living above the horizontal line, the world of souls below it. Angolan Kongolese myths featuring those who journey into the world of souls are based around it. Angolan Kongolese people understood the capture of Africans, their enslavement, and their transport to a new world in terms of this symbol. For example, the horizontal line not only separated the world of the living and the world of souls, but it also represented the Atlantic Ocean, where ships were said to emerge from beneath the horizontal line, then disappear with kinfolk below the line again. Rituals, dance, and music are based around the *yowa* and the *dikenga*.

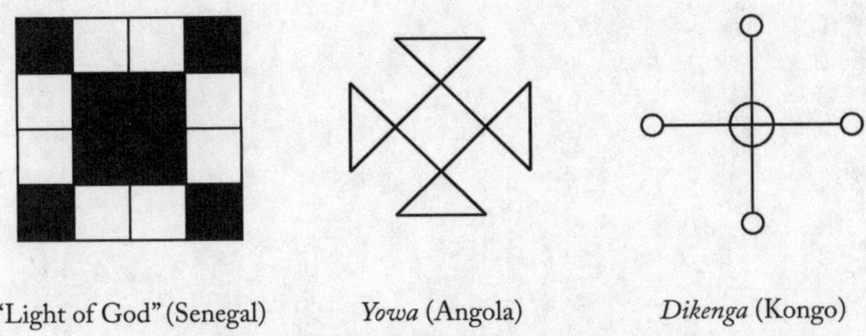

"Light of God" (Senegal) *Yowa* (Angola) *Dikenga* (Kongo)

African symbols related to the quincunx.

This sacred African symbol survived, intact, the brutality of the Middle Passage and enslavement, to be found many thousands of times drawn on walls, and pots, and drums, or simply on the ground throughout the African diaspora, in North America, in the Caribbean, and in Central and South America. In the essay for Chapter 6, "Music, Myth, and Stono," I describe how the *dikenga* found its way into the music, rhythms, and dance of America through its survival among Africans enslaved here. It was as if through this symbol enslaved men and women were calling back to an ancient source of spiritual strength they once knew, and they were calling forth this symbol to provide them spiritual strength for the struggles they now faced. I can only imagine that this symbol surfaced countless times in the dreams of the enslaved. Thanks to Benjamin Banneker, we know it surfaced in his dreams.

CHAPTER 3

الله أعظم ، أمريك

ALLAHU AKBAR, AMERICA: ISLAM AND THE BLACK FREEDOM STRUGGLE

"IN THE NAME OF ALLAH, THE MERCIFUL, THE COMPASSIONATE. May Allah grant his blessing upon our Prophet Muhammad."

Thus begins the preamble by Omar ibn Said, an Islamic marabout (spiritual teacher), writing of his life in Arabic, translated prior to publication in English. Only ibn Said did not write from somewhere in the modern-day Middle East; he wrote while enslaved by the governor of North Carolina in 1831. His essay "The life of Omar ben Saeed, called Morro, a Fullah Slave in Fayetteville, N.C. Owned by Governor Owen" opens a little-known chapter on the role of Islam in the history of the Black Freedom Struggle and on Islam's influence in early America.

Omar ibn Said continues his preamble in praise of Allah:

Blessed be He in whose hands is the *mulk* and who is Almighty; who created death and life that he might test You; for he is exalted; he is the forgiver (of sins), who created seven heavens one above the other.

Do you discern anything trifling in creation? Bring back your thoughts. Do you see anything worthless? Recall your vision in earnest. Turn your eye inward for it is diseased. God has adorned the heavens and the world with lamps, and has made us missiles for the devils, and given us for them a grievous punishment, and to those who have disbelieved their Lord, the punishment of hell and pains of body. Whoever associates with them shall hear a boiling caldron, and what is cast therein may fitly represent those who suffer under the anger of God—Ask them if a prophet has not been sent unto them. They say, "Yes; a prophet has come to us, but we have lied to him." We said, "God has not sent us down anything, and you are in grievous error." They say, "If we had listened and been wise, we should not now have been suffering the punishment of the Omniscient." So they confess they have sinned in destroying the followers of the Omniscient.

Those who fear their Lord and profess his name, they receive pardon and great honor. Guard your words, (ye wicked), make it known that God is all-wise in all his manifestations. Do you not know from the creation that God is full of skill? that He has made for you the way of error, and you have walked therein, and have chosen to live upon what your god Nasûr has furnished you?

Believe on Him who dwells in heaven, who has fitted the earth to be your support and it shall give you food. Believe on Him who dwells in Heaven, who has sent you a prophet, and you shall understand what a teacher (He has sent you). Those that were before them deceived them (in regard to their prophet). And how came they to reject him? Did they not see in the heavens above them, how the fowls of the air receive with pleasure that which is sent them?

God looks after all. Believe ye: it is He who supplies your wants, that you may take his gifts and enjoy them, and take great pleasure in them. And now will you go on in error, or walk in the path of righteousness.

Say to them, "He who regards you with care, and who has made for you the heavens and the earth and gives you prosperity, Him you think little of. This is He that planted you in the earth, and to whom you are soon to be gathered."

But they say, "If you are men of truth, tell us when shall this promise be fulfilled?"

Say to them, "Does not God know? and am not I an evident Prophet?"

When those who disbelieve shall see the things draw near before their faces, it shall then be told them, "These are the things about which you made inquiry."

Have you seen that God has destroyed me or those with me? or rather that He has shewn us mercy? And who will defend the unbeliever from a miserable punishment?

Say, "Knowledge is from God."

Say, "Have you not seen that your water has become impure? Who will bring you fresh water from the fountain?"

While this autobiographical preface may seem but a superfluous series of adulations to Allah, it actually represents Omar ibn Said's recollection and recitation of the sixty-seventh chapter, or *surah*, of the Qur'an known as the "Surah Al-Mulk." *Mulk* or *Al-mulk* means the Kingdom, the Dominion, the Authority, or the Sovereignty. From the translation of Said's Arabic:

Blessed be He in whose hands is the *mulk* and who is Almighty

Who created death and life that he might test You; for he is exalted; he is the forgiver (of sins), who created seven heavens one above the other.

From a modern translation of the Qur'an, verses one through three of the "Surah Al-Mulk":

> Blessed is the One in Whose Hands rests all authority. And He is Most Capable of everything.
>
> He is the One Who created death and life in order to test which of you is best in deeds. And He is the Almighty, All-Forgiving.
>
> He is the One Who created seven heavens, one above the other. You will never see any imperfection in the creation of the Most Compassionate. So look again: do you see any flaws?

For an Islamic scholar like Omar ibn Said, the "Surah Al-Mulk" was well-known and most likely recited by him often. But its inclusion as a preface to his autobiography also suggests he specifically chose it as a sacred protest to his secular status of being enslaved. In effect, ibn Said is saying to his enslavers, "You can chain my body, but you can never chain my soul because Allah has dominion over my soul," and furthermore, "as nonbelievers you will be judged harshly for the sins committed during your lives when you ultimately face the Almighty." In this respect, ibn Said joins a mighty lineage of enslaved Africans who drew on the spirituality—brought with them from Africa or given to them in America under the whip and chain—for the strength to continue on through the brutality and violence of their everyday lives, believing that redemption ultimately awaited them.

Enslaved Africans, for whom access to the spiritual supports they grew up with were violently forbidden, found a similar route in the Christianity forced upon them during enslavement. Spirituals, gospels, and blues songs picked up exactly the same theme as the one found in the "Surah Al-Mulk." Consider the first verse of the traditional Black spiritual "There Is a Balm in Gilead":

> There is balm in Gilead,
> To make the wounded whole;
> There's power enough in heaven,
> To cure a sin-sick soul.

This spiritual tells of a balm capable of making the wounded (the enslaved) whole and of curing the sin-sick (enslaver's) soul.

Ibn Said continues with "O, Sheikh Hunter," so his autobiographic account, then, is an apparent response to the entreaties of an unnamed individual whom he acknowledged as a cleric (*sheikh* is an Arabic honorific for a spiritual leader). Now, there were at least two constituencies with overlapping interests and memberships that may have benefitted by the autobiography of a literate enslaved man. One was the group of Southern slaveholders concerned about their portrayal as the monsters and brutes most of them were toward the men and women they enslaved. Another group, also of white Americans and many of whom were slaveholders, was the American Colonization Society (ACS), which was seeking a solution to the problem of race in America through the forced immigration of Blacks to West Africa, where the society had participated in the creation of the country of Liberia.

Around the time ibn Said's autobiographical essay was published in 1831, two very significant events rocked the slaveholding South. In Boston in 1829, David Walker published *Appeal to the Colored Citizens of the World*, and two years later, Nat Turner's Rebellion erupted in Southampton County, Virginia.

From his travels around America, David Walker, a free and learned Black man, chronicled the brutality and savagery of American slavery when compared to slavery depicted in the Bible or historically in other cultures of the world, like in ancient Greece or Rome. He took the American founders to task, particularly Jefferson, for establishing a country based on the principles of freedom and equality yet refusing to grant or acknowledge that Blacks were endowed with those same freedoms. Furthermore, Walker noted that the founders and white Americans, in general, believed Blacks to be inferior in body and mind simply because of their skin color. Walker appealed to the highest ideals of Christianity, asking, *If white Christians also believed in these biblical ideals, how could they hold Africans enslaved?* But David Walker went one step further. He called on the children of the African diaspora throughout the New World to act against their white oppressors, to fight for their freedom, unless those oppressors threw away their prejudices and treated them like human beings:

> We must and shall be free I say, in spite of you. You may do your best to keep us in wretchedness and misery, to

> enrich you and your children, but God will deliver us from under you. And wo, wo, will be to you if we have to obtain our freedom by fighting. Throw away your fears and prejudices then, and enlighten us and treat us like men, and we will like you more than we do now hate you; you are not astonished at my saying we hate you, for if we are men we cannot but hate you, while you are treating us like dogs.

Even some early abolitionists were opposed to the radical nature of David Walker's appeal. But still it was disseminated widely. Walker suggested that if Blacks couldn't read it because they had been barred from an education by their enslavers, then the *Appeal* should be read to them. He even enlisted Black Jacks—Black sailors, enslaved and free—to carry the *Appeal* to the Southern ports they visited.

Terror struck the hearts of slaveholders at the thought that those they enslaved might adopt such views and rise up against them. Southern states rushed to respond, passing even more draconian Black Codes, closing ports to ships with Black crews, and placing a bounty on Walker—wanted in Georgia, for example, dead or alive.

Then, two years after Walker's *Appeal*, the worst of white fears came to pass.

In Southampton County, Virginia, on August 21, 1831, a well-thought-out, well-planned rebellion led by an enslaved man named Nat Turner erupted. Turner led a core group of four—fellow enslaved men and free men—who went plantation to plantation, killing white slave owners and their families and liberating other enslaved men and women. The group swelled to around seventy, killing nearly sixty whites and accomplishing at least one of Turner's stated objectives: to spread "terror and alarm" among whites. Ultimately, the rebellion was put down by local militia, white mobs, and detachments from US naval ships stationed in nearby Norfolk, Virginia. Turner managed to escape and hide out in the Great Dismal Swamp bordering Virginia and North Carolina before he was caught. Turner—and anyone else whom white citizens deemed connected to the rebellion—was executed. In what may well be the worst of white depravity, Turner's body was flayed and his skin used to make souvenir purses.

Word, like white fear, spread quickly. Across the South, collective punishment of the enslaved ensued. More than one hundred enslaved people were slaughtered by white mobs and local white militia, even though most had nothing to do with the rebellion. Further laws were enacted against mass assemblies and unsupervised church gatherings of the enslaved—Nat Turner, a devout Christian, was often seen immersed in the Bible or prayer. Laws were also passed against free Blacks, whom Turner had recruited and whom Southern whites viewed as a present and future danger. Virginia, for example, passed a police bill that denied free Blacks the right to trial by jury and made them subject to being sold back into slavery, or relocation, if convicted of a crime.

Slavery and Southern society survived on a system of simple social status: If you were Black, you were enslaved. If you were white, you were free. Since the middle of the seventeenth century in America, the legal doctrine of *partus sequitur ventrem* (the status of the child follows the status of the mother) was in effect throughout most of the South. If your mother was a slave, so were you. But what if your mother was free? Maybe she was a white woman. Maybe she'd been manumitted by her enslaver. Maybe she was a descendant of a time when Blacks were also indentured servants, and her ancestors had worked off their indentures. There were many reasons a Black woman could be free, and therefore her children as well, and that threw a monkey wrench into the system's simple status based on skin color needed to support slavery and Southern society.

But an ever-resourceful America came up with a plan for that, too. Simply export the problem. Thus, the Society for the Colonization of Free People of Color of America was born officially in 1812, although it had roots in the American Revolutionary War. The society soon adopted the more benign name of the American Colonization Society (ACS), but the original objectives remained the same: to encourage and support the repatriation of free Blacks and emancipated slaves in the US to Africa. The ACS made for strange bedfellows. For the first time since the founding of the American colonies, a diverse group of people found common ground on the issue of slavery and race. Some early abolitionists, a few Blacks, and mostly Southern whites agreed on one of the first "back to Africa" movements. Run almost exclusively by white Americans (nearly all presidents were Southern white slaveholders), ACS was a prime example of the "we broke it, you fix it" philosophy of race relations in America that continued through the latter part of the twentieth century, with the society only officially dissolving in 1964.

This "go back to where you came from, and we'll help get

you there" approach, of course, suffered a great many problems, not the least of which was that there was no single country to repatriate Black Americans to, since they'd been stolen from a huge swath of Africa. From slavery, Christianity, and their experiences in America, by the nineteenth century, Black Americans also had evolved into an ever-growing more coherent and distinct amalgam of men and women, so the very notion of their blending back into African societies was faulty. Of course, none of this stopped the ACS from participating in the establishment of the colony, which eventually became the African country of Liberia. ACS backed federal and state laws in the US passed to support this repatriation effort, outfitted ships, bought supplies, and transported thousands of Black Americans to Liberia. Predictably, things did not go well. Relations between Black Americans and the indigenous Kru and Grebo peoples resulted in internecine strife, and for years Liberia was—some say it still is—a failed state.

Still, that did not stop white Americans from trying, and ibn Said's "Sheikh Hunter" may well have been the Reverend Eli Hunter of the New York branch of the ACS, who recruited for the organization throughout the South and perhaps encouraged ibn Said's autobiography. Although Said mentions a "Handah (Hunter?)" later in his autobiography, apparently connected to a church in Fayetteville, North Carolina, so "Sheikh Hunter" may have been a local reverend.

Since his escape from enslavement in South Carolina, ibn Said had always been something of a "freak show" or circus act for Governor Owen and his family. People traveled widely to meet this exotic man, a Muslim supposedly converted to Christianity, who spoke and wrote in a strange tongue and prayed several times daily on a small mat facing east.

Ibn Said begins his autobiography in a self-effacing manner, tinged with deep sadness:

> I cannot write my life because I have forgotten much of my own language, as well as Arabic. Do not be hard upon me, my brother—to Allah let many thanks be paid for his great mercy and goodness.
>
> In the name of Allah, the gracious, the merciful—Praise be to Allah, supreme in goodness and kindness and grace, and who is worthy of all honor, who created all things for his service, even man's power of action and of speech.
>
> You asked me to write my life. I am not able to do this because I have much forgotten my own, as well as the Arabic language. Neither can I write very grammatically or according to the true idiom. And so, my brother, I beg you, in Allah's name, not to blame me, for I am a man of weak eyes, and of a weak body
>
> My name is Omar ibn Said. My birthplace was Fouta Toro between the two rivers. I sought knowledge under the instruction of a Sheikh called Mohammed Seid, my own brother, and Sheikh Suleiman Kembeh, and Sheikh Gabriel Abdul. I continued my studies twenty-five years, and then returned to my home where I remained six years. Then there came to our place a large army, who killed many men, and

> took me, and brought me to the great sea, and sold me into the hands of the Christians, who bound me and sent me on board a great ship and we sailed upon the great sea a month and a half, when we came to a place called Charleston in the Christian language. There they sold me to a small, weak, and wicked man called Johnson, a complete infidel, who had no fear of God at all. Now I am a small man, and unable to do hard work so I fled from the hand of Johnson and after a month came to a place called Fayd-il.

Ibn Said remembered more than perhaps he even realized. Futa Toro was a state in the valley between the Senegal and Gambia Rivers with wavering allegiance to Islam. The "large army" that ibn Said writes of was most likely the confederated forces of the kingdoms of Bunda, Kaarta, and Khasso, which together invaded the kingdom of Futa Toro between 1806 and 1807. The people of this region are ethnically Fulbe (also known as Fula, Fulani, Peul, or Peuhl), and during American slavery they were simply grouped together by ignorant enslavers as Mandingoes or Mandinka, prized for their ability to cultivate rice and thus purchased principally in the rice-growing regions of the Sea Islands and New Orleans. The Fula occupy a wide swath of northern sub-Saharan Africa and the Sahel—from Senegal and Nigeria bordering the Atlantic to regions of Sudan and South Sudan near the Red Sea. Depending upon exactly how Fulbe ethnicity is measured, today some twenty-five to forty million people consider themselves Fulbe or Fulani. It's not hard to understand why estimates put the number of Fulbe or Fulani captured and enslaved in America at the height of the Atlantic slave trade at 30 percent of all enslaved people. Certainly not all Fulbe were Muslims, and not all West African Muslims were Fulbe, but many were.

"Sambo" (Samba), "Bailey" (Bilali), "Bullaly" (Bilali), "Bocarrey" (Abu Bakr), "Mustapha" (same in Arabic), "Momado" (Mamadu), "Wally" (Wali), "Homady" (Ahmad), "Mahomet" (Muhammad), "Mamoodie" (Madmudi), "Moussa" (Musa), "Alex" (Aliki), "Bram" (Ibrahim), and "Hammett" (Hamid or Ahmad). These are some of the anglicized Muslim names given to the enslaved by uneducated American enslavers found in advertisements for slave auctions, tax rolls of plantations, and wanted posters for runaways.

"Sambo," in particular, is an interesting name to further contemplate because it has been so long associated with the worst stereotypes and abject racism directed toward people of African descent in America. Yet, "Sambo," sometimes "Sam," is in fact a corrupted form of the Fulbe name Samba (meaning "second son") and represents a name given to men from areas of Africa where Islam was the principal religion. Once again, this does not mean that all men named Samba were Muslims, but most likely some were, as in this advertisement for a runaway enslaved man named Sambo in the January 9–12, 1782, edition of the South Carolina *Royal Gazette*:

> RUN away from the fubfcriber, on Chriftmas day laft, a NEGRO FELLOW, named Sambo, or Sam; he is about five feet high, flim made, and has a fmall limp or ketch in his walk; he is of a yellowifh complexion, and is a lit-

> tle pitted with the fmall-pox; his upper foreteeth comes a good deal over his lower ones, and his hair is pretty long, being of the Fulla country, fpeaks tolerable Englifh, is about 26 years of age, and fhoemaker by trade.

"Fula," of course, is that area of the Sahel where many people were Muslim.

An earlier advertisement in Georgia on May 24, 1775, in Savannah's *Georgia Gazette* also identified another enslaved man named Sambo with potentially Islamic roots, noting that of three runaways, one included a twenty-two-year-old "Sambo . . . of the Moorish country"—this reference probably suggests more of this enslaved man's identity as a Muslim than his origin in North Africa.

Certainly not all enslaved people in early America had their Islamic names preserved, even in corrupted forms. Salih Bilali of St. Simons Island in Georgia remained a devout Muslim all of his life, in full view of his enslaver, yet he was called Tom.

In surveying the names of enslaved people, a sharp distinction can be made concerning the names of the first generation of Africans captured and enslaved in the American colonies from roughly 1619 to 1660. Many of this first generation already had anglicized names from the kingdoms of the Kongo and the Ndongo, where Christianity, not Islam, had been adopted by African kingdoms by the middle of the fifteenth century.

Islam, like Christianity, is a proselytizing religion. Both grew larger through expansion into faraway lands by gun and by sword. Islam entered Africa around the eighth century and followed existing trans-Saharan trade routes to penetrate the semiarid Sahel and sub-Saharan Africa by the ninth century. Again, like Christianity three thousand miles to the south and six centuries later in the Angola–Congo region, rulers throughout the Sahel and as far south as Ghana used Islam to gain power, prestige, and wealth. Ruling elites often reserved Islam for themselves. Muslim ministers held court with local African kings, offering guidance based on Islamic teachings and laws while suggesting which kingdoms should make war with one another.

Human beings were the booty of such conflicts among warring African kingdoms, and Christian European powers like Britain, France, and Belgium reaped the benefits by purchasing these individuals from the winning sides, then shipping them off to European colonies, where they were sold into enslavement for profit. In all likelihood, ibn Said was the victim of just such a conflict, captured and then shipped by Britain, probably, to be sold in Charleston to an infidel whose last name was Johnson. If so, he was not alone.

Christian Europe, however, was not the only procurer and enslaver of Africans. A thousand years before the Portuguese slave trade began between the Angola–Congo region and Spanish and Portuguese colonies in Central and South America, a robust trans-Saharan slave trade thrived, principally run by Muslim Arabs who captured or bartered for slaves in sub-Saharan Africa, then transported them to slave markets in North Africa, from where they were sold to Mediterranean and Middle Eastern countries. The estimate for the number of people ensnared in this trans-Saharan trade is a staggering 7.2 million individuals from the seventh to the twentieth centuries, rivaling the transatlantic slave trade, although over a far longer period (the transatlantic slave trade lasted about four hundred years, from the mid-1400s to the mid-1800s). Instead of the dreaded Middle Passage across the Atlantic Ocean, these enslaved men and women were taken to Arab countries and faced an equally daunting crossing of the Sahara Desert, where as many as one in six of them died.

"Caravan" first entered English around the time of the Crusades through *caravana*, a Latin word with roots in the Arabic *qayrawān*, borrowed from the Persian word *kārawān*, meaning a column of soldiers or traders. With caravans of thousands of camels, traders crossed the Sahara from prehistoric times well into the twentieth century. Using an eastern route that began in Libya, a western route that started in Morocco, or a central route that left from Tunis, caravans from north to south carried cotton and silk clothes, weapons of war (guns, gunpowder, swords, and horses), European goods, and Arabic books. In exchange, caravans leaving the south of the Sahara and heading north carried gold, ivory, salt, and captured human beings, who would be enslaved.

While this trade satisfied the appetite for clothes and goods of war among sub-Saharan people, it also highlighted an oft-hidden aspect of sub-Saharan African culture—their appetite for learning. One of the first Islamic centers of learning in Africa was established in the late 600s at Qairawan, near Tunis, the city's name perhaps coming from its importance as a major terminus for the central route of caravans across the Sahara and also as a military outpost. The Great Mosque of Qairawan, also known as the Mosque of Uqba, a UNESCO World Heritage Site, is the first mosque built in Africa that is still standing. Occupying nearly one hundred thousand square feet, the Mosque of Uqba housed a major university, where scholars taught students the finer points of Islam and Maliki jurisprudence (one of four major Sunni Muslim schools of legal thought) but also mathematics, astronomy, medicine, and botany.

In Timbuktu, the principal terminus at the other end of the trans-Saharan trade route from Qairawan, a Maliki-inspired sister university emerged two to three hundred years later, around the campuses of the three main mosques at Sankoré, Djinguereber, and Sidi Yahya. Like the Mosque of Uqba, the University of Timbuktu was a major center of Islamic study, where students learned by writing down the dictation of their instructors, and all religious instruction occurred in Arabic rather than in local African languages. Graduates of the university received special turbans to wear and credentials attesting to their proficiency to teach various subjects.

Futa Toro, ibn Said's home, was also a center of learning, part of a network of madrassas and other Islamic educational centers that sprouted up across West Africa as satellites of major centers of learning like Timbuktu. Ibn Said said that he left his home for twenty-five years to study prior to returning to the Senegambia valley. Perhaps he traveled to Timbuktu. "I continued my studies twenty-five years, and then returned to my home where I remained six years." His brother Sheikh Mohammed Seid, Sheikh Suleiman Kembeh, and Sheikh Gabriel Abdul, all of whom ibn Said sought out for instruction, were, in all likelihood, teachers or graduates of a university like Timbuktu.

Believers of Christianity and Islam both perpetuate a notion that people with dark skin were ordained by God, or Allah, to be enslaved. As two of the three Abrahamic religions (Judaism being the third), Christianity and Islam both hold that Noah cursed Ham's son, Canaan, and as a result, the skin of Canaan's descendants blackened with sin, and they were forever condemned to be "servants of servants"—in other words, slaves.

Africans, therefore, were identified in both religions as the forever cursed descendants of Canaan. It was a convenient scriptural interpretation and justification for enslavement by Christians in America. But it was also a scriptural interpretation and justification for Muslim slave traders to continue the gruesome business of buying and selling human beings, even though the Qur'an forbids Muslims from holding other Muslims as slaves, as the Bible prevents the same for Christians. None of that seemed to matter in the face of profit and power.

Ibn Said ran away from his first enslaver, a man called Johnson, and made his way to Fayd-il (Fayetteville, North Carolina), from where he picks up his story:

> There I saw some churches. On the new moon I went into a church to pray. A lad saw me and rode off to the place of his father and informed him that he had seen a black man in the church. A man named Handah (Hunter?) and another man with him on horseback, came attended by a troop of dogs. They took me and made me go with them twelve miles to a place called Fayd-il, where they put me into a great house from which I could not go out.

I continued in the great house (which, in the Christian language, they called jail) sixteen days and nights. One Friday the jailor came and opened the door of the house and I saw a great many men, all Christians, some of whom called out to me, "What is your name? Is it Omar or Seid?" I did not understand their Christian language. A man called Bob Mumford took me and led me out of the jail, and I was very well pleased to go with them to their place. I stayed at Mumford's four days and nights, and then a man named Jim Owen, son-in-law of Mumford, having married his daughter Betsey, asked me if I was willing to go to a place called Bladen.

I said, Yes, I was willing. I went with them and have remained in the place of Jim Owen until now.

Before [after?] I came into the hand of General Owen a man by the name of Mitchell came to buy me. He asked me if I were willing to go to Charleston City. I said "No, no, no, no, no, no, no, I not willing to go to Charleston. I stay in the hand of Jim Owen."

O ye people of North Carolina, O ye people of S. Carolina, O ye people of America all of you; have you among you any two such men as Jim Owen and John Owen? These men are good men. What food they eat they give to me to eat. As they clothe themselves, they clothe me. They permit me to read the gospel of God, our Lord, and Savior, and King; who regulates all our circumstances, our health and wealth, and who bestows his mercies willingly, not by constraint. According to power I open my heart, as to a great light, to receive the true way, the way of the Lord Jesus the Messiah.

Before I came to the Christian country, my religion was the religion of "Muhammad, the Apostle of Allah—may Allah have mercy upon him and give him peace." I walked to mosque before day-break, washed my face and head and hands and feet. I prayed at noon, prayed in the afternoon, prayed at sunset, prayed in the evening. I gave alms every year, gold, silver, seeds, cattle, sheep, goats, rice, wheat, and barley. I gave tithes of all the above-named things. I went every year to the holy war against the infidels. I went on pilgrimage to Mecca, as all did who were able.—My father had six sons and five daughters, and my mother had three sons and one daughter. When I left my country I was thirty-seven years old; I have been in the country of the Christians twenty-four years.—Written A. D. 1831.

O ye people of North Carolina, O ye people of South Carolina, O all ye people of America—The first son of Jim Owen is called Thomas, and his sister is called Masa-jein (Martha Jane?). This is an excellent family.

Tom Owen and Nell Owen have two sons and a daughter. The first son is called Jim and the second John. The daughter is named Melissa.

Seid Jim Owen and his wife Betsey have two sons and five daughters. Their names are Tom, and John, and Mercy, Miriam, Sophia, Margaret and Eliza. This family is a very nice family. The wife of John Owen is called Lucy and an excellent wife she is. She had five children. Three of them died and two are still living.

O ye Americans, ye people of North Carolina—have you, have you, have you, have you, have you among you a family like this family, having so much love to Allah as they?

Formerly I, Omar, loved to read the book of the Qur'an the famous. General Jim Owen and his wife used to read the gospel, and they read it to me very much—the gospel of Allah, our Lord, our Creator, our King, He that orders all our circumstances, health and wealth, willingly, not constrainedly, according to his power—open thou my heart to the gospel, to the way of righteousness.—Praise be to Allah, the Lord of all worlds, thanks in abundance. He is plenteous in mercy and abundant in goodness.

For the law was given by Moses but grace and truth were by Jesus the Messiah.

When I was a Mohammedan I prayed thus: "Praise be to Allah, Lord of all worlds, the merciful, the gracious, Lord of the day of Judgment, thee we serve, on thee we call for help. Direct us in the right way, the way of those on whom thou hast had mercy, with whom thou hast not been angry and who walk not in error. Amen."

But now I pray in the words of our Lord Jesus the Messiah.

"Our Father, who art in heaven, hallowed be thy name, thy Kingdom come, thy Will be done, on earth as it is in Heaven. Give us this day our daily bread and forgive us our trespasses as we forgive those who trespass against us, and lead us not into temptation but deliver us from the evil one for thine is the Kingdom, the power, and the glory for ever and ever. Amen."

I reside in our country by reason of great necessity. Wicked men took me by violence and sold me to the Christians. We sailed a month and a half on the great sea to the place called Charleston in the Christian land. I fell into the hands of a small, weak and wicked man, who feared not Allah at all, nor did he read (the gospel) at all nor pray.

I was afraid to remain with a man so depraved and who committed so many crimes and I ran away. After a month Allah brought me forward to the hand of a good man, who fears Allah, and loves to do good, and whose name is Jim Owen and whose brother is called Col. John Owen. These are two excellent men—I am residing in Bladen County.

I continue in the hand of Jim Owen who never beats me, nor scolds me. I neither go hungry nor naked, and I have no hard work to do. I am not able to do hard work for I am a small man and feeble. During the last twenty years I have known no want in the hand of Jim Owen.

Today, Islam is so loathed by many Americans that it is hard for them to grasp the central role that Islam played in the history of Americans of African descent and in the history of America itself. Islam penetrated West Africa well before white Europeans did. As the slave trade shifted north from the Niger–Congo region of Africa to the Senegambia region, many of the men and women captured and transported to America were practicing Muslims. Some continued to practice Islam while in chains.

For Bilali Muhammad, life on the Sapelo Island plantation of Thomas Spalding in the Georgia Sea Islands was a world away from the life Omar ibn Said knew. Born a Fula in Timbo, Fouta Djallon (present-day Guinea), somewhere between 1760 and 1779, Bilali Muhammad, also known as Ben Ali, Bu Allah (possibly a corruption of Abu Abdullah), or simply the Old Man, was captured in West Africa and first purchased in the last decade of the eighteenth century by Dr. John Bell, a British Loyalist who'd sought refuge in the Caribbean from the American Revolutionary War. Bell owned a large cotton plantation on Middle Caicos, where he enslaved several hundred Africans, Bilali Muhammad among them.

In 1802—some reports say 1803—South Carolina politician and native Sea Islander Thomas Spalding purchased Bilali Muhammad along with other enslaved men and women from John Bell and brought them to one of his plantations on Sapelo Island. By the beginning of the nineteenth century, cotton had replaced tobacco as the American source of wealth. Power had shifted from the old tobacco money of the upper South to the new cotton money of the lower South. Georgian Eli Whitney had patented his new cotton gin and was mass-producing them in factories in the South while plantation owners and enslavers such as Spalding sought ways to cash in.

Spalding was a scientific and experimentalist farmer searching for the most effective ways to grow this new crop with the enslaved labor he needed. He pioneered new forms of enslavement, such as a task system, as opposed to the more traditional gang system, where enslaved people were assigned specific daily tasks. When an assigned task was finished, the enslaved person was free to pursue whatever they wished for the remainder of the day. Tobacco and sugar, which required considerable processing and inspection of the growing plants, had been traditionally done under the gang system of enslavement, where those enslaved worked as a group on a task with strict, often brutal oversight by a slave driver or an overseer. But coffee, rice, and cotton—crops that Spalding sought to cultivate on Sapelo Island—were hardier than tobacco or sugar and required less oversight. Spalding's ideal was a plantation of the enslaved run by the enslaved. A frequent contributor to *The Southern Agriculturist*, Spalding sent a letter to the editor on March 6, 1835, about his cultivation of rice on Sapelo Island, in which he wrote, "I manage my plantations without the intervention of any white men."

He managed this in several ways, starting off with the notion that he, like many white enslavers in the Sea Islands, did not wish to be on his plantation during the hottest summer months, when the risk of malaria ran high. Furthermore, Spalding believed that the four to five hundred men and women he enslaved would be better off and more productive if left in segregated ethnic groups based on the areas in Africa from which they had been captured.

Task system versus gang system. Segregation by African ethnicity. Enslaved supervising the enslaved. Taken as a whole, Spalding's approach, while economically beneficial to him, provided opportunities for the enslaved men and women he owned. Here, I am not suggesting that Spalding was an "enlightened enslaver" doing the very best he could for the sake of those he enslaved. Spalding was in the mold of the loose packer rather than the tight packer when it came to captaining slave ships. Loose packers reckoned that if they packed captured Africans into ships with more space among them, they would arrive at ports in America with fewer deaths and illnesses, and therefore they could command higher prices. Tight packers did not really care about how many Africans died or became ill during the dreaded Middle Passage, because they loaded their human cargo into every available space on their ship, figuring that whatever losses in human life they sustained could be made up when their captives were sold. To tight packers, loss was simply part of the risk of doing business.

Spalding's methodology followed that of the loose packers, and the enslaved men and women on his Sapelo Island plantation derived some benefits from this approach. Bilali Muhammad's family and friends were allowed to stay together. He was allowed to lead them in daily Islamic prayers and was even given permission to build a rudimentary prayer house or mosque. Bilali also rose through the ranks of the enslaved population, becoming the overseer of all the enslaved on Spalding's plantation, thus helping Spalding achieve his dream of a plantation run without "the intervention of any white men."

In turn, it must have been much easier for Bilali Muhammad to stick to a devout path based on the five pillars of Islam—the Muslim creed, daily prayer, charity toward the poor, fasting during Ramadan, and the hajj, a pilgrimage to Mecca for those who are able.

Katie Brown, granddaughter of Bilali Muhammad's daughter Margret (Mahgreb?), recollected Bilali's adherence to his faith in a series of 1937 interviews with Georgia Writers' Project writers under the supervision of Mary Granger. Here, the reader should be warned that quotes from Katie Brown were taken down by white interviewers with the intent of capturing the *flavor* of the dialect spoken by the formerly enslaved in the Sea Islands. While I applaud the effort, the transliteration into English at times borders on racist tropes of how Black Americans used English.

> Belali Mohomet? Yes'm, I know about Belali. He wife Phoebe. He hab plenty daughtuhs, Margret, Bento, Chaalut, Medina, Yaruba, Fatima, an Hestuh.
>
> Margret an uh daughtuh Cotto use tuh say dat Belali an he wife Phoebe pray on duh bead. Bey wuz bery puhticluh bout duh time dey pray ad dey bery regluh bout duh hour. Wen duh sum come up, wen it straight obuh head an wen it set, das deh time dey pray. Dey

> bow tuh duh sun and hab lill mat tuh kneel on. Duh beads is on a long string. Belali he pull bead an he say, "Belami, Hakabara, Mahamadu." Phoebe she say, "Ameen, Ameen." . . .
>
> She ain tie uh head up lak I does, but she weh a loose wite clat da she trow obuh uh head lak veil an it hang lose on uh shoulduh. I ain know wy she weah it dataway, but I tink she ain lak a tight ting ron uh head.
>
> She make funny flat case she call "saraka." She make um same day ebry yeah, an it big day. Wen dey finish, she call us in, all duh chillum, an put in hans lill flat cake an we eats it. Yes'm, I membuh how she make it. She wash rice, an po uff all duh wathu. She let wet rice sit all night, an in the mawnin rice is all swell. She tak dat rice and put it in wood mawtuh, an bet tuh past with wooden pestle. She add hone, sometime suhuh, and make it in flat cake wid uh hans. "Saraka" she call um.

Prayer mats. Prayer beads. Regular prayer times. Uttering Islamic prayer words. Bowing toward the sun. A veil. Honoring Islamic traditions like *sadaka* or *sadaqa* (*saraka*), the giving of alms in the form of food. Past the unfortunate transliteration of Black speech by white interviewers, Katie Brown presents us with a picture of an enslaved man attempting to honor his Islamic faith. With a prayer house erected, Bilali Muhammad, an overseer of other enslaved men and women, was most likely also an imam for other Muslims around him.

St. Simons Island lies a few islands south of Sapelo. There, Salih Muhammad, perhaps a biological brother of Bilali but certainly his spiritual brother in Islam and his friend, lived a life similar to Bilali's, only on the plantation of James Hamilton Couper, who apparently also purchased Salih from the plantation of Dr. John Bell on Middle Caicos.

The story of Abdul Rahman Ibrahima Sori reached all the way to the 1828 White House of President John Quincy Adams. Abdul Rahman was a Fulbe (Fula) prince born in Timbuktu, who later became commander of the Fouta Djallon region of Timbo, Guinea, under his father, Ibrahim Sori, a Fula leader. Educated at Timbuktu in 1788, Abdul Rahman was given command of a cavalry regiment with the duty of preventing the harassment of European ships, purchasing war captives from the Fulani, by a non-Muslim group known as the Hebohs. Call it karma, but Abdul Rahman was himself ambushed by the Hebohs, shot, captured, and subsequently sold to British slave traders, reportedly "for two bottles of rum, eight hands of tobacco, two flasks of powder, and a few muskets."

The slaver *Africa* took Abdul Rahman from Africa to the Caribbean island of Dominica, where another ship took him to New Orleans and farther upriver to Natchez, Mississippi, where he and his friend Samba were purchased by a planter named Thomas Foster for approximately $950 (almost $33,000 in 2024). Abdul Rahman's skills with horses and his command of the enslaved men and women on the plantation caused Foster to value him further, entrust him with greater authority, and even allow him to occasionally walk to a local market in Washington, Mississippi, to sell vegetables.

At the market in 1807, Abdul Rahman chanced to run into an old family friend, Dr. John Coates Cox. In 1788, while serving as a surgeon aboard an English slaver, Cox was injured while ashore, and the ship left without him. He was found by the Fula and taken to Timbo as a curiosity, where he healed in the home of Abdul Rahman's family. Cox immediately tried to buy Abdul Rahman from Foster in order to free him, but Foster refused to sell. Cox continued to seek Abdul Rahman's release, even bringing the governor of Mississippi into the campaign. Cox died in 1816, and his son continued the fight to no avail.

And Abdul Rahman's story might have ended there if it were not for New York–born Andrew Marschalk, who'd set up the *Mississippi Gazette* and the *Washington, Mississippi Republican*. Marschalk encouraged Abdul Rahman to write to his family in Arabic. In 1826, Abdul Rahman wrote a letter that was delivered to Sultan Abd'al Rahman (not the father) through the US consulate in Morocco. The Sultan proposed a prisoner swap to US President John Quincy Adams and Secretary of State Henry Clay—Abdul Rahman in exchange for several Americans held illegally in Morocco.

With an agreement in place by both governments, Thomas Foster consented to release Abdul Rahman to Andrew Marschalk and his wife without payment. The Marschalks immediately set Abdul Rahman free, then purchased his wife from Foster and set her free as well. Foster's one stipulation was that Abdul Rahman should not remain in the US and instead be sent to Africa by the US, which coincided with the terms of the swap.

On May 15, 1828, Abdul Rahman had an audience with President Adams, and prior to leaving the country, he and his wife went on a ten-month tour of the US, visiting various Northern cities in a quest for funds that would purchase the remainder of his family from Thomas Foster. In particular, Abdul Rahman was the most highly visible spokesman for the American Colonization Society and their efforts to immigrate freed slaves to Liberia. On February 9, 1829, Abdul Rahman and his wife, Isabella, boarded the *Harriet* out of Norfolk, Virginia, on a voyage to Liberia underwritten by the ACS. Though he professed conversion to Christianity in an effort to garner the funds needed to free his children, he declared his return to Islam once he got within sight of Africa. Along with thirty other passengers on the *Harriet*, Abdul Rahman succumbed to yellow fever within months of disembarking in Liberia. He died on July 6, 1829, without seeing Fouta Djallon or his children again.

Omar ibn Said, Bilali and Salih Muhammad, Abdul Rahman Ibrahima Sori—these are but a few of the thousands of enslaved Africans with a sad but similar story. Born as a Muslim in a region like Fouta Djallon, born as a Fula or other person of Muslim background, captured in war, then shipped off to a ready buyer in America.

From at least the middle of the seventeenth century, Islam was there in colonial America as the slave trade shifted north from the Angola–Congo region to the area of Africa the British called the Guinea Coast. Islam was there at the founding of the American republic, as names on the muster rolls of the Revolutionary War confirm—Yusuf ben Ali, a member of the Turks of South Carolina, an overlooked, tight-knit community still in existence today; Bamphett Muhamed; and possibly even Peter Salem. Islam was there in the life and work and writings of Omar ibn Said, Bilali, Salih Muhammad, and Abdul Rahman. But Islam may also have been present in slave rebellions, like the Stono Rebellion of 1739 in South Carolina (see Chapter 6), or in the life of Frederick Douglass, whose great-great-grandfather was an enslaved man named Baly and whose grandparents were Betsy and Isaac Bailey of Talbot County, along Maryland's Eastern Shore. There were no white Baileys in the area around Talbot, Maryland, and the name Baly or Bailey is a suggested corruption of Bilali or Belali. Islam was certainly present in the life of Noble Drew Ali, who founded the Moorish Science Temple in 1913 in Newark, New Jersey, considered a progenitor of Elijah Muhammad's Nation of Islam. Elijah Muhammad, born Elijah Poole, came from Sandersville, Georgia, not far from the coast. His father, Wali Poole, was a Baptist minister and sharecropper. *Wali* is an Arabic term or name that means "holy man" or "saint." Advertisements in Southern newspapers for runaway enslaved men include references to "Walley," nearly all of them further specifying they came from Gambia or Guinea.

Some enslaved people, like Bilali and Salih Muhammad, were able to practice Islam throughout their lives. Others, like Omar ibn Said and Abdul Rahman Ibrahima Sori, were probably wise enough to know that outwardly professing Christianity while inwardly holding on to Islam was a safer route in xenophobic America. But most enslaved men and women lacked the strength and training and luck of the few whose lives we have examined. They melded the local African spirituality they grew up with and the Islamic beliefs and practices given or forced upon them with the Christianity beaten into them at the hands of their enslavers. They fashioned a new, uniquely African American mixture that formed the underpinning of the Black church in America, a pillar of the Black Freedom Struggle.

Still, remnants hinting of an Islamic origin survive even in the Christian Black church. Some African Methodist Episcopal churches are built facing east, and churchgoers bury their dead in the same direction—both practices having shared roots in Christian and Islamic beliefs.

But by far the largest and most enduring contribution of Islam to the spirituality of Africans in America lies in the musical traditions and instruments brought with the enslaved to America. From ring shouts, to field hollers, spirituals, gospels, the blues, jazz, R & B, and hip-hop, subsequent chapters of this book delve more deeply into the Islamic roots of the music that formed the soundtrack of the Black Freedom Struggle and still deeply influences American culture today.

If nearly one in three enslaved Africans were Muslim, that

means thousands, perhaps hundreds of thousands, more than the enslaved men highlighted previously were of African and Islamic descent. It also means that the Black Freedom Struggle in America can never be understood absent the role of Islam in its founding and in the founding of America itself.

Allahu Akbar, America!

CHAPTER 4

BLACK BODIES, WHITE MEDICINE

TERROR SPREAD THROUGHOUT THE CITY, SPARKED BY A fourth wave of the virus, which had arrived by sea. One by one, crew members from a ship docked in the harbor fell ill, then passengers fell ill as well. One by one, crew members and passengers were confined. But the virus escaped quarantine to spread throughout the local population, causing the wealthy to flee the city.

No, this viral invasion was not the COVID-19 pandemic of 2020, nor the influenza pandemic of 1918. The city was Boston. The year was 1721. It was the variola virus, commonly known as smallpox. Smallpox had visited Boston in 1677, in 1690, and again in 1702. Now, in 1721, it was back.

Smallpox was an ancient, well-known enemy. Egyptians, ancient Turks, East Indians, and Persians all wrote about the disfiguring scourge of smallpox a millennium and a half before the rise of Judaism, Christianity, or Islam. But smallpox was unknown in the Western Hemisphere until European colonizers brought it with them to Hispaniola in 1507, where it decimated the local Taino population. Then Hernando Cortés's conquistadores spread the illness throughout Mesoamerica with a combined death toll, by some estimates, of more than two million Indigenous people.

The misadventures of Christopher Columbus and other explorers wiped out Indigenous American populations with smallpox, which contributed directly to the rise of the African slave trade. Left with no Native populations to enslave in their fields and mines, these early Spanish settlements turned to Africa for another source of enslaved labor, hardier and more resistant to European diseases.

This led one New England Puritan to reportedly observe, "The good hand of God favoured our beginnings in sweeping away the multitudes of the Natives by the small pox."

But an enslaved African purchased by a Boston Puritan congregation for their minister, the prominent Cotton Mather, proposed a way to prevent smallpox, which helped save citizens of Boston in 1721 and paved the way for saving the lives of countless millions ever since.

In December 1706, Mather's congregation gifted him a male slave, whom Mather named Onesimus, after the biblical figure who was most likely a slave to Philemon before his conversion to Christianity and probable rise to a bishopric in the church. Around 1716, Onesimus told Mather of an inoculation method to prevent smallpox, which had been used on him as child in Africa.

From the twelfth century onward, Ghana, from where Onesimus most likely came, had been conquered by and had extensive political and commercial contacts with the huge Islamic West African state that occupied a large portion of the Sahel. Arabic medical knowledge spoke of two practices seen throughout the Middle East and Africa: *Tishteree el Jedderi* ("buying the smallpox") and *Dak el Jedri* ("hitting the smallpox").

In "buying the smallpox," a mother with an uninfected child would visit the home of a newly infected child to haggle with the infected child's mother over the cost of a cloth tied around the infected child's arm that had come into contact with a smallpox pustule. After a price was reached, the mother would return home with the infected cloth and tie it around the arm of her uninfected child.

In "hitting the smallpox," fluid was collected from a smallpox pustule, often by means of a thorn, then scraped over the skin of the person to be inoculated. This is the method that Onesimus described to Cotton Mather, which Mather then reported, in Onesimus's words, in a letter: "People take juice of small-pox and cutty-skin and put in a drop; then by 'nd by a little sicky, sicky: then very few little things like small-pox; and nobody dy of it, and nobody have small-pox any more."

In other words, once infected material was introduced to the body of an uninfected person, it activated an immune response that provided the recipient with protection against the disease.

At first, Mather had trouble accepting Onesimus's wisdom, which he viewed as coming from an uncivilized and unconverted heathen. Mather verified the method by meeting with other

Africans and with other ministers, like Benjamin Colman, who had similar reports from slaves they owned or interviewed. From Colman, for example, Mather learned the practice Onesimus described was widespread throughout the Middle East, Far East, and Africa.

Mather, in a letter to the Royal Society, called Onesimus "a pretty Intelligent Fellow." Mather became a convert to the wisdom of inoculation—or variolation, as it is also known—which he advocated for from the pulpit and in his writings. This, in turn, drew the ire of his fellow white Bostonians, including other ministers, who resented the idea of any knowledge obtained from an "uneducated, uncivilized African." Newspapers inveighed against Mather. Ministers preached of his damnation. An explosive device was thrown through the window of his home.

All of this happened in the years before 1721, when the *Seahorse* arrived in Boston Harbor from the Caribbean. Said Mather in his diary on May 26 of that year:

> The grievous Calamity of the *Small-Pox* has now entered the Town. The Practice of conveying and suffering the *Small-pox* by *Inoculation*, has never been used in *America*, nor indeed in our Nation. But haw many Lives might be saved by it, if it were practised? I will procure a Consult of our Physicians, and lay the matter before them.

The pending smallpox epidemic presented Mather with an opportunity. He partnered with physician Zabdiel Boylston, and as the epidemic spread from those aboard the *Seahorse* to those living in the city, Boylston inoculated his son and his enslaved workers prior to inoculating other Bostonians. Only six of the 242 people inoculated using Onesimus's method died, a mortality rate of one in forty. That compared to a mortality rate of one in six for those who were not inoculated.

Mather was vindicated. Boylston was lauded a hero. A path was laid down for Edward Jenner to develop an effective vaccine against smallpox in 1796. And Onesimus was all but forgotten.

Finally, in 2016, nearly three hundred years later, readers of *Boston* magazine and experts in various fields voted Onesimus one of "The 100 Best Bostonians of All Time," at number fifty-two.

It is also worth noting that Onesimus's substantial contribution to the prevention of viral illness came in the form of homeopathic medicine. Three foundational principles of homeopathy are: (1) The human body can be stimulated to cure itself; (2) "like cures like"—the entity which causes a disease can be used to cure that disease; and (3) "minimum dosage produces maximal results." While most of homeopathy is dismissed as pseudoscience with little evidentiary effectiveness, vaccination against viral illness, long a staple of modern medicine, is one instance where homeopathic principles about disease and public health have been phenomenally successful.

While Onesimus may seem worthy of a prominent footnote in modern medical history, consider that an offshoot of this process of variolation is currently in use to deliver the influenza vaccine and is thought of as being on the cutting edge in immunization against COVID-19.

The process uses a patch of micrometer-size needles, not to

puncture the skin and inject the vaccine into muscular tissue, but to scratch the skin and deliver the vaccine to the outermost layer of skin, which contains an abundance of immune cells. Mark Prausnitz of the Georgia Institute of Technology describes the discomfort of applying a microneedle patch as similar to that of scratching the skin with Velcro.

Microneedle patches have many benefits: little pain for those averse to long needles; greater stability so that ambient temperature is not a problem and vaccines can be supplied anywhere in the world; and flexibility in delivery, as water-soluble microneedles can be made to dissolve at different rates so that one patch can handle the administration of multiple vaccines or a single vaccine that requires more than one dose days or weeks apart.

Here, the gee-whiz factor may have less to do with the technology behind microneedles and more to do with remembering that Onesimus, an enslaved African, first brought the notion of scratching the skin with a pathogen to raise immunity to the attention of American medicine more than three hundred years ago.

Onesimus was not the only enslaved person with whom the medical knowledge of traditional Africa survived the hardships and horrors of the Middle Passage. Enslaved Africans carried with them an extensive understanding of medicinal botanicals, food staples, and healing practices, which sustained them during the traumatic transatlantic passage, helped them survive centuries of brutal bondage, and found their way into early American medicine. Sometimes their European captors also took African flora and fauna with them. Sometimes Africans scoured the New World landscape for analogues of botanical medicines they knew from home. And while slaveholders might pummel the bodies of those they enslaved, they could not stamp out the knowledge of methods and practices in the minds of the enslaved.

Frequently, enslaved Africans with such medical knowledge gained the attention of their enslavers. Cesar was a slave from South Carolina whose botanical cures for poisoning and rattlesnake bites gained him his freedom, a one-time compensation of £500 (approximately $120,000 in 2021), and an annuity of £100 (approximately $24,000 in 2021) from the South Carolina Assembly in 1750.

Sometimes such medical knowledge made it more difficult for the enslaved to gain their freedom. A runaway slave named Simon was advertised for in the *Pennsylvania Gazette* in 1740 as possessing the ability to "bleed and draw teeth" and as "pretending to be a great doctor among his people." A similar ad for a fugitive slave in Charleston read, "He passes for a Doctor among people of his color and it is supposed practices in that capacity about town."

Barbers and surgeons share an interesting medical history that dates back to the Middle Ages in Europe, when barbers offered more than tonsorial services, including bloodletting, tooth extraction, and surgery. Barbers were, of course, well-known as men with skills using a blade. Joseph Ferguson, a Black barber, left Richmond, Virginia, in 1861 to study medicine in Michigan. Ferguson practiced in Michigan for many years.

And there were a number of Black men, some formerly enslaved, who rose to positions of great prominence in early American medicine prior to the Civil War, among them James

Derham, James McCune Smith, William Taylor, John V. DeGrasse, Martin R. Delany, and William Wells Brown.

⁘ ⁘ ⁘ ⁘

I had a taste of the power of traditional African medicine in my family. My grandparents used castor oil for treating a variety of conditions, from skin disorders, to gastrointestinal problems, to punishing my mother. Castor oil, with its powerful laxative effect, has long been used punitively. Belgium colonizers used it against Africans in the Congo to terrorize them into working harder. Mussolini's dreaded marshal Italo Balbo used it to humiliate opponents. Nazis used it to torture Jews. Thankfully, my mother forbade castor oil for use against her children.

The castor bean plant came to the New World from Africa in the early years of the sixteenth century. As a remedy for many ailments that afflicted Africans captured and confined in close quarters, such as the overpacked hold of a slave ship or the overcrowded room of a slave cabin, castor oil, pressed from beans produced by the plant, actually facilitated the slave trade. European enslavers used it on their captives as a powerful laxative and as a treatment for skin ailments and head lice. But then, Africans also used it, as they had for centuries, for the very same reasons.

Castor oil is emblematic of the bizarre relationship between enslavement and medical science. "Enslavement could not have existed and certainly could not have persisted," writes medical historian Harriet A. Washington, "without medical science."

On one side of this relationship, white slave traders and slaveholders relied on medical science to keep captive Africans healthy for sale, work, and breeding. While on the other side, enslaved Africans relied on medical science—retained from Africa or dispensed in the New World—to survive. But it was an unequal relationship where medical science profited and progressed often at the exposure and expense of Black lives.

Thomas Jefferson considered himself a "man of science" and a believer in the latest medical advances, such as British physician Edward Jenner's innovation that cowpox injections could provide immunity to smallpox. As president of the United States in 1801, Jefferson instituted trials of Jenner's method at his Monticello estate. On three occasions, Jefferson obtained shipments of cowpox material from Dr. Benjamin Waterhouse of Rhode Island, which he then sent to Dr. Edward Gantt for testing, but the cowpox material Jefferson received was not viable.

Jefferson proposed to Waterhouse a better containerized method of shipping, and Waterhouse then sent another sample of cowpox material. Unsure of its effectiveness, Jefferson first vaccinated fifty enslaved people at Monticello, then daringly challenged their immune systems by injecting them with a live smallpox virus. Only after they showed no symptoms did Jefferson allow the vaccination of two dozen of his own family members.

Enslaved Africans were exposed and expendable at the blunt, brutal end of this relationship with medical science. Most slave ships required a doctor aboard to examine African captives during the tumultuous transatlantic passage. Routinely, these doctors palpated the necks of their captives, searching for Winterbottom's sign, a swelling of lymph nodes associated with the parasitic disease trypanosomiasis (African sleeping sickness). Those found with such swelling were then summarily thrown overboard to the sharks. Medical doctors charged a premium for such services, but slave traders recouped these fees by demanding higher prices for their healthier captives at market.

"Negro medicine," as white American doctors called the practice of attending to the enslaved, was not only profitable for doctors but, after 1807, essential for slaveholders. Britain passed the Act for the Abolition of the Slave Trade in 1807 (the Slave Trade Act of 1807), formally prohibiting the trade anywhere in the British Empire. After debate at the Constitutional Convention of 1787, the US Congress passed the Act Prohibiting the Importation of Slaves in 1807 to take effect in 1808.

The net result of these two laws was to curtail the external slave trade to America but ramp up the slave trade within America. A dwindling supply of slaves coming into the country from Africa meant that those already enslaved were more valuable.

Thomas Jefferson was more concerned with breeding slaves than having them as laborers. "I consider the labor of a breeding woman as no object," he said in a 1819 letter to Joel Yancey, "and that a child raised every two years is of more profit than the crop of the best laboring man."

"Negro medicine" thus became the lucrative basis for a form of animal husbandry applied to human beings. The compact between medical science and enslavement was clear: Keep slaves healthy so they can work more and bear children. In this way, crops and children will fetch higher profits at market.

Into this intersection of American medicine and slavery stepped a doctor whom some laud as the "father of modern gynecology," while others condemn as an American version of the Nazi "angel of death," Josef Mengele. His name was J. Marion Sims.

Sims was born in Hanging Rock, near Lancaster, South Carolina, in 1813. He attended South Carolina Medical College in the early 1830s and graduated from Jefferson Medical College in Philadelphia in 1835 as "a lackluster student who showed little ambition after receiving his medical degree."

Sims felt little conviction for medicine and wrote quite openly of his desire to pursue any profession that might make him a fortune. When he realized that "Negro medicine" held out the hope of such a fortune, he settled on work in Macon County, Alabama, as a "plantation physician" to rich slave owners.

Sims first made his mark treating neonatal tetanus (*trismus nascentium*, *tetanus neonatorum*, seven-day sickness, nine-day fits, lockjaw of infants), an often-fatal neuromuscular disease of newborns characterized by failure to thrive, convulsions, muscle spasms, and frequently death from bacteria entering a child's immunologically immature body through an unhealed umbilical stump, especially when the cord is cut with a nonsterile instrument.

But Sims blamed neonatal tetanus on the moral and intellectual inferiority of the enslaved:

> Wherever there are poverty, and filth, and laziness, or wherever the intellectual capacity is cramped, the moral

> and social feelings blunted, there will it be oftener found. Wealth, a cultivated intellect, a refined mind, an affectionate heart, are comparatively exempt from the ravages of this unmercifully fatal malady. But expose this last class to the same *physical* causes, and they become equal sufferers with the first. [Sims's emphasis.]

In some regards, Sims was correct. Unsanitary conditions and poor nutrition were causative factors, but he blamed the wrong parties. Slave owners rarely cared where the enslaved were housed as long as they were out of sight, and therefore they frequently lived on the worst tracts of plantation land. Slave quarters were built near barns or livestock pens. They were inherently unsanitary, even during childbirth. And the enslaved rarely had the benefit of proper nutrition.

Sims's medical solution to neonatal tetanus was barbaric. He operated principally on enslaved babies by exposing their undeveloped craniums, then prying apart their cranial bones with cobblers' tools in an attempt to arrest the muscle spasms. Harriet A. Washington provides some context for Sims's surgeries:

> Sims's attempt to "open" the skull was based upon a scientific myth that the bones of black infants' skulls, unlike white infants', grew together quickly, leaving the brain no space to grow and develop. This premature closing of the black skull was held to cause low intelligence and perpetual childishness in adult blacks.

If a baby died, Washington notes, Sims "castigated the sloth and ignorance of their mothers and the black midwives who attended them."

It also would be difficult to conclude that Sims had any great conviction for the health of women. "If there was anything I hated," he wrote in a half-completed autobiography, "it was investigating the organs of the female pelvis."

Yet planters needed slaves to breed, as Jefferson pointed out so clearly, and Sims realized he could help them, to his great financial reward, by specializing in complications associated with enslaved females giving birth.

To perform the vaginal examinations he clearly detested, Sims devised an examination instrument, the speculum, from a bent spoon, and an examination position, the Sims' position, in which the patient lies on her side with her lower arm behind her back and her thighs flexed, the upper right thigh more so than the lower left one.

He had a steady stream of patients to examine and experiment on among the enslaved women given to him by willing plantation owners.

Using enslaved Black men and women for medical research was widely accepted in the antebellum South. In 1831, a year or so before Sims studied there, a South Carolina Medical College prospectus advertised:

> Some advantages of a *peculiar* character are connected with this Institution, which it may be proper to point

> out. No place in the United States offers as great opportunities for the acquisition of anatomical knowledge, SUBJECTS BEING OBTAINED FROM AMONG THE COLORED POPULATION IN SUFFICIENT NUMBER FOR EVERY PURPOSE, AND PROPER DISSECTIONS CARRIED ON WITHOUT OFFENDING ANY INDIVIDUALS IN THE COMMUNITY!! [Capitalization in the original.]

The college also touted its ability to improve the dissection skills of students:

> . . . since each can have as many human bodies as he pleases to experiment upon—and as to the fathers, mothers, husbands, wives, brothers, and sisters, of those whom they cut to pieces from day to day, why, they are not "individuals in the community," but "property," and however *their* feelings may be tortured, the "public opinion" of slaveholders is entirely too "chivalrous" to degrade itself by caring for them! [Italicization in the original.]

And from where were the cadavers for these dissections obtained? From exhuming Black bodies from graves without permission. This brazen dehumanization of Black bodies, both alive and dead, gave rise to a ghoulish mythology among antebellum enslaved Black communities and postbellum freed ones of the "night doctors." Fused with the post–Civil War terror of Black Codes, Jim Crow laws, and the Ku Klux Klan, night doctors were also known as night witches, Ku Klux doctors, night riders, student doctors, bottle men (for the camphor or ether supposedly used to disable victims), and needle men (for the syringes with which victims were killed).

Experimenting on enslaved females given to him willingly by slaveholders, J. Marion Sims would have been properly called a night doctor.

Many of the enslaved women given to Sims had a condition known as vesicovaginal fistula (VVF), in which an opening develops between the bladder and the vaginal wall, allowing for continuous and unremitting urinary incontinence. Such fistulae are often the result of pregnancy, when a woman's bladder, cervix, and vagina are pinched between her pelvis and her child's skull. Blood flow to the trapped tissue is cut off. The tissue dies and the dead cells slough off, leaving an opening that did not exist before. Symptoms of VVF include incontinence, depression, social isolation, and infertility. For slave owners, the principal symptom of VVF was less revenue from selling the offspring of slaves.

Sims and his wife, Theresa, owned slaves. From 1845 to 1849 in Montgomery, Alabama, he performed experimental surgeries on Black women with fistulae in a hospital he built behind his office. In at least one case, when he could not convince a slave owner to consign a female slave with a fistula to him, Sims purchased the slave outright "expressly for the purpose of experimentation."

In his surgical notes, Sims named three enslaved women, Anarcha, Betsy, and Lucy, though he actually experimented on many more. All surgeries were done without the benefit of anesthesia, which Sims claimed he knew little about and was too new during the years of his surgical experimentation. Besides, it was a common belief among medical doctor then—and still is now—that Black people do not feel as much pain as white people. Sims did administer opium to his patients post-surgery, though some reports suggest they then became addicted, which helped Sims keep them as experimental subjects.

Sims refused to heed the American Medical Association's Code of Medical Ethics and the counsel of lawyers advising him to suspend his experimentation. He operated on Anarcha thirty times before declaring her fistula repair a success. For his work on fistula repair and other vaginal surgeries, Sims was one of the most revered surgeons of the late nineteenth century. During the Civil War, he moved to Europe, where by most accounts he worked for the Confederacy as a spy. After the Civil War, he moved to New York City, where he continued to practice gynecological surgery until his death in 1883.

A statue of Sims, standing nearly nine feet tall, was cast in bronze by the German sculptor Ferdinand Freiherr von Miller and first erected in New York City's Bryant Park in 1894 behind the main branch of the New York Public Library. Subway construction forced the moving of the statue to Central Park in 1934, where it stood for nearly eighty-five years near the New York Academy of Medicines. Protests against Sims's experimentation on powerless, enslaved Black women caused New York City to move the statue in 2018 from Central Park to the Green-Wood Cemetery in Brooklyn, where Sims is buried.

So, was Sims a Satan or a Savior?

Perhaps the better question is, How does a society give rise to medical professionals like J. Marion Sims? We cannot simply say that Sims was a man of his times and that those times were racist but behind us. A 2016 study reported in the *Proceedings of the National Academy of Sciences* showed that 40 percent of first- and second-year medical students believed patently false notions such as "Black people's nerve endings are less sensitive than white people's," "Black people's skin is thicker than white people's," and "Black people's blood coagulates more quickly than white people's." These are the same outdated, absurd claims that allowed Sims to believe he was doing nothing wrong by performing experimental surgery without the benefit of anesthesia on enslaved Black women.

The medical racism of Sims's day is still very much alive in doctors today.

The Tuskegee Syphilis Study monitored the natural course of the disease in untreated Black men from 1932 to 1972. It was conducted by the US Public Health Service (headed by the US Surgeon General) and by the Centers for Disease Control and Prevention. How was this any different from the experimentation engaged in by Sims?

Henrietta Lacks succumbed to cancer, but her cells were harvested by researchers at Johns Hopkins University without her consent or knowledge, and they continue to live on as the source of the HeLa cell line, one of the most important cell lines in medical research. How was this any different from the night doctors of Sims's era who treated enslaved Blacks not as human beings but as property, using them for medical study and experimentation without a thought?

It is not surprising, then, that today Black Americans have a deep, inbred distrust of American medicine with its horrific history of partnering with the worst racist inclinations of society to treat their bodies as if they were less than human, to be used and experimented on at will.

J. Marion Sims was problematic, but he was not **the** problem. The problem was, and still is, an American medical system that Black lives and bodies helped to create, a medical system that has used Black men and women in the worst way—as human guinea pigs—while denying them the care, treatment, and respect human beings deserve.

Even as the COVID-19 pandemic threatened the world, the idea of night doctors is still with us, only now built in to medical technology. Pulse oximeters, a primary instrument used to measure oxygen levels in the blood through the skin, do not read correctly for people with dark skin, which had major implications for treating COVID-19 in an already vulnerable population. The authors of one large-scale study conducted at the University of Michigan Medical School concluded that Black patients had nearly three times more incidents of "occult hypoxemia" than white patients and that pulse oximetry to triage patients, especially during the COVID-19 pandemic, placed Black patients at greater risk.

A subsequent letter to the *New England Journal of Medicine* is reminiscent of those who excused the work of men like J. Marion Sims. Thomas Whitehead-Clarke, the British medical doctor who authored that letter, argued, "Medical devices such as pulse oximeters are blind to color and cannot exhibit such a bias. It is worrisome that the study findings have been disseminated across social media as proof of 'structural racism in health care.'"

And therein lies the problem. Dr. Whitehead-Clarke is right: Pulse oximeters are color-blind, and they cannot exhibit bias. But pulse oximeters are designed and constructed by other human beings who are not color-blind and who do exhibit racial bias. Software is written to control how the instruments read oxygen levels through the skin. Those instruments and that software are then tested on subjects. If the end result is a pulse oximeter that does not read dark skin well, then the makers of the instrument have not designed and tested it on a wide-enough cross section of people with different skin colors.

It was a monumental error of commission for Cotton Mather, Zabdiel Boylston, Thomas Jefferson, Edward Gantt, J. Marion Sims, the US Public Health Service, the Centers for Disease Control and Prevention, Johns Hopkins University, and all those doctors and scientists who advanced medical science through freely experimenting on Black bodies. For pulse oximetry, the problem is omission—that Black bodies are not included in medical testing. But in either case, the problems point to underlying structural racism in health care.

Night witches still fly, carrying with them the bones of Black people for unsanctioned experimentation and study. On May 13, 1985, Philadelphia Mayor Wilson Goode ordered police to bomb a building that housed MOVE, a Black nationalist group. A police officer in a helicopter dropped an explosive device that leveled an entire city block, killing six MOVE members and their five children, ages seven to fourteen. Bones belonging to one or possibly two of those children came under the control of a University of Pennsylvania privately hired consultant, anthropologist Alan Mann, after he consulted with the city's medical examiner in an attempt to identify the bone fragments. When Mann transferred to Princeton University, he took the bones with him.

Astonishingly, the bones became part of an online course called "Real Bones: Adventures in Forensic Anthropology" taught by Janet Monge, an adjunct professor in anthropology at the University of Pennsylvania, and a visiting professor at Princeton.

Monge's course, which enrolled nearly five thousand students, used the bones of these murdered children, which she described in great detail. For her part, Janet Monge has disputed what occurred during this course. She has filed legal proceedings challenging the media's reporting on her course, which, at the time of this writing, remain ongoing in the courts.

In an effort at damage control, the universities involved apologized for their handling of these remains. The Philadelphia City Council had already apologized in 2020 for the bombing of the MOVE complex. Still, it is hard not to hear in this story words similar to those reported earlier from the prospectus of the South Carolina Medical College in 1831: These children were not "INDIVIDUALS IN THE COMMUNITY," but property.

Black bodies, often at their own expense, saved white lives. Voices and figures from the African American past lie hidden beneath advances in medicine and health care, even as today those same advances are not equitably distributed among the very people who made them possible. The yawning health gap between Black and white Americans, in terms of both treatments and outcomes, must be closed, and truth and reconciliation are needed as part of that process.

Truth and reconciliation in medicine have already begun. In 2023, the estate of Henrietta Lacks settled a lawsuit against Thermo Fisher Scientific for decades of making profits from using her cells for scientific research. But this settlement is only a small first step in what will ultimately be a long, arduous journey.

Penn Museum, an archaeological and anthropological museum that is part of the University of Pennsylvania, returned the remains of one MOVE child to her family in 2021, but then announced in 2024 that it had discovered additional remains of MOVE members in its holdings after denying for years that it held any further such remains. Still left unexplained are how these remains had been treated by university and museum staff.

While the movement of Sims's statute from Central Park was a good first step, much more needs to be done to reverse the long history of medical racism that gave rise to his experiments in the first place and continues in the form of misperceptions about and mistreatments of Black people today.

The truth-and-reconciliation process implies there can be no reconciliation without first revealing the truth, however inconvenient or uncomfortable. Onesimus's role in the history of vaccine science has been little revealed, Jefferson's use of the enslaved people he owned as human guinea pigs even less so. The dead speak to us from beyond the grave as Henrietta Lacks's cell line so clearly demonstrates. But only the living can listen to these buried voices and act upon their messages so that the terrible mistakes of the past will not proliferate into the future.

CHAPTER 5

WE KNOWED WHAT WAS GOIN' ON

IT TOOK TWO AND A HALF YEARS FOR THE GOOD NEWS OF freedom to reach the last enslaved men and women in Texas. On June 19, 1865, US Major General George Granger informed the formerly enslaved that, based on Lincoln's Emancipation Proclamation, all enslaved men and women were now free, and that included them, right there in Galveston and throughout the state of Texas. A time of jubilation ensued as the formerly enslaved celebrated their freedom. The name of that day became the name of the celebration and eventually the name of a US national holiday: Juneteenth. Glory, Alleluia!

What a wonderful day that first Juneteenth must have been. Fetters gone. Shackles removed. Whips silenced. Uninformed formerly enslaved men and women reveling in their newly found freedom. But there's a problem with this idyllic picture of Juneteenth—most of the above events never happened, even though they are taken as unquestioned truth by Americans Black and white. General Granger was not in Texas to inform uninformed Black people of their freedom. Lincoln's Emancipation Proclamation did not free all enslaved men and women in the US. We have simply come to accept a number of lies about Juneteenth because they fit the convenient truths we would like to believe about the day.

⁂ ⁂ ⁂ ⁂

"Is you a white man, or is you a Black man?" Felix Haywood asked.

"I'm Black," Fred Dibble said. "Blacker than you are."

The blind eyes of the ninety-two-year-old Haywood twinkled. "No, you ain't." He chuckled. "I knewed you was white man when you comes up the path and speaks. I just always asks that question for fun. It makes white men a little insulted when you don't know they is white."

On July 6, 1937, Dibble, a writer for the WPA, interviewed Haywood, a formerly enslaved Texan. Haywood dressed in overalls, with white hair and a white mustache standing in sharp contrast to his dark skin. From the steps of a run-down wooden shack in San Antonio, a hand-hewn walking stick at his side, the tall, lanky Texan spoke about being enslaved and about the end of the Civil War.

"It's a funny thing how folks always want to know about the war," Haywood said. "The war weren't so great as folks suppose. Sometimes you didn't knowed it was goin' on. It was the ending of it that made the difference. That's when we all wakes up that somethin' had happened. Oh, we knowed what was goin' on in it all the time, 'cause old man Gudlow went to the post office every day and we knowed. We had papers in them days jus' like now."

Almost a century ago, a blind, formerly enslaved man exposed a central canard about slavery in Texas, the end of the Civil War, and the holiday we know today as Juneteenth. The falsehood is that formerly enslaved Texans did not know they were free until Union General Granger arrived in Galveston on June 19, 1865, to deliver that news. As Felix Haywood said, "Oh, we knowed what was goin' on in it all the time."

Two thousand Union troops were in Texas, not to deliver the good news to formerly enslaved Black men and women that they were free, but to deliver the bad news to white Texan slaveholders that they had to stand down and release those they'd continued to enslave. Much like today, in 1865 Texas was a pariah state, where Southern whites dreamed of a white supremacist homeland.

In what should be called the "Second Slavery Trail of Tears," during the Civil War, white slaveholders across the South forcibly marched tens of thousands of Black men and women to Texas, attempting to keep them enslaved and out of the Union Army's hands. Slaveholders and their families frequently escaped the Union's advances with their human property. The First Slavery Trail of Tears happened in the 1830s, as the economies of Southern states shifted from tobacco to cotton, and a domestic slave trade flourished. Slave merchants sold Black men and women from tobacco states like Virginia and Maryland to slaveholders in the cotton South, then marched them to states like Louisiana and Texas.

Sir Arthur Lyon Fremantle, a British Army officer who traveled throughout the South during the Civil War, was a contemporary observer of this Second Slavery Trail of Tears.

"We met several planters on the road," Fremantle wrote in his diary, which was later published as a book, "who with their families and negroes were taking refuge in Texas after having abandoned their plantations in Louisiana on the approach of Banks [Union General Nathaniel P. Banks and his troops]. One of them had as many as sixty slaves with him of all ages and sizes."

Estimates of the number of enslaved forced to march this Second Slavery Trail of Tears range from fifty thousand to one hundred fifty thousand. Even after Robert E. Lee's surrender to Ulysses S. Grant at Appomattox on April 9, 1865, Texas Governor Pendleton Murrah refused to surrender the state, instead fleeing to Mexico and leaving control of the state government, and the eventual surrender, to Lieutenant Governor Fletcher Stockdale and Confederate Lieutenant General Edmund Kirby. Murrah succumbed to asthma shortly after fleeing.

How ironic it was that he fled across the Rio Grande, where many enslaved Black Texans also stole away to freedom.

"There wasn't no reason to run up North," said Felix Haywood. "All we had to do was to walk, but walk South and we'd be free as soon as we crossed the Rio Grande. In Mexico you could be free. They didn't care what color you was, Black, white, yellow or blue. Hundreds of slaves did go to Mexico and got on all right. We would hear about them and how they was goin' to be Mexicans. They brought up their children to speak only Mexican."

While many know of the Underground Railroad leading enslaved people to freedom in Canada, few know of what was called the southbound Underground Railroad. In the years before and during the Civil War, somewhere between ten thousand and thirty thousand enslaved people crossed over the southern US border into Mexico.

Mexico opened its northern frontier state of Coahuila y Tejas (from which Texas gets its name) to white American settlers in 1821 after winning its independence from Spain. These settlers sought to establish Southern-style cotton plantations in East Texas and brought with them enslaved Black men and women, thus setting up a conflict with the Mexican government, which promoted universal equality and outlawed the importation of enslaved people in 1824. White settlers responded by either ignoring Mexican law or, in a throwback to early American colonial times, imposing contracts of lifetime indentured servitude on the people they enslaved. Mexico countered by limiting indentured servitude contracts to ten years and, in a law known as the "free womb" law, guaranteeing freedom to the children of slaves.

White settlers revolted, resulting in the Texas Revolution, in which they fought for independence from Mexico. Jim Bowie, Davy Crockett, "Remember the Alamo"—these men, this slogan, and the seesaw contest between the forces of Mexican General Santa Anna and Texan troops under the control of Sam Houston were key features of the Texas Revolution, fought in large part over the issue of slavery.

Ultimately, Houston's forces prevailed at the Battle of San Jacinto in April 1836. Texas thus secured its freedom from Mexico, enshrined slavery in its constitution, and joined the United States in 1845 as a slave state. In 1849, the Mexican Congress ruled that simply by setting foot on its national territory an enslaved person would become free, and that news spread quickly throughout the United States.

While enslaved men and women sought freedom south of the border, slave hunters also sought them there, in violation of Mexican sovereignty. For years, American diplomats unsuccessfully pressured Mexico to sign an extradition treaty guaranteeing a return of runaways to their enslavers, much as Northern states had such agreements in place with Southern states.

Unlike Harriet Tubman and the northbound Underground Railroad, there were no organized conductors or stations, but some Texans, like Nathaniel Jackson, did aid runaways. Jackson, originally from Alabama, married a woman he once enslaved, then moved to Texas with her.

"The runaways knew they could get help here," said Diana Cardenas, great-great-great-granddaughter of Jackson. "Food, clothing, and work if they wanted it. Nathaniel was a nice, generous, courageous man, a humanitarian. He would cross them into Mexico in boats."

The Nueces Strip was the most treacherous portion of the southbound Underground Railroad. It was one hundred to one hundred fifty miles of parched, thorny brush country between the Nueces River and the Rio Grande, with little food or water, few human settlements, and an infestation of rattlesnakes. With the chances of enslaved men and women escaping to Mexico so great, there actually was no slavery in the Nueces Strip. If you were Black and found there, it was assumed you were a runaway. Slave catchers, military patrols, Native Americans, and Texas Rangers patrolled the Nueces Strip and were likely to capture or kill any Black person they found there.

With Texas's reputation for independence and a disdain for the government in Washington, DC, it's no wonder that even after Appomattox, white slaveholders in Texas kept Black men and women enslaved, and killed many trying to escape to freedom. So when Granger read General Order No. 3 to the public on Galveston Island on June 19, 1865, he was delivering a message not so much to enslaved men and women but to their enslavers, and he was backing up that message with the force of the Union Army.

"The people of Texas are informed that, in accordance with a proclamation from the Executive of the United States, *all slaves* are free," newspaper accounts reported Granger saying, emphasizing the word "all" and referring to the Emancipation Proclamation.

Only the Emancipation Proclamation, which went into effect two and a half years before Granger read General Order No. 3 in Galveston, did not free *all* slaves. That, too, is a popular misconception. A close reading of the Emancipation Proclamation reveals it only freed slaves in Confederate states: those states at war with the Union, which never recognized Lincoln's authority to begin with.

The Emancipation Proclamation was largely a war tactic meant to intimidate the South, much as Dunmore's Proclamation—the proclamation issued on November 7, 1775, by John Murray, the Fourth Earl of Dunmore and royal governor of the Virginia colony, that declared freedom to all slaves who left their owners and aligned with the British royal forces—was meant to intimidate the colonists. This enraged slave owners like Jefferson, hence his words in an early draft of the Declaration of Independence about King George III "now exciting those very people to rise in arms among us." Dunmore was soon after forced from his post, and he took three hundred former slaves with him.

After the Emancipation Proclamation, slavery was illegal in Mississippi but permitted in Massachusetts. New Jersey did not sign the Thirteenth Amendment to the Constitution abolishing slavery until January 23, 1866. Mississippi did not sign it until 2013.

British newspapers had been quick to point out the hypocrisy. In the fall of 1863, the *London Spectator* decried the Emancipation Proclamation as "half consciously pressing along a road which ends in emancipation," then continued that the "principle asserted is not that a human being cannot justly own another but that he cannot own him unless he is loyal to the United States."

Lincoln himself was ambivalent about ending slavery. His overarching concern was preserving the Union at any cost. In

1862, he said as much in response to abolitionist and editor of the *New-York Tribune* Horace Greeley:

> If there be those who would not save the Union, unless they could at the same time save slavery, I do not agree with them. If there be those who would not save the Union unless they could at the same time destroy slavery, I do not agree with them. If I could save the Union without freeing any slave I would do it, and if I could save it by freeing all the slaves I would do it; and if I could save it by freeing some and leaving others alone I would also do that. What I do about slavery, and the colored race, I do because I believe it helps to save the Union; and what I forbear, I forbear because I do not believe it would help to save the Union.

Granger was in Galveston to enforce the Emancipation Proclamation, Lincoln's "psyops" measure against the Confederacy.

Years later, WPA writer Fred Dibble asked Felix Haywood about this moment.

"Everybody went wild," Haywood said. "We all felt like heroes and nobody had made us that way but ourselves. We was free. Just like that, we was free."

But freedom came with a high price. Lincoln had no plan for what to do with the four to five million enslaved people the Emancipation set free. All he said was "I hereby enjoin upon the people so declared to be free to abstain from all violence, unless in necessary self-defence; and I recommend to them that, in all cases when allowed, they labor faithfully for reasonable wages."

Eschewing violence? Working for reasonable wages? That's not a plan; that's a prayer.

Surprisingly, the Confederacy actually did have a plan for what to do if they prevailed. Out of desperation, in March 1865, the Confederate States Congress authorized ardent slaveholder President Jefferson Davis to recruit as many as three hundred thousand slaves for the Confederate forces. No more than 25 percent of male slaves between the ages of eighteen and forty-five were to be drawn from any given state. Called Black Confederates, they trained in segregated regiments, though the war was over before they ever saw battle. Many more enslaved men and women populated the Confederate ranks, bound to white officers as cooks and on the staff of field hospitals.

Confederate Secretary of State Judah Benjamin drew criticism from slaveholders for laying out what would happen to Black Confederates after the South won its independence. They would be manumitted from slavery, and then:

> The next step will then be that the States, each for itself, shall act upon the question of the proper status of the families of the men so manumitted. Cautious legislation providing for their ultimate emancipation after an intermediate state of serfage or peonage would soon find advocates in different States. We might then be able, while vindicating our faith in the doctrine that the negro is an inferior race and unfitted for social or political equality with the white man, yet so modify and ameliorate the existing condition of that inferior race by providing for

> it certain rights of property, a certain degree of personal liberty, and legal protection for the marital and parental relations, as to relieve our institutions from much that is not only unjust and impolitic in itself, but calculated to draw down upon us the odium and reprobation of civilized man.

The South's plan can be summed up in a few words: maintain white supremacy and slavery under the guise of serfage and peonage. But the North won the war. The emancipation of slaves did take place.

"We knewed freedom was on us," Felix Haywood said. "But we didn't know what was to come with it."

Haywood's uncertainty lingered over the nation.

Haywood had little knowledge of those working to resolve his uncertainty affirmatively. In particular, an eloquent former slave, a principled New England abolitionist, a stalwart senator from Massachusetts, and a rough-and-tumble congressman from Pennsylvania—the Republican Gang of Four, as they were known—led the charge for what some called a Second American Revolution that radically refashioned the nation after the Civil War.

That's right, the Republican Gang of Four. To better understand the tumultuous times Felix Haywood lived through, one must come to terms with Republicans as the progressive party and Democrats as the conservative party. Just the opposite of modern-day Republicans and Democrats. It's amusing when a Republican politician today describes their roots as the "party of Lincoln" without the slightest understanding of the progressive agenda the party of Lincoln championed in the nineteenth century—ideas about equality and social justice that members of the party of Donald Trump would find anathema today.

While few know the name of Republican Wendell Phillips, many are heir to his legacy. Phillips, one of the "Gang of Four," was a Harvard-trained lawyer and a scion of an old American family that emigrated from England to New England in the early 1600s. Phillips left the ranks of Boston's privileged and powerful to lead a radical progressive movement in the nineteenth century that fought for abolition, then for the rights of the formerly enslaved. He had a falling-out with the better-known William Lloyd Garrison over the goals of abolition. Garrison saw no further than the emancipation of slaves. Phillips had a much grander vision for racial justice after the North's victory. "All the negro asks is justice," he demanded. "The right to vote. The right to an education. And, most of all, the right to land."

Phillips wanted to take land from vanquished slave owners and redistribute that land wealth to poor Blacks and poor whites. "Confiscation is mere, naked justice to the former slave," he said. "Who brought the land into cultivation? Whose sweat and toil are mixed with it forever? Who cleared those forests? Who made those roads? Whose hand reared those houses? Whose wages are invested in those warehouses and towns? Of course, the Negro's. Why should he not have a share of the inheritance?"

Phillips understood the debt America owed to those it had enslaved, and he wanted to repay that debt. He wanted Black folks to share in the power and wealth their labor had created. One hundred years later, one hears a similar urgency in the words of Dr. Martin Luther King Jr., who spoke often of the "fierce urgency of now" and opined that "too late" is too often written over the residue of great civilizations.

"Harmony purchased at any sacrifice of the absolute need of the hour is dangerous," Phillips said one hundred years before.

At six feet tall, with a lion's mane of salt-and-pepper hair and a matching beard and mustache, Frederick Douglass was the only formerly enslaved member in the Gang of Four. The visionary of the group, Douglass was Wendell Phillips's longtime friend. Intelligent, articulate, passionately desirous of freedom for all Black men and women, Douglass spoke with words that thundered with the same intensity of purpose set in his eyes.

Abraham Lincoln approached the Civil War too tepidly, according to Douglass, who, among many others, was unimpressed by the Emancipation Proclamation. The old Union, with its appeasement of the South and tolerance for slavery, was not worth the fight.

"What business, then, have we to fight for the old Union?" Douglass asked. "We are not fighting for it. We are fighting for something incomparably better than the old Union. We are fighting for unity; unity of idea, unity of sentiment, unity of object, unity of institutions, in which there shall be no North, no South, no East, no West, no black, no white, but a solidarity of the nation, making every slave free, and every free man a voter."

One cannot help but hear in Douglass's oration similar words spoken at the Democratic National Convention in 2004: "There is not a liberal America and a conservative America—there is the United States of America. There is not a Black America and a White America and Latino America and Asian America—there's the United States of America." The speaker then was Barack Obama.

For Douglass, the work America faced through and after the Civil War was not simply "reconstruction" but "national regeneration . . . a radical revolution in all modes of thought which have flourished under the blighting slave system."

Within the 39th US Congress, Frederick Douglass and Wendell Phillips found faithful friends and powerful allies in a cadre of Radical Republicans, led by Senator Charles Sumner and Representative Thaddeus Stevens.

Tall and handsome, Sumner, like Phillips, was a Harvard-trained Boston Brahmin. Also like Phillips, Sumner was principled. Sumner even sounded much like Phillips, a century ahead of his time, when he declared there was no place for anything but equality in America: "It is not enough to provide separate accommodations for colored citizens, even if in all respects as good as those of other persons. Equality is not found in any pretended equivalent, but only in equality; in other words, there must be no discrimination on account of color."

Nearly seventy years old at the start of the Civil War, Thaddeus "Thad" Stevens, a Republican representative from Pennsylvania, was a driving force of this Gang of Four. Given chairmanship of the powerful House Ways and Means Committee, Stevens had a vision of the country after the Civil War that was at odds with those of presidents Lincoln and Johnson. Not surprisingly, he placed his faith in the power of the purse—economics. That meant, after the war, the confiscation and redistribution of land to newly freed Black men and women. Stevens brought the Fourteenth Amendment to the House floor for a vote. The Amendment granted all citizens of the United States, including former slaves, "equal protection of the laws." Stevens exhorted his fellow House members to pass it.

> In my judgment, we shall not approach the measure of justice until we have given every adult freedman a homestead on the land where he was born and toiled and suffered. Forty acres of land and a hut would be more valuable to him than the immediate right to vote. Unless we give them this we shall receive the censure of mankind and the curse of Heaven.

The April 3, 1861, edition of *The New York Times* ran a piece on the inside masthead page that was critical of Lincoln's indecisiveness with regard to the events unfolding at Fort Sumter. But appearing next to it, two columns over, was a story about emancipation and reparations in Russia. If the story on Lincoln caught the attention of the Gang of Four, the article on Russia must have as well.

In his recent emancipation of serfs, Russian Czar Alexander II had also granted them houses and land. Why not in America? Alexander's actions mirrored the vision the Gang of Four had for the formerly enslaved at the conclusion of the Civil War as part of reconstructing America. Andrew Johnson, congressional

Democrats, and the former Confederate states branded this vision "Radical Reconstruction" and were staunchly opposed.

"Is this great conquest to be in vain?" Stevens asked rhetorically on September 6, 1865, in a speech in Pennsylvania, referring to the Union's victory in the Civil War. "That will depend upon the virtue and intelligence of the next Congress. To Congress alone belongs the power of Reconstruction—of giving law to the vanquished," he answered.

Never one to shy away from strong-arming Congress, he hit politicians where it hurt: their power. Did the gentlemen realize that the Emancipation Proclamation now nullified the three-fifths clause of the Constitution? Did they really want Southern states to return to the Union more powerful than before, with a larger voting block? Was this to be the reward for secession? If the answers were no, then the gentlemen must join with him in passing the Freedmen's Bureau Act and the first-ever Civil Rights Act, which extended citizenship and the vote to Black Americans.

Against this backdrop of Radical Republican ideas about national reconstruction and regeneration, Union General William T. Sherman and Secretary of War Edwin M. Stanton seemed to recognize that President Lincoln needed a plan to deal with the four to five million men and women who would be freed by the Emancipation Proclamation if the Union prevailed in the war.

On the evening of January 12, 1865, Sherman and Stanton met with a group of Black Baptist and Methodist ministers at Sherman's second-floor headquarters in a private mansion bordering a lush tropical square in Savannah, Georgia. Major General Edward Davis Townsend, one of Lincoln's military advisors, took extensive notes of the meeting, which began at eight o'clock.

Sixty-seven-year-old Reverend Garrison Frazier had been selected to speak for the group. Born in North Carolina, Frazier had been enslaved until 1857, when he bought his freedom and his wife's for one thousand dollars in silver and gold. An ordained Baptist minister for thirty-five years, Frazier, an elder spokesman of America's nascent African American community, had the full support of the men in this room.

Sherman questioned Frazier's understanding of Lincoln's actions and the wartime goals of the United States before getting around to the most urgent matter—the need for a plan.

"State in what manner you think you can take care of yourselves, and how can you best assist the Government in maintaining your freedom?" Sherman asked.

"The way we can best take care of ourselves is to have land," said Frazier, "and turn in and it by our labor—that is, by the labor of the women, and children, and old men—and we can soon maintain ourselves and have something to spare; and to assist the Government the young men should enlist in the service of the Government, and serve in such manner as they may be wanted . . . We want to be placed on land until we are able to buy it and make it our own."

"State in what manner you would rather live, whether scattered among the whites or in colonies by yourselves?" asked Sherman.

"I would prefer to live by ourselves, for there is a prejudice against us in the South that will take years to get over, but I do not know that I can answer for my brethren."

To a man, every minister gathered agreed.

Two years after issuing the Emancipation Proclamation, Lincoln finally had the makings of a plan. Four days after this meeting, from the self-expressed desires of Black men long held in bondage, General Sherman issued Special Field Order No. 15, accepted by Abraham Lincoln and otherwise known as "forty acres and a mule." Mules were not actually in Sherman's original order. He later requisitioned the US Army to lend them to newly freed Black landholders.

The scope of Special Field Order No. 15 was astounding: Distribute four hundred thousand acres of prime coastlands stretching from Charleston to the St. Johns River in Florida and extending some thirty miles inland to newly emancipated slaves. The acreage, which formerly belonged to Southern white slaveholders, was among the most agriculturally productive in the South. Within this area, African Americans would be allowed to organize and govern their own communities.

Two hundred fifty years after arriving in bondage to America's shores. Two hundred fifty years after enduring the brutality, indignity, and inhumanity of slavery. Two hundred fifty years after being cast adrift on a sea of prejudice and intolerance. After these long two hundred fifty years, America's citizens of color were finally receiving their fair due. Special Field Order No. 15 was nothing less than an order for reparations for slavery. For the first time in its history, America, it seemed, had not turned away from its dark past but instead confronted the issue of race head-on and then taken "the road not taken" before.

The federal government got to work!

Brigadier General Rufus Saxton, a Massachusetts native and West Point graduate, immediately began processing thousands of requests by Black families for land. By June 1865, forty thousand Black Americans had settled on the first four hundred thousand acres of land, called derisively by Sherman's critics "Sherman's Reservation." Six weeks before Lincoln's assassination, Congress passed the first Freedmen's Bureau Act of 1865, placing General Oliver O. Howard (for whom Howard University is named) in charge of land grants. Saxton ordered Howard to continue the land redistribution program, and another five hundred thousand acres of land were under consideration to be taken from slaveholders and redistributed to slaves. Nearly one million acres of land, one million acres of wealth, were up for redistribution in this way.

"We thought we was goin' to be richer than the white folks," Felix Haywood said, "'cause we was stronger and knowed how to work, and the whites didn't and they didn't have us to work for them anymore. But it didn't turn out that way. We soon found out that freedom could make folks proud but it didn't make 'em rich." Special Field Order No. 15 seemed determined to do both: make the formerly enslaved proud and redistribute wealth, which would ultimately make them rich.

"Damn the negroes," President Andrew Johnson said. "I am fighting these traitorous aristocrats, their masters."

And what a fight Johnson put up! After assuming the presidency upon the assassination of Abraham Lincoln on April 15, 1865, Johnson issued fourteen thousand pardons to wealthy Southern slaveholders, forgiving them of any crimes against the United States, including a sweeping pardon to Confederate President Jefferson Davis. Within seven weeks of taking office, coinciding almost exactly with the first Juneteenth, Johnson rescinded Special Field Order No. 15, ordering any confiscated lands redistributed to the formerly enslaved to be returned to their original white owners. Andrew Johnson was not fighting against "traitorous aristocrats"; he was fighting for them.

Saxton now commanded Howard to about-face. As head of the Freedmen's Bureau, Howard had already overseen the redistribution of land to thousands of the formerly enslaved. Crops had been planted. Schools and churches had been opened. Votes had been cast for leaders. Now Howard was in South Carolina to deliver the news from Washington to ex-slaves on Edisto Island that they would be evicted and their land returned to former slave owners. An old Gullah woman in the back of the crowd that day listened intently. As the general struggled for words, she found her voice in the Sea Islands' version of a spiritual:

Nobody knows de trouble I've had,
Nobody knows but Jesus,
Nobody knows de trouble I've had,
(Sing) Glory hallelu!
What makes ole Satan hate me so?

> Because he got me once and he let me go.
> Nobody knows de trouble I've had . . .

Howard broke down and wept.

Not long after the rescission of Special Field Order No. 15, Representative John Winslow Chanler of New York, one of Johnson's minions in the House of Representatives, read into the Congressional Record a letter from General Sherman to President Johnson, in which Sherman said, in part:

> I knew of course we could not convey title and merely provided possessory titles, to be good as long as War and our Military Power lasted. I merely aimed to make provision for the Negroes who were absolutely dependent upon us, leaving the value of their possessions to be determined by after events or legislation.

Lincoln's plan, it turned out, was no plan at all. Like the Emancipation Proclamation itself, Special Field Order No. 15 was a wartime psyops maneuver, this one meant to appease the formerly enslaved. With Special Field Order No. 15 rescinded, the formerly enslaved were forced to work as sharecroppers and tenant farmers—in other words, reduced to serfage and peonage. One could not be faulted for believing that the South lost the war but won the peace, at least with regard to the welfare and status of the formerly enslaved.

All of which begs the question of why Juneteenth is a national holiday.

General Granger was in Texas to tell white enslavers to stop enslaving Blacks, while back in Washington, President Andrew Johnson was rescinding the only plan for reparations for slavery ever put forward by the federal government, thus firmly establishing and enshrining a huge wealth gap between Blacks and whites in this country. Aren't both questionable acts to commemorate?

Still, there is something commemorable that could come from the truth of that first Juneteenth: a national plan for reparations for slavery. Reparations is a contemporary yet contentious issue. But the Republican Party, the party of Lincoln, which would certainly line up against reparations now, can truthfully claim ownership of the idea. Famed General William Tecumseh Sherman devised the plan for Lincoln. Special Field Order No. 15 can be resurrected and modified for a modern age. A map of the nine hundred thousand acres originally set aside to be allocated to the formerly enslaved still exists. That land should not be confiscated from its present owners; instead, the value of that land should be computed, and that value should be the basis of the dollar amount for reparations. The trillions of dollars that land is worth today would significantly close the racial wealth gap in America.

How that dollar amount is distributed should be up for negotiation. Housing grants. Education grants. Business grants. Outright payments. Tax credits. A mixture of the above. Along with this, whoever is president at the time of this national reparations for slavery act should issue a broad, unequivocal national apology.

America has done this before. At the start of World War II,

Democratic icon President Franklin Delano Roosevelt issued Executive Order No. 9066, which took land and property away from Japanese Americans, while placing these citizens en masse in internment camps. These loyal Americans were declared enemies of the United States. In 1988, Congress passed the Civil Liberties Act of 1988, which included a financial payment to Japanese Americans interred during the war. Republican icon President Ronald Reagan signed the bill into law, and issued along with it an unequivocal blanket apology for Japanese American internment.

In memory of Felix Haywood, who said, "We knewed freedom was on us. But we didn't know what was to come with it," America could then proudly say to the descendants of the formerly enslaved, "This is what was to come with freedom." Now, that would be a day worthy of commemoration as a national holiday.

CHAPTER 6

MUSIC, MYTH, AND STONO

"WHY I SING THE BLUES," WRITTEN BY B. B. KING AND MUSIC promoter Dave Clark, is a historical tour de force of the political, cultural, social, and economic struggles of Black men and women in America. Reminding us that the song's narrator has been around a long time is simply to point out that this way of embracing history is different, reminiscent of Native American lore where the "long body" represents the history of an individual uniquely understood through the history of a group, and the history of a group is more than the sum of the history of single individuals. Rather, it is a collective history of the group understood as a single individual.

King sings of how the blues first began in Africa, from where he was brought over to America on a ship. In short order, each epoch of the Black struggle for freedom is given voice—from enslavement, to Jim Crow segregation, to the Great Migration north and the challenge of living in cities, to the economic wealth gap, to police brutality, to personal transformation. In a verse he sings on looking in the mirror and watching himself age, one gets the sense that B. B. (and by extension Black Americans) has the blues not just because Father Time is catching up with him but because even at the end of his life, the very issues that have given him the blues will still be present.

Moreover, "Why I Sing the Blues" points to a deep and abiding connection between song and the struggle for freedom, between music and the movement toward change, for Black Americans—from the struggle against enslavement, to resistance in the face of Jim Crow, to the push for equality within American democracy, to demands for a different kind of law enforcement, to the dictates of personal change.

From gospel, to spirituals, to R & B, to blues, to jazz, to orchestral suites, to folk music, to hip-hop, and even to country and western, nearly every genre of American music has been influenced by the Black Freedom Struggle and vice versa—that struggle has been influenced by the music that emerged from the people deeply committed to achieving freedom.

But to truly get a feeling for these many epochs, listening to the related music of the age is required. Music provides a soundtrack of the struggle for freedom.

⁘ ⁘ ⁘ ⁘

A plausible explanation for the origins of Indigenous music is that it first emerged as humans attempted to mimic and communicate with the natural world around them. Walk anywhere beyond the noise-polluted corridors of a city and you will be greeted with a symphony of sound. The fluted trills of birds. The steady hum and buzz of insects. The rat-a-tat drumbeat of a woodpecker. The staccato rasp of a squirrel. The rattle of leaves by a deer. The eerie hooting of an owl. The sonorous percussion of antlers during the rut. The laughing cluck of a raven. Now multiply these sounds tenfold and add to them the high-pitched cackling of a hyena. The deep bass roar of a lion. The trumpeting of an elephant. The clacking of the jaws and teeth of a crocodile. The shrill shrieks of monkeys. The sound of coconuts hitting the ground. The clap of thunder. The patter of rain over tree leaves and into water. And if you have ever mimicked one of these sounds—a raven's call, for example—and had the sound call back, then you know the exhilaration that derives from that deep sense of merging with nature in this way, in this use of the human voice to communicate with and imitate nature.

Communicating with nature, the theory goes, may have emerged at the same time, or even before, humans began to verbally communicate with one another. We may have sung before we spoke, vocalized before we verbalized, intoned before we informed, and hummed before we harangued. Music and language are fundamentally connected. In fact, ethnomusicologists have noted since the late 1800s that African rhythmic and tonal musical patterns match the language patterns found in a given area of Africa. So much so that "talking drums" really do "talk," in the sense that speakers of the language from which the drumbeats come can actually "understand" what the drums are saying because the beats match the rhythmic and tonal patterns of words in that language.

Myth and ritual present yet another way in which music is deeply embedded in African culture. Myth, in this context, implies more than phantasmagoric tales that are plainly falsehoods. Myths are tales constructed by African societies to reflect the many ways these societies attempt to come to terms with the realities of life: birth and death, the maturation process, the relationship of individuals to society and vice versa, the relationship of individuals and societies to the Earth and the cosmos they find themselves in—the cosmologies of inner and outer space. Rituals, then, are enactments of myths, while myths are encodings of rituals, and within traditional African societies, there are few rituals, if any, that are devoid of music and dance. Music scores myth as the soundtrack for ritual, and myth may be one of the most powerful elements of Africa that enslaved men and women brought with them. Mythology gave them strength when they needed it most.

We know for certain that Africans who were captured and transported across the Atlantic through the dreaded Middle Passage carried myths with them. Identical iconography has surfaced on both sides of the ocean, identical rituals as well. Along with the shared iconography and rituals is a shared musical tradition that animated people in Africa and throughout the African diaspora.

Some of the most powerful and enduring iconography of myth and music to survive the Middle Passage are contained in a form known in Kongolese as the *dikenga* or *yowa*. In its most basic version, the *dikenga* is simply a cross, appearing in Africa millennia before the advent of Christianity. But this cross encodes a deep cosmology that some researchers have suggested informed the Egyptian cross known as the *ankh*, which in turn,

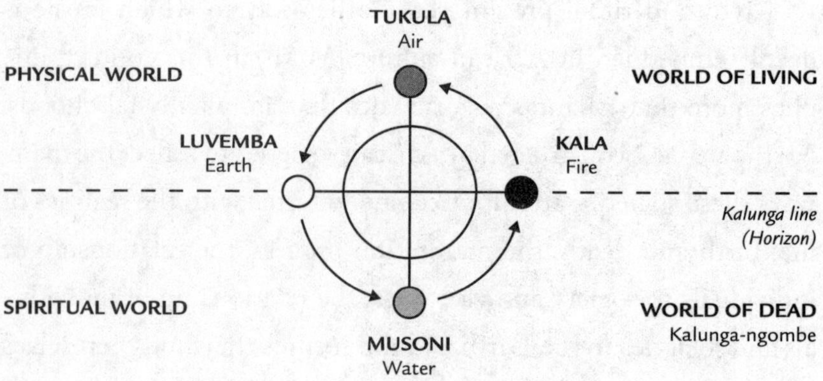

The Bakongo cosmogram: the *dikenga* or *yowa*.

through the Romans, informed the Christian version of the cross, symbolizing Jesus. Often the *dikenga* appears drawn on the ground, at the base of a pot, on a tree, on a wall, or on an altar with circles at the end of each crossarm.

The *dikenga*, in multitudinous shapes and forms and embellishments, has been found everywhere throughout the African diaspora and in North, Central, and South America, sometimes alone, sometimes fused with the iconography of other African societies. Though drawings of the *dikenga* have been found less often in North America, here a more enduring version of this cosmogram has survived embodied in human form, embedded in the bones and bodies of the enslaved. This living cosmogram first appeared on American soil as the ring shout.

In traditional African societies there exists a ritual associated with the *dikenga*, which consists of a turning or dancing around the form, often drawn on the ground, with the movements through each phase of the cosmogram directed and interpreted by the celebrant. Questions are called out by the celebrant while answers are shouted back by the participants. Clapping, body slapping, drumming, and the playing of instruments are also involved. Such counterclockwise circular rituals are known in nearly every region of Africa, particularly those from which Africans were captured for enslavement in America. Even Islam, which many of the enslaved counted as their faith, has within it a form of circular address to the sacred known as the *tawaf*, in which adherents engage in a counterclockwise circumambulation of the Kaaba, the most holy of Islamic mosques, seven times as part of their hajj, or spiritual journey to Mecca, located today in Saudi Arabia. Since there really is not much actual shouting done during a ring shout, the suggestion has been further made that "shout" comes from the Arabic *shawt*, meaning "a single run" or a one-time circumambulation of the Kaaba.

In the early years of enslavement in America, prior to the establishment of a formal Black church, enslaved men and women would gather in self-constructed buildings on plantations known as "praise houses," or in the woods, moving in a counterclockwise circle while singing, dancing, stomping, or shuffling and clapping their hands in an ecstatic, transcendent spiritual ritual called a ring shout.

With this counterclockwise circular address to the sacred found in so many African cultures, the ring shout may well have served as a unifying element for enslaved Africans in America, as scholar Sterling Stuckey suggests, from which over time emerged field hollers, work songs, freedom songs, gospels, spirituals, blues, jazz, R & B, pop, and hip-hop. Scatting, call-and-response, bending notes, syncopated beats, spiritual address, and rhythmic dance. All the elements that would eventually evolve into these various other genres of Black musical expression in America, and then move beyond Black culture to American culture in general, trace their roots to the ring shout. In recent years, the traditional ring shout has been preserved among the Gullah people of the Sea Islands off the coast of South Carolina and Georgia through performance recordings made by the Black men and women of the McIntosh County Shouters.

If music is myth, it is also memory. Tones and beats are not easily chained or beaten or aged away. Play a song from a person's youth, and often that person will be transported back to the time when they first heard that song. Along with the memories and emotions that song evokes will come also the sights and sounds and colors and other people of the song's time.

Playing music is also an act of protest, defiance, and rebellion. On most slave ships crossing the Atlantic, enslaved men and women were allowed exercise by dancing on deck, accompanied by sailors' whips but also by the beat of drums, or the clang of chains, or the clap of shackles on wooden decks, and the occasional strumming of an African string instrument purchased by a captain or crew member as a souvenir of the gruesome voyage. While the crew was entertained, the enslaved men and women aboard were unwittingly offered an opportunity to not only carry their culture forward to an uncertain and fearful future but build community as they did. Africans aboard a slave ship frequently came from different societies with different languages but from similar regions. While there are thousands of African languages, there are only a handful of major language families. And each language family is united through the sharing of similar myths, rituals, musical rhythms and beats. Music aboard a slave ship was a means by which the enslaved communicated when speaking in their native tongue was forbidden and often beaten out of them.

On May 10, 1740, the South Carolina General Assembly passed An Act for the Better Ordering and Governing of Negroes and Other Slaves in This Province, also known as the South Carolina Slave Code of 1740 or the Negro Act of 1740. While such slave codes were not unheard of in colonial America, the reasons behind the passage of this act in 1740 have a clear connection to the role Black music played in the struggle for freedom in America.

Section 36 of the law, captioned "Slave Meetings," states:

> And for that as it is absolutely necessary to the safety of this Province, that all due care be taken to restrain the wanderings and meetings of negroes and other slaves, at all times, and more especially on Saturday nights, Sundays and other holidays, and the using and carrying wooden swords, and other mischievous and dangerous weapons, or using and keeping of drums, horns, or other loud instruments, which may call together or give sign or notice to one another of their wicked designs and purposes; and that all masters, overseers and others may be enjoined diligently and care-

> fully to prevent the same, be it enacted: That it shall be lawful for all masters, overseers and other persons whomsoever, to apprehend and take up any negro or other slave that shall be found out of the plantation of his or their master or owner, at any time, especially on Saturday nights, Sundays or other holidays, not being on lawful business, and with a letter from their master or a ticket, or not having a white person with them, and the said negro or other slave or slaves correct by a moderate whipping.

Many would trace these slave codes back to the Stono Rebellion of the preceding year (which we will examine shortly), and there is no question that the ability of slaves to use music—in particular drums—as a means of communication weighed heavily in favor of the language in this bill. Yet an earlier report of a slave uprising near Charleston that featured music and dancing is seldom mentioned in connection to this bill, or the role of traditional African singing and dancing in the quest of enslaved men and women for freedom.

The July 1757 edition of the *London Magazine* printed a very short article on an event that took place twenty-seven years earlier in the British colony of Carolina, which would in 1732 be split into the colonies of Georgia and South Carolina. The magazine reported that in August 1730, enslaved people had conspired

> to affemble all together at a time to be appointed, and, at a certain place in the neighbourhood of Charles-

> Town, under pretence of a folemn dancing-bout, from whence they were to rufh all at once into the town, and make themfelves mafters of all the arms and ammunition therein, after which they were immediately to maffacre all the white men in the town, and the fpread the deftruction thro' all the plantations in the country.

Now, the key phrase in this report is a "solemn dancing-bout," from which the enslaved would then rush to take over the city, and kill their white enslavers. The term "dancing-bout" is not a simple term to understand because its current, limited use is no doubt very different from its usage in 1730. Currently, the term "dance-bout" is used in three different contexts: Ornithologists use the term to describe the dance-mating rituals of some birds. Apiarists use it to describe the flight of dancer honeybees. And occasionally it is used to describe a dancing contest (i.e., a bout). None of these current usages seems appropriate in describing a gathering of enslaved people prior to striking a blow for their freedom in 1730. More than likely, the term had another meaning in the English of 1730, when it may have been a contraction of "dancing about." The modifier "solemn" further suggests that this "dancing-bout" may have been related to an event considered serious, even sacred, to the enslaved Africans, and also in the eyes of the white Southerners and the European media writing about it. That "dancing-bout" was more than likely some form of a ring shout. In all likelihood, music attended this "dancing-bout."

While the music, and even the details, of this 1730 uprising reveal little in the way of source references other than the 1757 magazine article, the uprising of the enslaved that unfolded near the Stono River, southwest of Charleston, South Carolina, in 1739 has been well-documented and well-reported, along with the roles of drums and music in the affair.

⁘ ⁘ ⁘ ⁘

Sunday, September 9, 1739, dawned as most Sundays did in South Carolina. The esteemed gentlemen owners of the plantations and their families sat in church pews, having left behind the troubles of enslaving so many of African descent. They'd whipped their human property into a fine and subservient workforce. Hadn't they earned this right to take a few hours off to worship God for sanctioning their efforts and rewarding them with power and wealth?

Rumors circulated among these gentlemen that agents of the Spanish Crown lurked in Charles-Town, reminding the men and women they enslaved of King Philip V's revised edicts of October 1733. The first Spanish royal edict prohibited compensation for their runaways, which many rightly shrugged off because such compensation had rarely, if ever, occurred. But the second edict troubled the gentlemen more because Philip V commended the valor of their fugitives in defending Florida against the English attack of 1728 and then reiterated Spain's offer of freedom to any slave who fled British colonies for Florida after four years of service to the Crown.

After all, just the previous year, hadn't nearly a hundred slaves escaped their plantations and, making it to Florida, established themselves in the city of Fort Mose with the blessings of the Spanish Crown?

Philip V's interference with the domestic policies of colonial America stoked unease among these gentlemen of a rebellion and march to freedom by the Black men and women they owned. Rumors of conspiracy swelled. Earlier in 1739, the secretary of the governing body of the newly formed colony of Georgia, in between them and Spanish Florida, warned "that a Conspiracy was formed by the Negroes in Carolina." That plot, which William Stephens, an administrative official in Georgia, warned of, was uncovered before any actions were taken.

Outside the church but not far away, Jemmy Cato mused. Cato, an enslaved man whose African name was stripped from him and has since been lost to the passing of time, understood that Sundays gave him and his twenty-odd compatriots the best chance of striking a blow for their freedom. Cato ordered the strike, and the Stono Rebellion began.

In a late 1930s WPA interview, George Cato, Jemmy Cato's great-great grandson, relates the family's version of how the rebellion unfolded.

> Yes sah! I sho' does come from dat old stock who had de misfortune to be slaves but who decide to be men, at one and de same time, and I's right proud of it. De first Cato slave we knows 'bout, was plum willing to lay down his life for de right, as he see it. Dat is pow'ful fine for de Catoes who has come after him. My granddaddy and my daddy

tell me plenty 'bout it, while we was livin' in Orangeburg County, not far from where de fightin' took place in de long ago.

My granddaddy was a son of de son of de Stono slave commander. He say his daddy often take him over de route of de rebel slave march, dat time when dere was sho' big trouble all 'bout dat neighborhood. As it come down to me, I thinks de first Cato take a darin' chance on losin' his life, not so much for his own benefit as it was to help others. He was not lak some slaves, much 'bused by deir masters. My kinfolks not 'bused. Da[t] why, I reckons, de captain of de slaves was picked by them. Cato was teached how to read and write by his rich master.

How it all start? Dat what I ask but nobody ever tell me how 100 slaves between de Combahee and Edisto rivers come to meet in de woods not far from de Stono River on September 9, 1739. And how they elect a leader, my kinsman, Cato, and late dat day march to Stono town, break in a warehouse, kill two white men in charge, and take all de guns and ammunition they wants. But they do it. Wid dis start, they turn south and march on.

They work fast, coverin' 15 miles, passin' many fine plantations, and in every single case, stop, and break in de house and kill men, women, and children. Then they take what they want 'cludin' arms, clothes, liquor and food. Near de Combahee swamp, Lieutenant Governor Bull, drivin' from Beaufort to Charleston, see them and he small a rat. Befo' he was seen by de army he detour into de big woods and stay 'til de slave rebels pass.

Governor Bull and some planters, between de Combahee and Edisto [rivers], ride fast and spread de alarm and it wasn't long 'til de militiamen was on de trail in pursuit of de slave army. When found, many of de slaves was singin' and dancin' and Cap. Cato and some of de other leaders was cussin' at them sumpin awful. From dat day to dis, no Cato has tasted whiskey, 'less he go against his daddy's warnin'. Dis war last less than two days but it sho' was pow'ful hot while it last.

I reckon it was hot, 'cause in less than two days, 21 white men, women, and chillun, and 44 Negroes, was slain. My granddaddy say dat in de woods and at Stono, where de war start, dere was more than 100 Negroes in line. When de militia come in sight of them at Combahee swamp, de drinkin' dancin' Negroes scatter I de brush and only 44 stand deir ground.

Commander Cato speak for de crowd. He say: "We don't lak slavery. We start to jine [join] de Spanish in Florida. We surrender but we not whipped yet and we is not converted." De other 43 men say: "Amen." They was taken, unarmed, and hanged by de militia. Long befo' dis uprisin',

> de Cato slave wrote passes for slaves and do all he can to send them to freedom. He die but he die for doin' de right, as he see it.

George Cato's narrative of the Stono Rebellion, reported two hundred years later to a WPA writer in 1937, reads well when compared to contemporaneous accounts of white observers.

An anonymous white official wrote "An Account of the Negroe Insurrection in South Carolina," a contemporary report of the rebellion. This account corroborates and also adds some details missing in George Cato's narrative. From the two accounts, we can summarize the principal details of the rebellion.

On the morning of Sunday, September 9, 1739, while many plantation owners were in church, a small group of about twenty Africans, under the leadership of an enslaved man named Cato, overtook a warehouse, raiding it for weapons and powder and killing two white guards. This armed band of enslaved men then proceeded south toward Florida, burning homes and murdering plantation owners and their families while sparing others, such as a tavern owner by the last name of Wallace, who the Africans claimed had been kind to the men and women he enslaved. They marched south under "colors" (flags), shouting "Liberty" as they went, and either coerced or convinced other enslaved Africans to join them.

On horseback, returning home from official state business, South Carolina's lieutenant governor William Bull and several other men encountered Cato's group and narrowly escaped. Bull raced back toward Charles-Town to raise a militia, which set out on horseback after the rebels. The unnamed white official continues this account:

> By this time many of them were drunk with the Rum they had taken in the Houses. They increased every minute by new Negroes coming to them, so that they were above Sixty, some say a hundred, on which they halted in a field and set to dancing, Singing and beating Drums, to draw more Negroes to them, thinking they were now victorious over the whole Province, having marched ten miles & burnt all before them without Opposition, but the Militia being raised, the Planters with great briskness pursued them and when they came up, dismounting, charged them on foot. The Negroes were soon routed though they behaved boldly, several being killed on the Spot, many ran back to their Plantations thinking they had not been missed, but they were there taken and Shot, Such as were taken in the field also, were, after being examined, shot on the Spot; and this is to be said to the honour of the Carolina Platers, that notwithstanding the Provocation they had received from so many Murders, they did not torture one Negroe, but only put them to an easy death.

The battle between the rebels and the white militia actually raged on for at least a week, with several skirmishes between the sides. Ultimately, most of the rebels were captured and executed, with perhaps only a handful making their way to Florida.

Still, the Stono Rebellion is a hallmark in the history of early uprisings of the enslaved in colonial America. First, because it showed the agency that enslaved Africans knew they possessed, and second, because of the role that music and dance played.

Two phrases from the anonymous report cited above stand out as the centerpiece of the study, analysis, and conjecture about the rebellion and its legacy. The anonymous reporter wrote, "Many of them were *drunk with the Rum they had taken in the Houses.* They increased every minute by new Negroes coming to them, so that they were above Sixty, some say a hundred, on which *they halted in a field and set to dancing, Singing and beating Drums, to draw more Negroes to them.*" (Italics added.)

For some, like George Cato's family, the wanton nature of Cato's forces was forever to be eschewed, suggesting that had the band not stopped in a field and engaged in such merriment and drinking, their chances for success would have increased. Some scholars, like Peter C. Hoffer, agree, depicting the rebellion as an unorganized, unplanned, and spontaneous event with little intention behind it.

But historian John K. Thornton, in a well-reasoned paper, notes that everything about the rebellion, including stopping in the fields to dance and sing, points to an army of soldiers with a history of being well-trained in African battle tactics prior to their capture as slaves. Thornton argues persuasively for a Kongolese origin of Cato and his core group of rebels. "Dancing in preparation for war was so common in Kongo," Thornton writes, "that 'dancing at a war' (*sangamento*) was often used as a synonym for 'to declare war' in seventeenth-century sources." From "hit and run" rather than the "stand and fight" tactics used by Cato and his rebels, to the marching under colors, Thornton demonstrates that they can be traced back to African roots.

Still others see the most important legacy of the Stono Rebellion not in the rebellion itself or the rebels but in the development of Black music. This way of thinking comes from a sharper focus on "dancing, Singing and beating Drums, to draw more Negroes to them" and the reaction of the South Carolina legislature a year later to pass a law prohibiting enslaved Africans from the "using and keeping of drums, horns, or other loud instruments, which may call together or give sign or notice to one another of their wicked designs and purposes."

Drumming as a form of communication has been well-documented in various regions of Africa from which slaves were taken. Particularly for those from the same or a similar African society, one that shared a language, drumming could actually be interpreted as communication in that language. Cato's men, this line of reasoning goes, stopped in a field to drum not just to make noise that would attract other enslaved people to them, but to send a specific message of what had occurred and what would come next.

With the rebellion put down and drumming now outlawed, enslaved Africans turned to other means of percussive communication and expression, particularly those involving the body in the absence of drums. These other means included the Juba dance—or hambone or Pattin' Juba—which involved stomping and slapping or patting the arms, legs, chest, and cheeks as a rhythm for various dance movements. Juba was originally brought to America by the Kongolese arriving in South Carolina.

The most prominent proponent of this Stono "drum thesis" was Marian Hannah Winter, a dance historian who published an article in 1947 entitled "Juba and American Minstrelsy." She writes:

> Substitutions for the forbidden drum were accomplished with facility—bone clappers in the manner of castanets, jawbones, scrap iron such as blacksmiths' rasps, handclapping and footbeats. Virtuosity of foot-work, with heel beats and toe beats, became a simulacrum of the drum. In modern tap-dancing the "conversation" tapped out by two performers is a survival of African telegraphy by drums.

Choreographer Mark Knowles, writing in 2002, cites Winter and specifically references the Stono Rebellion and its influence on tap dancing. He observes that banning drumming deprived the enslaved of their traditional, sacred methods of communication and expression. They responded with the use of "bone clappers, tambourines, and most importantly, hand and body slaps, and foot beats. The most primitive of all instruments, the human body, became the main source of rhythm and communication."

I don't believe that Stono was the catalyst for the emergence of new forms of Black music or dance. I do believe that Stono was one in a long series of events that communicated to people of African descent in America that American culture despised them, even if it reveled in the music and dance they created in struggling against the effects of that despisement.

CHAPTER 7

HOLLERIN' FOR FREEDOM

IN THE EARLY 1990S, MY GRANDMOTHER, ELSIE V. HILL, passed away. She was born and raised in rural Surry County, Virginia, but spent most of her life in the Bronx in New York City. In the later years of her life, she returned to her home along the Blackwater Swamp, close to the James River. Grandmother was "Mother Hill" to the sisters and brothers of the Refuge Temple Annex, not far from her home in the Bronx, a devoutly Pentecostal denomination led by Elder Reverend William George Fields. She was "Mother" because she'd nursed the church from a small storefront on East 225th Street to occupying a former bank building eight blocks away, which she'd helped to purchase.

At my grandmother's homegoing, my nephew Juma was sitting with me in the pews of Mount Nebo Baptist Church in Surry, Virginia, when several school buses full of her church sisters from the Refuge Temple Annex arrived late, having lost their direction along the way. With Elder Fields at the lead, these

Black women dressed in all white marched into Mount Nebo dancing, clapping, pounding tambourines, and singing praise songs to the Almighty. I leaned over to Juma and said, "You're about as close to witnessing a traditional African ritual as you will ever be here in America." Juma sat enthralled.

During her life, my grandmother also dressed in all white and danced and clapped and played the tambourine at funerals and other special occasions. Though Grandmother would disown any mention that the white color she wore and the percussive rhythms she swayed to could be traced directly back to West Africa.

"Hush, boy," she'd say. "That's blasphemy. Africa ain't got nothing to do with the way we worship the Lord!"

Sorry, Grandmother. Africa had everything to do with the way you sang and danced and worshiped the Lord.

Martin Luther King Jr. may have said it best in a single short sentence that encapsulates a long portion of Africa and the history of America. In his "How Long? Not Long!" speech delivered on March 25, 1965, at the conclusion of the last Selma-to-Montgomery march, King drew a parallel between slavery and Reconstruction, observing that slavery gave Black people Christianity, while Reconstruction (that period after the Civil War) gave poor white people Jim Crow. In each case leaving both groups without the political and economic power they really needed.

That, in a nutshell, is the history of race in America.

King went on to unpack the meaning of the last clause in his speech. But in the first clause lies answers to my grandmother's deeply held beliefs that nothing within the Refuge Temple Annex had anything to do with Africa. My only quibble with King is that Jesus wasn't "given" to most Africans captured and sold to white Americans; he was "forced" upon them at the point of a gun, a whip, or a cattle prod.

Jesus had already been "given" to the first generation of captured Africans long before they arrived in irons on American shores. By the early sixteenth century, Christianity was well-established in Africa thanks to Portuguese missionaries in the Angola–Congo region, from where this first generation came.

Christianity in early America bore witness to strange and contradictory doctrinal truths. On one hand, the religion quickly became a justification for enslavers, while on the other hand, it represented a "balm in Gilead" for the enslaved, holding out the hope of freedom not just in the hereafter but in the now, as if the enslaver and the enslaved were reading from two different Bibles.

In fact, they were.

When it came to slavery, enslavers read from the Old Testament while the enslaved read from the New. Enslavers seized upon the Old Testament curse of Ham, misinterpreted by many Christian, Jewish, and Islamic writers to suggest that Ham was the father of Africans, condemned forever to subservience and enslavement. Enslaved Africans, meanwhile, held on to the Sermon on the Mount from the Gospel of Matthew in the New Testament, where Jesus speaks of such ideals as "loving one's enemies" and "turning the other cheek" rather than "an eye for an eye," as found in the more violent Old Testament verses.

Christianity was forced upon enslaved Africans, but they found within it a salve for the soul that supported them—and still does support them—through their dark, brutal nights in America. What emerged from this bifurcated theology was not a wholesale adoption of Christianity by the enslaved but a hybrid theology: what scholars call "syncretism," in which elements of traditional African spirituality were fused with Christian precepts to create a novel theology uniquely adapted to the needs and circumstances of enslavement in the land of the free. Although my grandmother would never have believed or accepted it, the music she sang to, the ecstatic dances she swung her hips to, and the rhythms she clapped her hands to were fundamental African parts of this brew, which found their way into places such as the Refuge Temple Annex.

Black Christianity moved seamlessly—and still does move seamlessly—between the pews of spirituality and the streets and fields of the social, political, and economic struggles to throw off oppression. It represented, in the early nineteenth century, one of the first forms of what today is called "liberation theology" (now most closely associated with the Catholic Church in South America). But it also represented a widespread belief among African societies—and Indigenous people worldwide—of a deep and abiding unity between the sacred and the secular. The spiritual world, as the *dikenga* referenced in previous chapters shows, is but a reflection of the secular world and vice versa. Thus, in a similar manner, the new music central to the liturgy of this new theology of the enslaved, of this experience of captured Africans in America, also moved seamlessly between the profound and the profane.

Black spirituals and Black gospels are two of many musical

forms that emerged from this mélange of Christianity, African spirituality, and the lived experience of enslavement. Where Black spirituals are reworkings of traditional biblical stories and themes to more closely fit the experience of struggling under the yoke of oppression while attempting to heave it off, Black gospels are new sacred hymns and lyrics, not grounded in specific biblical tales but seeking to accomplish the same. Although the specific term "gospel" was not in widespread use for Black sacred music until the beginning of the twentieth century, it is certainly appropriate in describing earlier sacred Black musical forms.

Black gospel music also supported the social, political, and economic struggle mounted by enslaved Africans against their oppression in the use of songs with encoded messages. Perhaps the most popular belief along these lines is that "Follow the Drinking Gourd" is a Black gospel song with specifically encoded messages about timing, routes, hazards, and aids that would help an enslaved person in Texas escape all the way north to Canada and to freedom. The outlines of this song and its encoded message are widespread and commonly held. The "drinking gourd" is the constellation the Big Dipper, whose stars at the front edge of the ladle point to Polaris, the polestar, which, regardless of time or season, points north; thus, following the star would lead an enslaved person to freedom and, as the song's lyrics say, "an old man waitin'," whom many identify as a white sailor and conductor of the Underground Railroad, Peg Leg Joe, whom H. B. Parks, an amateur folklorist and school administrator, claimed first created the song.

Gloria D. Rall at the New Jersey State Planetarium produced a children's planetarium event called Follow the Drinking Gourd, which traced the astronomical events associated with the story. She also has two accounts in refereed astronomical journals detailing the apparent facts behind her planetarium show. Recently, governmental agencies have gotten involved. NASA created a web page devoted to the song and the astronomy behind it. The National Park Service (NPS) and even the National Security Agency (NSA) have attested on their websites to its "coded message." Both NASA and NPS have reproduced the song's full lyrics with interpolated text meant to prove the fidelity of the song's message. With acknowledgment and support from governmental agencies and with widespread public belief in the "coded message" theory, it must be true. Right?

Not so fast, cautions historian James B. Kelley, who authored an important paper in 2008 that attempted to get to the truth behind this story. Just because a story has worked its way into popular imagination does not guarantee its veracity. Kelley points out that all of the source references to this song and its use go back to H. B. Parks, who recorded the song in writing from memory, based on encounters with several itinerant Black musicians. Parks published "Foller de Drinkin' Gou'd" in *Publications of the Texas Folklore Society* in 1928. Parks admitted that he was not able to record all the verses because some of his Black informant musicians could not recall them. Parks further admitted to being told by one informant musician that the lyrics had been changed over time to better bring the song into accord with Christian beliefs and views. Gloria Rall, then, according to

Kelley, in her written publications embellished the story with astronomical and naturalistic observations (such as the movements of birds during different seasons) that, while they gave the "coded message" theory a patina of truth, did nothing to get at the core of the song's provenance or even the manner by which it was passed along as oral history.

Kelley's point, and I fully agree, is that one cannot simply accept a fact because most people believe it or want it to be true, regardless of the skin color of the believers. That would be a dangerous prospect, yet it's one too often seen. The story behind Juneteenth reported earlier in this book, for example, shows how popular wisdom of what happened on June 19, 1865, is far removed from the recollections of a man who was actually in Texas that day. My sense is that unquestionably accepting a popular truth leads to obscuring an even deeper truth for which evidence can be found. That is certainly the case with Juneteenth, and I fear that may also be the case with "Follow the Drinking Gourd."

Kelley is not saying that the song contains no encoded message about navigating one's way to freedom. It well might, but there is no evidence to that effect. Even if "Follow the Drinking Gourd" is more myth than truth, that does not lessen the song's importance. Myth, after all, is not the same as falsehood. Myth is an encoding of experience such that it can be transmitted in ritual and story. Myth does not have to be literal to be powerful symbolically. Whether any enslaved person actually used the verses of this song as a road map to freedom may not be as important as what the song does encode about significant aspects of Black life in antebellum America and the desire of enslaved people for freedom.

Why, Kelley asks, should this song about Black freedom trace its roots back to an old white sailor named Peg Leg Joe, who, so it's claimed, instructed enslaved people to look to the stars for a road map to freedom? Doesn't that fact alone transpose agency away from the enslaved? Kelley then offers an alternative, very compelling interpretation based on West African mythology. "The puzzling 'peg leg' reference," Kelley observes, "might signal the name Papa Legba through both consonant patterning (the 'p-,' 'l-,' and 'g-') and the visual cue of the wooden leg."

Papa Legba is a *lwa* (pronounced like the French term for "law," *loi*), a principal spirit in Voodoo, found across a wide swath of the American South, and Central and South America. Voodoo itself is syncretic or diasporic religion, emerging from a fusion of diverse West African spiritual traditions (such as those practiced by people in the present-day nations of Benin, Togo, Ghana, and Nigeria, all locations from which many enslaved Africans came) with Catholicism. Papa Legba is an intermediary, a "go-between" through the spiritual and secular worlds. Most mythologies have such figures or paracletes who move between these realms, whether it is Mercury of Roman mythology, Raven in the spiritual systems of Native Americans in the Northwest, the Holy Spirit in Christianity, or Eshu of the Yoruba. What, then, is Papa Legba's *veve*—the Voodoo term for "icon"? It is none other than an embellishment of the *dikenga* or *yowa* or quincunx, as shown here:

Papa Legba's *veve*, or icon, an embellishment of the *dikenga*. Might it unlock a deeper meaning to "Follow the Drinking Gourd"?

"Follow the Drinking Gourd" does encode what I have come to describe as the "mythic cartography of freedom." Almost all traditional societies, and certainly African societies from which enslaved individuals came, practiced a form of "land naming" (after the Old Norse practice of *landnám*), where unoccupied land was first sacralized by marking its directions and noting the psycho-emotional aspect each direction held. The *dikenga* or *yowa* discussed earlier, when drawn on the ground, is a form of sacralizing the ground beneath one's feet, even if those feet are in shackles.

The mythic cartography of freedom was literal even if it was not expressed freely. In your mind, draw a cross, a *dikenga*, or a *yowa*. At the top, at north, envision the word "Freedom." Now turn ninety degrees, and at east, see the word "Home." Turn another ninety degrees, and in the south, mentally write "Bondage." Turn a final ninety degrees and see the word "Unknown." The

Underground Railroad ran north to freedom. Yet even this belies what is known about the mythic cartography of freedom. For the Underground Railroad had at least two southern and one eastern division. If an enslaved person lived far enough south, then north was not necessarily the direction of freedom—south was, for passengers on the Underground Railroad often escaped by foot to Mexico and by boat to the West Indies. And if the enslaved lived along the Eastern Seaboard, then farther east by boat to Bermuda might be the direction to freedom they took. The point here is simply that north was not always the direction of freedom, as suggested by popular interpretations of "Follow the Drinking Gound." Cato and the rebels of Stono, for example, sought freedom by heading south.

Furthermore, "Follow the Drinking Gourd" has gone through a number of iterations that reflect more on the need for soothing the souls of white Americans than reflecting the deeper truths of the Black American past. Folk singer Lee Hays of the Almanac Singers and later the Weavers performed and published the song beginning in the late 1940s—he said it was from a melody given to him by an elderly Black woman named Aunty Laura, with lyrics from the version originally transcribed by H. B. Parks. Singer-songwriter Randy Sparks claimed he heard the song from an elderly Black street musician named John Woodum. The Sparks version, which he later recorded with his group the New Christy Minstrels, included new lines: "Think I heard the angels say, Stars in the heaven gonna show you the way."

Thanks to Parks, Hays, and Sparks, we have the tune and the lyrics and much of the meaning we attribute to this song today, but like James B. Kelley, I would also caution, "Not so fast!" There's more to this Black gospel song than popular wisdom—based on a history of transcription, interpretation, and additions by white ethnographers and musicians—admits.

With the burgeoning Black church as its incubator, the Black gospel tradition only grew stronger during the first half of the nineteenth century, through the Civil War and into the post–Civil War period, reaching a zenith of stylistic excellence in the early twentieth century through the work of Chicagoan Thomas A. Dorsey. Considered the "father of gospel music," Dorsey wrote more than one thousand gospel songs. But like so many Black musicians across genres before and after him, and like the Black musical tradition from which they emerged, Dorsey embodied the spirit of Papa Legba, even if, as a devout evangelical Christian, Dorsey would have abhorred any association with Voodoo as blasphemous. He moved between the sacred and secular musical realms, highlighting through his songs the deep, abiding unity between spirituality and everyday reality that is a cornerstone of Black music as a soundtrack of the struggle for freedom. He "combined the good news of gospel with the bad news of the blues," summarized Anthony Heilbut, a Grammy award–winning producer of gospel music.

Dorsey's musical career began in the juke joints and at the rent parties of early twentieth-century Atlanta. He played piano and wrote and arranged popular jazz and vaudeville scores. He accompanied blues singer Ma Rainey on tour. But after a two-year bout with depression, during which he contemplated suicide, Dorsey had a spiritual awakening in 1928, leading him to transition to gospel music. Despite going church door to church door, as well as to the doors of music publishers, to sell his newly inspired songs, gospel music was not in vogue with Black churches, which were attempting to become more like mainstream white churches and offering classical European music in their liturgies. So Dorsey returned to the blues.

Known as "Georgia Tom," Dorsey and Hudson "Tampa Red" Whittaker collaborated on and recorded more than fifty successful blues songs under the name of Tampa Red and Georgia Tom, the Famous Hokum Boys, between 1928 and 1932. Dorsey claimed that "hokum" was a neologism the pair created.

Slowly, Black churches in Chicago saw how Dorsey's music and his spirited piano playing—he once jumped up from his stool and continued playing and belting out a tune while standing—moved congregants. In 1932, Pilgrim Baptist, then one of Chicago's largest Black churches, hired Dorsey as its musical director. While it allowed him to devote his time to composing gospel music, it also brought him into conflict with other Black churches, ministers, and congregants who objected to Dorsey's energetic sound, how his music often overshadowed the messages of preachers, and his showcasing of female lead singers at a time when most in the Black religious hierarchy were male.

The list of Black musicians inspired by Dorsey and who, like him, moved between sacred and secular music is legendary and long, and includes such luminaries as James Cleveland, Mahalia

Jackson, Dinah Washington, Sam Cooke, Ray Charles, Little Richard, James Brown, the Coasters, and Aretha Franklin.

In 1932, Dorsey's wife, Nettie, formerly Ma Rainey's wardrobe mistress, died in childbirth. The son she gave birth to, Thomas A. Dorsey Jr., passed away that next day. These twin tragedies prompted Dorsey to compose one of his most moving, beautiful, and internationally acclaimed songs, "Take My Hand, Precious Lord."

The song calls out for guidance through challenging times, as it did to Martin Luther King Jr. during the years he was among the leaders of the Black struggle for freedom in America. King often asked Mahalia Jackson to sing it at rallies and meetings to inspire those in attendance. She sang the song at the March on Washington in 1963, bringing King to tears. Later that day, standing behind King as he spoke, she whispered loudly, insistently, "Martin, tell them about the dream," whereupon King ad-libbed one of the most powerful and memorable portions of his "I Have a Dream" speech. Mahalia Jackson also performed "Take My Hand, Precious Lord" at King's funeral in April 1968. The last words King spoke before his assassination were a request to musician Ben Branch: "Ben, make sure you play 'Take My Hand, Precious Lord' in the meeting tonight. Play it real pretty." King never made it to that meeting.

"Work songs," an early form of Black gospel music, present before the widespread usage of the term "gospel," represent yet another way in which African music emerged in America to support the plight of the enslaved and their path toward freedom. On tobacco and cotton fields, from the decks of small crafts plying the riverine highways of the great southeast deltas, from the gangs pounding on iron to lay thousands of miles of railroad tracks, these were songs of enslaved men and women seeking not only to relieve the boredom of the relentless, brutal conditions under which they were forced to work to build the foundations of this country, but to communicate with others bound by a similar fate.

Enslaved and free Black men who laid and maintained thousands of miles of railroad tracks beginning in the antebellum South belonged to a group known as "gandy dancers." While this group of railroad workers included their white counterparts, it was the Black men who developed a unique style to their work. They tapped their long crowbars on the metal tracks in rhythm with the upward jerking motion needed to straighten a section here and there. Some say the word "gandy" came from the Gandy Tool Company of Chicago, which made the tools the workers/dancers used, though no company by the name "Gandy" has been shown to have existed. Others claim the name comes from the wobbling, gander-like motion of the men while walking the tracks. Still others say the term is a neologism of "Ghana," the West African nation from which early enslaved men were captured for work along US railways.

Field hollers, or field calls, or the closely related arwhoolie were another form of work songs with roots in Africa. Frederick Law Olmsted, the landscape architect who laid out Central Park in Manhattan and Prospect Park in Brooklyn, among many other parks across the country, in 1853 observed such hollers on one of his many journeys through the American South, describing the caller as making "a long, loud, musical shout, rising, and falling, and breaking into falsetto, his voice ringing through the woods . . . like a bugle-call. As he finished, the melody was caught up by another, and then, another, and then, by several in chorus."

"Bile [Boil] dem Cabbage Down" is an enslaved women's work song from St. Simons Island of the Georgia Sea Islands that has since become a fiddle-and-banjo standard of bluegrass and country and Western music, its African roots seemingly forgotten.

> Possum up in a 'simmon tree,
> Raccoon on the ground.
> Raccoon say to possum,
> Won't you shake that 'simmon down.
> Bile them cabbage down, down,
> Bile them cabbage down.
> Look here, gal, don't want no fooling,
> Bile them cabbage down.
> Went to Susy's house,
> Bile them cabbage down.
> Susy wasn't home.

Look here, gal, don't want no fooling,
Bile them cabbage down.
My old missus promise me
When she die she going to set me free.
She live so long till her head got bald,
She give up the idea of dying at all.
Bile them cabbage down, down,
Bile them cabbage down.

Play the "Levee Camp Holler" recorded by Alan Lomax in 1947 at the Mississippi State Penitentiary against a recording of a muezzin call to prayer. These eerie concordances—the melody, the fluctuating note changes, the praise of God, the quivering and shaking of the singer's voice, the nasal intonation, the sharp changes in musical scale—have not gone unnoticed by ethnomusicologists such as Sylviane Diouf at the New York Public Library's Schomburg Center for Research in Black Culture, who has been doing groundbreaking research in this area for years.

Field hollers were sung by the enslaved in the antebellum South and also by Black Americans jailed and forced to work under slave-like conditions in the postbellum Jim Crow era. Even in this modern age, when electronic recordings of the muezzin calling the faithful to prayer play from huge speakers atop mosques throughout Istanbul, the playback is staggered, and the call thus echoes and reverberates throughout the city and across the Bosphorus, giving the impression of one mosque or one person calling out to another, then another. This eerily beautiful effect reminds me of what Olmsted must have heard many years ago in Southern cotton fields. Reports stated that, with the right conditions of wind and air pressure, the voice of a man or woman hollerin' on one plantation would be picked up by the enslaved on another; that call then echoed and returned with a new call from a distant voice. These field hollers communicated the pain and suffering and sorrow of the enslaved but also the joy and the hope.

This deep Islamic influence on the music of America's enslaved African people is not surprising. The first generation of the enslaved came from the Angola–Congo region of Africa, many of whom had already been baptized Catholic prior to their capture. But succeeding generations largely came from farther north and west, an area roughly from present-day Senegal to Nigeria and as far inland as Mali; many of the people were devoutly literate in Arabic, highly educated, and Muslim (see Chapter 3 for more on the Islamic influence in early America). Through the horrors of the Middle Passage and the barbarism of the plantation, the muezzin's call to prayer morphed into field hollers; African and Islamic instruments such as the oud and banjer morphed into the guitar and banjo; and the quivering notes of Africa and Islam morphed into the bending of notes ubiquitous to Black American musical forms—really, American musical forms—found in work songs and spirituals and blues and jazz and R & B and pop and country and Western and hip-hop.

I've listened to saxophonist John Coltrane for more than sixty years, yet recently, thanks to the work of Moustafa Bayoumi, a professor of English at Brooklyn College, City University of New York, I've heard one of 'Trane's classic albums, *A Love Supreme*, recorded in 1964, with new ears. Six minutes and five seconds into the first track, "Acknowledgement," 'Trane, along with pianist McCoy Tyner, bassist Jimmy Garrison, and drummer Elvin Jones, breaks into chanting the album's title. While the men are mostly repeating "A Love Supreme," there are a few times, right at the beginning and about ten chants in, when Bayoumi suggests—and it's hard to dispute—it sounds like someone, perhaps 'Trane himself, has slipped in the words "Allah Supreme" atop the chant. I've replayed this section a great many times and cannot decide for certain if Bayoumi is correct. But whether this chant to Allah is, in fact, true, the very thought now gives me pause to contemplate the deep and abiding role that Africa and Islam have played in the roots of Black American music.

CHAPTER 8

BLUE NOTES

CALL-AND-RESPONSE, IN WHICH ONE PERFORMER OFFERS a phrase and a second then answers, is a form of communication derived from Africa and a foundational element of Black American music. West African drumming provides many examples. In a drumming ensemble, one drummer may break out in a high-pitched beat, striking close to the rim of the drum. Upon finishing, another drummer answers with a lower-pitched beat from the center of the drumskin. The first responds by quickening the tempo of the beat, while the second answers by slowing the beat down. To which the first replies with an intricate, syncopated beat, and the second answers with a straight rhythm. Thus, a conversation ensues. If the rhythm of the drumming reflects the language of the drummers and the audience, both performers and listeners may actually understand what messages are being sent back and forth.

As an art form, call-and-response extends well beyond drumming, both in Africa and in America.

Call-and-response is a form of democratic participation in any given matter—social, political, or spiritual. Frequently, the call is phrased as a question, the response as an answer. When a leader calls out about their beliefs, the other members of the group respond with theirs. Black American preachers developed a call-and-response style of oration, certainly adopted by others outside of the Black community. But no one better represented a call-and-response style of preaching than Martin Luther King Jr. In his short but famous "How Long? Not Long!" speech, he asks rhetorically, *How long must Black Americans wait for the freedoms and rights they deserve?* At first, he answers for himself, "Not long!" It is both a legitimate answer to his question and a means of priming the twenty-five thousand people King looked out on. As he continues asking, "How long?" and then answering, "Not long!" the crowd picks up the message, so that when King asks, "How long?" the crowd now answers, "Not long!"

Call-and-response is a hallmark of protest, resistance, and struggle. "Whaddya want?" yells the speaker. "Peace!" roars the crowd. "Whendya want it?" asks the speaker. "Now!" answers the crowd.

Call-and-response is found in every Black musical form, from work songs, to blues, to spirituals, to jazz, to R & B, to hip-hop. It's evident in a jazz ensemble when one member of the group—say, the saxophonist—rises above the others in a riff, answered with another riff of similar cadence by the drummer or the bassist. But this democratic form of musical performance is even present between jazz musicians and their audience, as when an ensemble leader signals each member of the group to take a solo, and after each solo, the audience applauds.

⁘ ⁘ ⁘ ⁘

Blues emerged as a musical form in the 1890s, an address to the failures of the Civil War and Reconstruction. Blues, because of emancipation, represents one of the first movements of individual Black people away from families or groups. Blacks were enslaved on plantations together, but lone Black men were seen as a threat to the preferred social order of white America. An itinerant Black man wandering the streets and byways of the postbellum American South is not only emblematic of the blues but symbolic of the formerly enslaved, especially in the South, freed but cast aside by American democracy, wandering in search of direction.

Blues, though often sung by individuals, are not only about individuals down on their luck, but about a people down on their hope that American democracy will ever extend to them. The crossroads that bluesman Robert Johnson stood at may well have represented a personal life crisis, but in a larger context, after emancipation and the Civil War, all Black men and women in America stood at the crossroads of democracy. America chose a direction, and as Robert Johnson later put it so eloquently, "Didn't nobody seem to know me, babe, everybody pass me by." Blues are odes to this passing-by of the formerly enslaved.

In the aftermath of Lincoln's assassination, the KKK and other white supremacist groups rose, lynching, killing, and intimidating

Blacks away from voting Republican. In a few short years, America witnessed yet another instance when violence trumped justice, so that by 1877, a political compromise gave Republicans the presidency in Rutherford B. Hayes, with the agreement that all federal troops would be pulled from the South so that Southern states could continue their violent wresting of political power from Blacks with impunity. The antebellum laws of slavery were ultimately replaced with the laws of Jim Crow.

The economic situation faced by the formerly enslaved unfolded as brutally as the political. Beginning around the turn of the nineteenth century, the economics of American slavery had substantially changed. Tobacco as a "cash crop" had cratered, and gone were the vast rolling hills of the large southeastern riverine tobacco plantations run by patricians like Jefferson, Washington, and Madison.

Where once the death of tobacco had signaled to some the demise of slavery, "Ginny" turned that around. Eli Whitney's cotton gin breathed new life into American slavery, and an explosion in the population of the enslaved took place in the first decade of the nineteenth century. Only that explosion did not take place in the upper South; it took place in the Deep South, with its soil more favorable for cotton.

The US Congress in 1807 passed the Act Prohibiting the Importation of Slaves, which Jefferson had promised in his 1806 State of the Union Address. Like the eclipse of tobacco by cotton, the act of cutting off the importation of enslaved men and women had just the opposite effect on slavery. With no international slave trade permitted, the domestic trade boomed in America. Slaves were raised, bred, and sold like cattle to the profit of men like Jefferson. This domestic trade brought Black men and women from the north farther south, where cotton plantations prospered with their free labor. After the Civil War, after the end of Reconstruction, slave labor was simply replaced with sharecropping and tenant farming, where Black Americans often worked the same fields they had as slaves, only now deeply in debt to the owners of those fields. Sharecropping was little more than Slavery 2.0.

W. E. B. Du Bois captured the period between the end of the Civil War and the turn of the nineteenth century succinctly when he wrote, "The slave went free; stood a brief moment in the sun; then moved back again toward slavery." Of all the blues musicians, Robert Johnson may have captured the essence of this period best. America stood at the crossroads and, for about ten years, took the road leading to the full participation of all Americans, Black and white, women and men, until backtracking quickly to take the more familiar road that led not to greater freedom for the formerly enslaved, but to greater oppression and hardship.

Music reflected this transition. Black spirituals and gospels had little reason to change. The "Pharaoh" in the spiritual "Go Down Moses" may have once stood for slavery but now stood for Jim Crow, the KKK, and the political disenfranchisement of the formerly enslaved. The trouble seen that nobody knows, while once slavery was now embodied in these same racist organizations and practices. All of which left ample room for new musical forms to emerge that represented these new trials and tribulations, these new reasons for singing the blues.

Jim Crow cast a long shadow over the blues. Not only did

it fuel the music, but it also fostered the segregation around its history, how the blues was recorded, and to whom the music was marketed.

Blues and country music (also known as country and western music) share a long, if forgotten, common history. Both emerged in the American South, and both drew heavily from earlier African influences, not only in musical form but in the musical instruments used.

The banjo, that signature instrument of country music, for example, came to America by way of enslaved Africans. The banjo was known by various names throughout West Africa—the *banjul* of the Mandinka, the *bangoe* of Ghana, or the *banza* of the Kongolese—and transcribed by European writers who first encountered the instrument in Africa, and it was known among the Caribbean enslaved as the *bangil*, *banshaw*, *bangelo, banjer*, *banjar*, *bangie* or *bonjaw*. African-made banjoes were constructed around a gourd body with a fitted animal skin (the sound box), to which was affixed a wooden stick as a neck, with one to five strings fashioned from gut or vegetable fibers, and one string, a drone note, shorter than the others.

White banjo players learned to play this African instrument from the enslaved who taught them. Many, like Joel Walker Sweeney, credited with advancing the design of the five-string banjo, turned around and mocked the enslaved by performing in blackface during minstrel shows. Uncle Dave Macon, a banjoist and darling of the Grand Ole Opry, had a similar disdain for African Americans, although he sang and plucked their songs to success. As banjoes began to be made in America, wood replaced gourds, plastic eventually replaced skin, and the neck was fitted with frets and tuning pegs.

Then, at the turn of the twentieth century, the recording industry began to grow, and with that the blatant injection of Jim Crow into early American music. Just as water fountains and restrooms and cafeteria counters existed as "Whites Only" or "Colored Only," recording companies presented early American music as "race music" or "hillbilly music." The bending notes from Islamic Africa, call-and-response, and syncopated beats from traditional Africa all found their way to the banjo. As just one of many commonalities between the music of poor, rural Black America and equally poor, rural white America, the banjo could have come to symbolize unity around common musical influences and instruments; instead, it came to symbolize divisiveness. Recording companies sold Black people race music and white people hillbilly music, even though they emerged from the same African ground and used the same African instruments, which neither the companies nor the white musicians dared to admit. White music and white Americans ultimately rejected the term "hillbilly music" in favor of "country music" or "country and western music," and with that, a genre of American music was born with little acknowledgment of its deep African roots. Yet another reason to sing the blues.

At Super Bowl LVIII in Nevada in 2024, Beyoncé shocked her fans and those cheering on her rousing performance in a Verizon commercial when, at the end of the commercial, she said, "Okay, they ready. Drop the new music." Afterward she dropped two singles, one of them being "Texas Hold 'Em," a country music song that rocketed to the top of Billboard's Hot Country Songs chart. Topping the country music chart was a first for Beyoncé and for a Black woman, but it was not the first time a Black woman had an outsize influence on the genre. Beyoncé's success came by standing on the shoulders of other great Black female country artists. Francesca Royster, PhD, author of *Black Country Music: Listening for Revolutions*, suggests that Linda Martell might be a good place to start looking, and listening, for Black women and their country music roots.

In the 1960s and 1970s, Martell released three commercially successful singles that charted on Billboard and a lone album, *Color Me Country*. She played the Grand Ole Opry a dozen times and appeared on country music television shows like *Hee Haw*. But she also battled the headwinds of racism, prejudice, and hatred throughout her career. At a gig in Poplar Bluff, Missouri, Martell was taunted and called the N-word so loudly and so often that it interrupted her performance, forcing the show's white promoter to join her onstage and tell the audience to either shut up or leave. To release her singles and her album, Martell was forced to sign with Plantation Records. Prior to a live television appearance, a network executive suggested how she might better pronounce her words. Martell's career ended prematurely. Still, Linda Martell was a trailblazer who paved the way for other female Black country musicians, like singer-songwriter Rissi Palmer, host of the radio show *Color Me Country*, named after Martell's album.

Jazz is yet another musical genre deeply connected to the experience of Africans enslaved in the Americas, and it is impossible to speak of the emergence of jazz as a Black musical form without simultaneously speaking of the triangular trade. Only this is not the triangular trade that brought enslaved Africans to the Americas and the goods and products they made to Europe, but a triangular trade of music among New Orleans, Havana, and New York City.

For more than a hundred years, from the first half of the nineteenth century up until the American embargoes against Cuba beginning in the late 1950s, regular ferry service existed between the American mainland and the island. This was not just service between ports in Florida and Cuba with a distance of, at most, a few hundred miles. This was also service between the port of New Orleans, Louisiana, and Havana, Cuba, nearly seven hundred miles away. For many years, a twice-daily ferry ran between New Orleans and Havana.

Where people and trade flow, art and culture follow.

"Now, in one of my earliest tunes, 'New Orleans Blues,'" Jelly Roll Morton said, "you can notice the Spanish tinge. In fact, if you can't manage to put tinges of Spanish in your tunes, you will never be able to get the right seasoning, I call it, for jazz."

Though Jelly Roll Morton, one of the earliest progenitors of jazz, spoke of the "Spanish tinge," what he really meant was the syncopated rhythmic patterns in Cuban music brought over from Africa by the enslaved, such as the *tresillo* and its many variants. *Tresillo* (pronounced *tray-see-yo*) is a beat absolutely fundamental to sub-Saharan music, which appears over and over in jazz and modern-day Black music. It's clapped—1-2-3, 1-2-3, 1-2—to a four-beat measure, or simply heard in the driving groove and hook of the well-known song "Stand by Me," written by Ben E. King, Jerry Leiber, and Mike Stoller. Wynton Marsalis sees in *tresillo* a fundamental key to unlock New Orleans jazz. When *tresillo*, a simple rhythm that survived the Middle Passage, hit New Orleans, it helped birth jazz. When jazz hit New York City and other urban centers, it helped birth a renaissance.

Jazz is, by its nature, subversive and taboo. The very term derives from a mid-nineteenth-century slang word, "jasm," meaning energy, vigor, or spunk. "Jasm" derives from an early nineteenth-century slang word, "jism" or "gism," with the same meaning, but also connoting semen or seed—hence the modern slang word "jizz." Some have also suggested that an earlier spelling, "jass," refers to the jasmine perfume popular with prostitutes in New Orleans during the early twentieth century, and thus slang for a woman's behind. Most etymologies of the word place its first American musical use sometime between 1912 and 1915.

Blue notes accompanied the dawn of jazz. A dismal economic reality faced Black Americans as the South moved back toward slavery under the guise of sharecropping and tenant farming and Jim Crow laws. Black Americans seeking to escape headed north in what is known as the Great Migration, occurring in two major waves, one before and another after the Great Depression of the 1930s. New York City was a major destination of the Great Migration, and Harlem was then the center of gravity for Black New Yorkers. By 1924, nearly three hundred thousand Black folks heading north had flocked there.

Service in segregated military units, like the Harlem Hellfighters, during World War I resulted in Black American soldiers returning to a country that despised them, even lynched them in uniform, after they had seen a more tolerant and accepting world abroad. The influenza pandemic of 1918 and the age of Prohibition gave rise to the release of the pent-up energies of speakeasies and the Roaring Twenties. The 1915 hurricane season hit New Orleans hard. The Great Flood of 1916 struck North Carolina.

And then, on May 15, 1916, Jesse Washington, a seventeen-year-old farmhand, was castrated, burned, and lynched in Waco, Texas, to the delight of a crowd of white onlookers, including young children. The gruesome spectacle was photographed by Fred Gildersleeve, who later provided the images as postcards.

Bright notes accompanied the dawn of jazz, too. The National Association for the Advancement of Colored People (NAACP) had been founded in 1909. British-born suffragette Elisabeth Freeman was hired by the NAACP to travel to Waco and investigate Washington's death, at great risk to her own safety. In 1915, the US Supreme Court delivered a unanimous decision in the little-known *Guinn v. United States* case, striking down a portion of literacy tests for voting put in place by Oklahoma to limit Blacks from registering to vote. At first an apparent victory for Black Americans, Oklahoma and other states skirted the court's decision by implementing new and sometimes more onerous literacy tests. Still, the decision in *Guinn v. United States* was the first step in a long march that, fifty years later, would lead to Selma and the 1965 Voting Rights Act.

Slowly, in a few areas of American life, Black men and women appeared to be "breaking the color line," as a popular phrase went. The Negro Actors Guild of America (NAG) was formed. In Hollywood, not an early accepter of Black actresses and actors, Ethel Waters and Mantan Moreland found their ways into films. Bessie Smith and Ma Rainey sang to sold-out crowds. Black writers such as Langston Hughes, Zora Neale Hurston, Countee Cullen, and Jean Toomer had their books published by major New York houses. Jobs like Pullman porters peaked; even though placed in subservient roles, men like Claude McKay, Malcolm X, Gordon Parks, and E. D. Nixon worked the rails. Nixon, for example, was able to finance and plan much of the Montgomery bus boycott due to his job as a Pullman porter. That boycott, between 1955 and 1956, brought Martin Luther King Jr. and Rosa Parks to fame.

In the post–World War I years, something was brewing in Black America, which could especially be seen in Harlem. Rejecting old barriers to fuller participation in America, embracing new opportunities for the same, the outlines of a "New Negro," in the words of Black intellectual Alain Locke, whose groundbreaking book bore the same title, were emerging. Jazz both announced and participated in this emergence.

Formally, this emergence was called the Harlem Renaissance, and it touched many areas of Black American society and culture. Intellectuals, activists, and journalists; writers, performers, and entertainers; musicians, composers, and painters—all seemed to move together, to create together, to inspire together in the decades before and after the Great Depression. Duke Ellington, Count Basie, and Louis Armstrong were there. So, too, were Marian Anderson, Billie Holiday, and Lena Horne. Paul

Robeson, Florence Mills, and Bill "Bojangles" Robinson were part of this renaissance. Writers of the Harlem Renaissance included Zora Neale Hurston, Claude McKay, and Langston Hughes. Visual artists counted among their ranks Romare Bearden, Jacob Lawrence, and James Van Der Zee.

Writers like Hughes and Hurston found homes in magazines like *Opportunity*, founded by Charles S. Johnson; *The Crisis*, the official magazine of the NAACP; *FIRE!!*, started by Harlem Renaissance patron Carl Van Vechten; and New York publishing houses willing to take a chance on fresh Black talent. For many visual artists of the Harlem Renaissance, death gave birth to fame through posthumous showings in major museums.

But for musicians of the Harlem Renaissance, their work was consumed nightly in the speakeasies, theaters, and clubs of New York City, especially in Harlem. The Apollo Theater, the Savoy Ballroom, and the Cotton Club ranked among the most popular of these venues. Amateur Night at the Apollo began in 1934 and featured unknown performers in front of one of the toughest audiences in the world, who ruthlessly determined their fate. Luther Vandross was booed offstage four times before he finally succeeded. James Brown didn't make the cut his first try at the Apollo. But the theater helped bring many young or unknown artists to the public's attention, including Harlem Renaissance artists like Ella Fitzgerald and Billie Holiday.

Fresh from winning the top spot at the Apollo Theater's Amateur Night in 1934, Ella Fitzgerald moved twenty blocks uptown to the Savoy Ballroom, where she became a teenage vocalist in front of Chick Webb's famous house band. Duke Ellington, Billie

Holiday, Louis Armstrong, Cab Calloway, Fletcher Henderson, Lena Horne, King Oliver, Count Basie, Coleman Hawkins, Erskine Hawkins, Benny Carter, Earl "Fatha" Hines, Jimmie Lunceford, Dizzy Gillespie, Art Blakey—all the kings and queens, dukes and duchesses, counts and priestesses of Harlem Renaissance jazz played the Savoy at least once, which distinguished itself as one of New York's first large integrated dance halls in Harlem. Still, Jim Crow would not die, even in Harlem. White patrons who fancied Black music and dance and a trip uptown to exotic Harlem could patronize the Cotton Club there. The same Black musicians who performed at the Savoy also performed at the Cotton Club, but only white patrons were allowed.

The Harlem Renaissance emerged as one of the first large-scale, post-enslavement consciousness-raising movements among Black Americans, or, as the poet Langston Hughes simply put it, a time "to express our individual dark-skinned selves without fear or shame." But "the personal is political," argues that oft-repeated slogan from the 1960s. The Harlem Renaissance altered the social and political landscape of America well beyond the contributions of its member artists.

"Dean" of the Harlem Renaissance and its philosophical leader, Alain Locke, a Rhodes Scholar with a PhD in philosophy from Harvard, taught for many years at Howard University. He wrote prolifically and influenced many young people who would later step into leadership roles in the Black Freedom Struggle. Locke had a vision of profound human togetherness beyond superficial segregation, based on his deeply held Bahá'í spirituality. He encouraged a young student named Ossie Davis to pursue acting in New York City, which led to his landmark Hollywood career. Martin Luther King Jr., in a March 19, 1968, speech in Mississippi, said, "We're going to let our children know that the only philosophers that lived were not Plato and Aristotle, but W. E. B. Du Bois and Alain Locke came through the universe."

A. Philip Randolph, another intellectual pillar of the Harlem Renaissance, founded the Brotherhood of Sleeping Car Porters in 1925, one of the first large unions organized to enhance the welfare of Black workers. Randolph would go on to organize the first march on Washington in 1941, which eventually led to the desegregation of the US military under President Harry S. Truman. Twenty years later and with Randolph well into his seventies, Martin Luther King Jr. and other prominent leaders of the Black Freedom Struggle tapped him to be the nominal head of the 1963 March on Washington. This was in part out of deep respect for Randolph's contributions throughout his life and in part from knowing that Randolph's protégé, Bayard Rustin, would actually do the organizing work.

During the Harlem Renaissance, Black music, which had hitherto chronicled the struggle for freedom and equality, now also led that struggle. Billie Holiday mesmerized many with the song "Strange Fruit." When performing what became a protest anthem against lynching, she would request that all food and beverage service be stopped and the houselights turned off except for one on her. Upon completing her performance, that spotlight, too, would go dark. When the houselights would finally come back on, Billie Holiday would have disappeared from the stage, and she took no encores.

While many would applaud wildly, some white audience members would leave in disgust. Her refusal to back down from performing "Strange Fruit" led directly to conflicts with the federal government, in particular with the head of the Federal Bureau of Narcotics, Harry Anslinger, an avowed white supremacist who believed that jazz was the "devil's music." Anslinger promised to ruin her, and he made good on that promise. He set up a sting operation that caught her in a drug bust and an arrest that led to imprisonment for eighteen months. After her release, Anslinger ensured she was not issued a cabaret performer's license. In 1959, an emaciated and ill Holiday checked herself into a New York City hospital. Though she was starting to show signs of recovery, Anslinger had her chained to her hospital bed and forbade doctors from providing her any further treatment. Billie Holiday died several days later.

A newfound agency had arisen in the souls of Black folks without "fear or shame." White men like Harry Anslinger may have hastened the death of the messenger, but they could not kill the message that freedom and equality were unalienable rights in the land of liberty, and that message spread far beyond the well-known names of the Harlem Renaissance. Those who came of age during this time not only swung to music but also continued carrying the message forward.

Pauli Murray, a legal scholar and advocate for civil rights and human rights, born in 1910, wrote a landmark book, published in 1950, entitled *States' Laws on Race and Color*, which then–NAACP chief legal counsel and later Supreme Court justice Thurgood Marshall declared the "bible" of the Black Freedom

Struggle. Bayard Rustin, born in 1912, protégé of A. Philip Randolph and committed practitioner of nonviolence, became the silent driving force behind many of the seminal moments of the civil rights phase of the Black Freedom Struggle. Black men and women began stepping out of the shadows as "hidden figures" and into the spotlight as "the first" in many fields. My father, John S. Ford, born in 1919, was another child of the renaissance. He later went on to become the first Black software engineer in America, hired by IBM in 1946.

Beyond race, the Harlem Renaissance stood at the forefront of new conversations about sexuality and gender. Many of the renaissance's leading writers were women, though during their lives, their contributions were too often discounted, and they, like many visual artists, received due acclaim only after death. Many Harlem Renaissance figures were also queer, with varying degrees of openness about their sexuality. Alain Locke, Countee Cullen, Claude McKay, Langston Hughes, Ethel Waters, Ma Rainey, and Bessie Smith are just a few of the Harlem Renaissance creative geniuses who led only partially disclosed lives as queer men and women in same-sex relationships.

By no means did the Harlem Renaissance fully embrace or address the issues of race, gender, and sexual orientation. Insisting that Black men and women should be able to define themselves in the absence of fear or shame often put the Harlem Renaissance at odds with prevailing social norms, even in the Black community. Christianity was, and still is, the dominant religious force among Black Americans, and Christianity was, and still is, deeply conflicted about queerness and the role of women. But the Harlem Renaissance, by accepting queer men and women, even if still in the shadows, paved the way for the continued advancement of equality around gender and sexual orientation.

Pauli Murray was surely a child of the Harlem Renaissance. But, based on her personal writings and private life, she has also often been described as a transgender man in an age where there were no such descriptors of sexuality. No one can ask Murray what pronouns she preferred—he, she, they. Yet she figured mightily in the struggles for Black freedom and women's rights. Bayard Rustin, more openly gay than many in the Harlem Renaissance, was arrested for his homosexuality. Championed by A. Philip Randolph, one of the renaissance's towering figures, Rustin became one of the most influential, if most unsung, heroes of the civil rights era of the Black Freedom Struggle, befriending, tutoring, and placing before him Martin Luther King Jr. and other more well-known figures of that time. In part, because of a focus on race, gender, and sexuality (see the essay in Chapter 11 for more on Rustin), the Harlem Renaissance was criticized by some for appealing more to the Black middle class and to white Americans than to the Black lower class.

The Great Depression, then the advent of World War II, prefigured the denouement of the Harlem Renaissance. But the ideas advanced by this convergence of creativity, talent, and intellect continued. Jazz did not die, either, although new expressions of jazz arose in the post–World War II era. And wholly new musical forms pushed their way onstage, like rhythm and blues.

CHAPTER 9

THE MINISTER AND THE MAHATMA

FOR THE FOUR BLACK AMERICANS VENTURING INTO THE heart of the British colonial empire in South Asia in 1935, visas would have never been granted in any ordinary way. Permission needed to be obtained from the British Home Office in London rather than a local consulate. Initially, the Home Office balked. "You do not know what you are asking," a British official, issuing visas to India, told the YMCA, which, along with the YWCA, was sponsoring the travelers. "If an American-educated Negro just traveled through the country as a tourist, his presence would create many difficulties for our rule—now you are asking us to let four of them travel all over the country and make speeches!"

Eventually, the visas were granted for a four-month sojourn known as the Pilgrimage of Friendship. Howard Thurman and his wife, Sue Bailey Thurman, and Edward Carroll and his wife, Phenola Carroll, would travel to India, Burma, and Ceylon, despite the British government's objections. They would listen and give speeches. They would be interviewed and constantly trailed by British spies. And consequently, a seminal moment in the history of the Black Freedom Struggle in America would unfold in the heart of India.

An unassuming and humble man, Howard Thurman expressed surprise when asked by the national YWCA and YMCA International Committee on behalf of the World Student Christian Federation to chair this delegation sponsored by the Student Christian Movements of India, Burma, and Ceylon. Although by 1935 Thurman was a deeply respected Christian minister and renowned religious philosopher, he felt conscientiously unable to represent a religion that had been the basis of so much hatred and division toward people of color in both America and Asia.

"My central concern was whether I could in good conscience go to India," Thurman would later write in his autobiography, "as a representative of the Christian religion as it was projected from the West, and primarily from America. I did not want to go to India as an apologist for a segregated American Christianity, yet how could I go under the auspices of the Student Christian Movement without seeming in fact to contradict my intention?"

After many hours of discussion with his wife, companion, and intellectual equal, Sue, Howard came to the conclusion that he should not lead this delegation, that he should not go to India. He notified the YWCA and YMCA organizing committee.

Yet had Thurman not gone to India, there would likely have been no Martin Luther King Jr. as we knew him, no Montgomery bus boycott, no Rosa Parks, no Freedom Summer, no Mississippi Freedom Democratic Party, no Birmingham, no Selma, no

March on Washington. Had Howard Thurman not traveled to India, there likely would have been no Black Freedom Struggle, no Civil Rights Movement in America as we knew it. Thus, the next steps taken by the YWCA and YMCA were crucial.

Instead of responding to Thurman by mail, the organizing committee sent his good friend Winnifred Wygal from New York City to Atlanta to speak with Thurman and his wife. Wygal understood Thurman's concerns and conveyed to him that it was precisely because of these concerns about a "segregated American Christianity" that the committee wished for him to go. For a central question in non-Western Christianity was how and why Black Americans adopted the religion of their oppressors as a tool of survival and faith. And in 1935, there was no better person to answer that question than Howard Thurman.

Howard Washington Thurman was born on November 18, 1899, in Daytona Beach, Florida, the only child of Saul Thurman and Alice Ambrose Thurman. He spent most of his childhood in the Black community of Waycross, where his family lived. His father, a railway worker, died of pneumonia when Howard was just seven. His mother went back to work washing clothes and cleaning homes to support the family, leaving Howard to be raised by his grandmother Nancy Ambrose. Thurman frequently told of how his grandmother pointed him in the direction of his faith, giving him the "contagion" of religion.

For twenty years, Nancy Ambrose had been enslaved on a plantation in Madison County, Florida. Once a year, the enslaver permitted a Black preacher to give a sermon to the enslaved. And while all the enslaved men and women gathered around for the preacher's words, he ended his preaching each year with three sentences that struck them the most, Nancy Ambrose told Howard: "You are not slaves. You are not niggers. You're God's children!" Howard's grandmother's words provided him with an identity that racism and white supremacy could never take away.

Thurman described himself as more interested in Jesus than in Christ, by which he meant he was more interested in finding the divinity within his humanity rather than finding beliefs which, if he adhered to them, would by themselves guarantee his being saved. He was more attuned to the direct experience of divinity rather than in experiences mediated by doctrines, practices, or beliefs. As a young preacher, Thurman studied with Quaker Rufus Jones, and he found great solace in silence and meditation. He frequently spoke of his connection to nature and how he discovered deep spiritual fulfillment in sitting against and talking to an oak tree in his family's front yard. "We thought we'd found our Moses," some said of Howard Thurman. "Instead, we found our mystic."

Thurman may well have been a mystic, but this quality of seeking within for spiritual fulfillment served him very well in India, a country of mystics and "inner seekers" for millennia.

Thurman and the delegation were surprised to discover how well-informed many Indians were about Black history and the Black struggle for freedom in America. But over and over, Thurman also encountered those questions that had originally caused him to consider not going to India: *How could Black Americans adopt the religion of their oppressors? How can you travel to India as a representative of that oppressive religion?*

One questioner went so far as to relay the story of a white American Christian congregation released in the midst of worship to participate in the lynching of a Black man. After the lynching, they returned to their church to continue their worship service. That man questioned if Thurman was a "traitor" to people of color the world over who were struggling against the yoke of such oppression and brutality.

Howard Thurman was not someone to shy away from tough questions, and reportedly, his conversations with his Indian audiences lasted many hours. He was not in India as a representative of Christianity, Thurman said many times. He was there because he and many Black Americans had found meaning and comfort in the New Testament life of Jesus the man, a disinherited, persecuted Jew oppressed by Romans. Jesus's response to his persecution is what sustained Black Americans through the dark years of slavery. Jesus's response to his persecution is what might ultimately raise the yoke of persecution off the backs and necks of people of color around the world. Jesus's response to his persecution is what their own Mahatma Gandhi found so uplifting and meaningful and filled with lessons that Gandhi's followers might emulate.

Those challenging exchanges were never far from Thurman. Years later, he authored a book exploring them in great depth. That book was entitled *Jesus and the Disinherited* rather than *Christianity and the Disinherited*. In separating the man from the religious institution, Thurman offered an understanding of how his faith was so deeply connected to his belief in the Black Freedom Struggle in America and the worldwide struggle of people of color against white supremacy and oppression. Little wonder that Martin Luther King Jr. and his close disciples carried *Jesus and the Disinherited* with them whenever they traveled.

On September 9, 1935, Thurman wrote to Mahatma Gandhi, "For years I have read about you and there are many things I should like to talk through with you and covet the privilege very, very much."

Thurman's delegation arrived in Colombo to a postcard from Gandhi dated October 6, 1935:

Dear Friend, I thank you for your letter of 9th September, just received. I shall be delighted to have you and your three friends whenever you can come before the end of this year. After that my movement will be uncertain though you will be welcome at this place whenever you come. Reverend Ralla Ram will be able to tell you how simply we live here. If therefore we cannot provide western amenities of life, we will be making up for the deficiency by the natural warmth of our affection. Muriel Lester had prepared me to receive you here.

Muriel Lester appeared at several key moments in the history of Gandhian nonviolence and the Black Freedom Struggle in America. Lester was an Englishwoman, a close friend of Gandhi, and the traveling secretary of the International Fellowship of Reconciliation (IFOR). In the early 1930s, while lecturing in the US on Gandhi, she met Howard Thurman and, upon her return to India, informed Gandhi of the impressive Black American religious thinker.

The story, as it is usually told, is that from that initial meeting with Gandhi, Thurman inspired other Black leaders at Howard University, like Martin Luther King Sr. ("Daddy King"), his classmate and friend, and Benjamin Mays, dean of Howard's School of Religion, with Gandhi's commitment to nonviolent activism. Some, like Mays, made trips to India to meet directly with Gandhi. Then, two decades later, a young preacher named Martin Luther King Jr. established nonviolence as the central premise of the struggle for the freedom and equality of Black Americans.

That story truncates the truth. Thurman was not the first Black American to make a connection with Gandhi and the Black Freedom Struggle in America. In the decade before Thurman's trip, Marcus Garvey's Universal Negro Improvement Association (UNIA) actively consulted with representatives of the Mahatma, even though Garvey and Gandhi never met.

Yet even Garvey's connection with Gandhi was not the only one. Perhaps the most important connection between Gandhi and Black Americans came with a very unlikely character, George Washington Carver of the Tuskegee Institute.

Many remember Carver as the "peanut scientist" who discovered hundreds of uses for the peanut—from making soap to insulating homes. But Carver's real mission lay in helping poor Black farmers survive the withering oppression of Jim Crow.

In 1929, Anglican priest Charles Freer Andrews, who'd been at Gandhi's side as an advisor in South Africa, China, and India for a quarter century, came to America to tour historically Black colleges and universities (HBCUs), where he lectured on *satyagraha*, Gandhi's word for nonviolent action. Andrews met

George Washington Carver while lecturing at the Tuskegee Institute, where the renowned scientist had been for almost fifty years. As they talked and became friends, Andrews realized that Carver shared much in common with Gandhi.

Both were deeply spiritual. Both were working to liberate the disinherited of society. And both believed that self-sufficiency and self-determination sprang from a deep, spiritual connection to the land; hence, they focused much of their efforts on elevating the plight of poor farmers. Carver created a series of pamphlets he sent to Black farmers to help them learn how to replenish the land they farmed, land that had been stripped of nutrients from many years of only growing cotton. Carver also wrote pamphlets on making goods and materials that many poor farmers once bought and on improving the physical conditions of farmers' dwellings, thereby enhancing self-sufficiency, increasing savings, and improving the lives of farmers and their families.

Carver also forwarded his simple, illustrated pamphlets to Gandhi, who distributed them to the poor farmers of India. The two developed a strong bond of mutual affection and a correspondence that lasted through the last decade of Carver's life. When Howard Thurman met Mahatma Gandhi, he encountered someone who already understood much about the plight of Black Americans and recognized the common struggle against white supremacy that Indians and Black Americans faced.

Howard Thurman and his delegation had been in India for five months but had been unable to arrange a meeting with Gandhi. Then, with the help of Mahadev Desai, Gandhi's longtime secretary, two weeks before they were to depart, Howard and Sue Thurman and Edward Carroll (Carroll's wife was not feeling well) boarded a train at night and then, four hours later, disembarked at Navsari Station, two hundred miles north of Bombay, where Mahadev Desai met them. They rested for the remainder of the night, then at dawn, the trio stepped into a battered Model T Ford for a dusty twenty-mile trip over rutted roads to Dharampur. Gandhi uncharacteristically sprang from his tent to greet the delegation.

Gandhi consulted a watch and informed Thurman he knew they did not have much time, since the delegation needed to leave soon. Then Gandhi launched into an intense questioning of Thurman, who would later write in his autobiography, "Never in my life have I been a part of that kind of examination: persistent, pragmatic questions about American Negroes."

Voting rights, lynching, education, Black churches, various schools of Black thought—Gandhi wanted to know about it all. Thurman obliged him with a brief history of Black Americans since emancipation and more detailed answers to Gandhi's pointed questions. Then it came time for the guests.

"Did the South African Negro take part in your movement?" Sue Bailey Thurman asked, for Gandhi had lived in South Africa from 1893 to 1914.

"No," said Gandhi. "I purposely did not invite them. It would have endangered our cause. They would not have understood the technique of our struggle, nor could they have seen the purpose or utility of nonviolence." It was his honest answer, yet it was difficult for the delegation to hear, since it implied that Gandhi held stereotypes of Black Africans as prone to violence and unable to grasp the significance of nonviolence, which was precisely what Thurman had been interested in bringing home to Black Americans.

Ultimately, the conversation turned to *satyagraha* (nonviolence), the principal reason all parties wished to convene. Gandhi expressed regret that he chose "nonviolence" as an English translation of *satyagraha* because the English word began with a negation ("non-"). *Satyagraha* is "no negative force," said Gandhi; rather it is "the greatest and the activest force in nature."

"Nonviolence overrides all other forces?" Thurman asked.

"Yes," Gandhi replied, "it is the only true force in life."

Gandhi believed that *satyagraha* was so powerful that one dedicated *satyagrahi* (a person living a nearly ascetic life adhering to the principles of *satyagraha*) could accumulate enough "soul force" to free millions from their oppression. Gandhi lamented to Thurman that though he had tried to be a dedicated *satyagrahi*, he'd fallen far short of the mark.

Sue Bailey Thurman interjected, "How am I to act, supposing my own brother is lynched before my eyes?"

"I must not wish ill will to these [lynchers], but neither must I cooperate with them," said Gandhi, "even to touch food that comes from them, and I refuse to cooperate even with my brother Negroes who tolerate the wrong."

Thurman left Gandhi with his thoughts that Black Americans were ready to embrace nonviolence.

"Well," said Gandhi, "if it comes true, it may be through the Negroes that the unadulterated message of nonviolence will be delivered to the world."

One is, of course, tempted to skip ahead twenty years to the Montgomery bus boycott, Rosa Parks, and a young Martin Luther King Jr.; skip ahead and affirm, as Bayard Rustin did with King after the success of Montgomery, that Gandhi's prophecy had come true. The only problem with skipping ahead is that it leapfrogs over too many important and interesting moments that, like a trail of potent breadcrumbs, link that fateful meeting in Dharampur and Gandhi's earlier correspondence with George Washington Carver to the swell of the Black Freedom Struggle in America.

Only months after Thurman departed India in 1936, Benjamin Mays arrived on his own pilgrimage to meet the Mahatma. Mays was Martin Luther King Sr.'s friend, Martin Luther King Jr.'s teacher and mentor, and dean of the School of Religion at Howard University. If Howard Thurman before him had received the first part of Gandhi's teachings on nonviolence, then Benjamin Mays received the second part.

Nonviolent resistance "is much more active than violent resistance," Gandhi said to Mays. "It is direct, ceaseless, but three-fourths invisible and only one-fourth visible. Nonviolence is the most invisible and the most effective. . . . A violent man's activity is most visible while it lasts. But it is always transitory."

By "invisible," Gandhi meant the rootedness of *satyagraha* is within each participant in a nonviolent resistance campaign. Gandhi—then later, King—called this invisible portion of nonviolence "soul force."

When Mays asked about what to do if nonviolent resistance broke down and became violent, Gandhi was firm that the welfare of the opponent should always be of utmost consideration. Violence toward and humiliation of an opponent led to division, not unity, in Gandhi's mind. Leaders of nonviolent resistance needed to be ready to call off an action and regroup if nonviolence turned into violence.

"How is a minority to act against an overwhelming majority?" Mays asked, knowing that, unlike the Indian people, Black Americans were far outnumbered by whites.

After recalling that his own movement on behalf of Indian people began in South Africa, where Indians were, by far, a tiny minority, Gandhi also espoused the notion that nonviolence is so powerful that when others see a people committed to nonviolent action, it will move many to join their ranks.

Like Thurman, Mays came away from his meeting with Gandhi humbled and deeply impressed. "The Negro people have much to learn from the Indians," he wrote. "The Indians have learned what we have not learned. They have learned how to sacrifice for a principle. They have learned how to sacrifice position, prestige, economic security, and even life itself for what they consider a righteous and respectable cause." Though Mays pondered whether nonviolent resistance could free India, he knew that Gandhi had given his followers an immensely valuable gift. "The fact that Gandhi and his nonviolent campaign have given the Indian masses a new conception of courage, no man can honestly deny," Mays wrote. "To discipline people to face death, to die, to go to jail for the cause without fear and without resorting to violence is an achievement of the first magnitude. And when an oppressed race ceases to be afraid, it is free."

Now would be the moment to say that Mays would be a future teacher of Martin Luther King Jr., and that Howard Thurman, a friend of King's father, was a constant visitor in their house, and that Gandhi had been following the Black Freedom Struggle in America at least since the time of George Washington Carver. But there is still so much history that took place for Black Americans in the twenty years between 1936 and 1956, between the meetings with the Mahatma and Montgomery: a world war in which Black Americans fought in overwhelming numbers, the US Army desegregated by presidential order for the first time since the Revolutionary War, the first march on Washington, *Brown v. Board of Education* successfully argued before the Supreme Court. But one of the aims of this book is to lift up and make visible some of the many hidden voices of the Black American past. None speaks more cogently to this deep connection between Gandhi, nonviolence, and the Black Freedom Struggle in America than the Gandhian ashram established in Harlem from 1940 to 1946.

Somehow, an ashram in Harlem, the gravitational center of Black America in the twentieth century, seems almost like an oxymoron. When I graduated from college in 1970, I helped to establish a branch of the Satchidananda Ashram at a communal living center, called Aquarius, on 148th Street in Harlem, between Amsterdam and St. Nicholas Avenues. Aquarius was founded by nutritionist and yoga teacher Daya Quander, and a group of us worked to have a portion of Aquarius certified as an Integral Yoga Institute, making it part of the Satchidananda Ashram community. For years, I told how we had established the first ashram in Harlem. And for years, I was wrong.

The first ashram in Harlem, an offshoot of IFOR, incorporated the Gandhian principles of *satyagraha*. Located at 2013 Fifth Avenue (around the corner from 125th Street), the Harlem Ashram, as it was called, included single men, women, and families. Presbyterian pastor James Herman Robinson called for the Fellowship of Reconciliation (FOR) to create an interracial spiritual community modeled after a Hindu ashram, where members could live in community and employ the principles of nonviolence to advocate for interracial justice.

Members of the Harlem Ashram lived in voluntary poverty. From their income, ashram members gave to a common fund according to their ability and took from this common fund according to their need. Members served the larger Harlem community through:

- Helping to find housing for Black men and women migrating to New York City from the South
- Investigating violence against Black men and women by the New York City Police Department
- Establishing a credit union run by and for the Harlem community
- Organizing a local cooperative buying club
- Supervising activities for children of the Harlem community

Muriel Lester, who'd first alerted Gandhi about Howard Thurman, taught a course on *satyagraha* at the ashram, and ashram members participated in several important and first-of-its-kind nonviolent actions, including a successful campaign to desegregate all New York City YMCAs and a 250-mile pilgrimage to the Lincoln Memorial in 1942 in support of anti-lynching and anti–poll tax bills.

Unique and rarely spoken of, the Harlem Ashram was a laboratory for injecting Gandhian nonviolent methods into the Black Freedom Struggle and for incubating future leaders of the movement.

Activist and legal crusader Pauli Murray, perhaps one of the first Black people to be open about their gender dysphoria, lived at the ashram. She would later go on to personal involvement in desegregation suits and professional involvement as a lawyer in civil rights and gender discrimination cases. Murray labeled discrimination against women "Jane Crow." Murray was a cofounder of the National Organization for Women (NOW).

Bayard Rustin, himself openly gay, lived nearby and studied at the ashram. Rustin, a dedicated IFOR member who would become a confidant and close advisor to Martin Luther King Jr., spent a month in India not long after Gandhi's assassination, studying *satyagraha* with the intention of developing a nonviolent movement upon his return to America. Once back, in a plan strongly opposed by Walter White and Thurgood Marshall of the NAACP, who thought it was too dangerous, Rustin proposed and executed a Journey of Reconciliation, the first-ever Freedom Ride through fifteen cities in Virginia, North Carolina, Kentucky, and Tennessee.

From April 9 to 23, 1947, an integrated team of IFOR members rode together. They were trained in Gandhian nonviolent methods, and they stopped along the way to speak and teach about nonviolent action at churches and universities and to civil rights groups. The Freedom Riders were arrested in North Carolina, where local judge Henry Whitfield ruled they had violated Jim Crow laws. The white members of the group were particularly objectionable to Whitfield.

"It's about time you Jews from New York learned that you can't come here bringing your niggers with you to upset the customs of the South," Whitfield said. "Just to teach you a lesson, I gave you black boys thirty days, and you whites ninety."

James Farmer, also an IFOR member, trained in nonviolence at the Harlem Ashram. While at Howard University, Farmer studied under Howard Thurman. Nonviolent social change was a core tenet of Farmer's belief. He founded the Congress of Racial Equality (CORE) and signed on to Gordon Carey's idea for a second Journey of Reconciliation in 1961, which Farmer dubbed the Freedom Ride. In the early 1960s, Farmer was considered one of the "Big Four" leaders of the Black Freedom Struggle, along with Martin Luther King Jr.; Roy Wilkins, head of the NAACP; and Whitney Young, head of the Urban League.

And then there was Reverend James Lawson, whom Martin Luther King Jr., on the eve of his assassination, called "the leading theorist and strategist of nonviolence in the world." While Lawson did not have direct contact with the Harlem Ashram, he did have a profound impact on bringing Gandhian nonviolent methods to the Black Freedom Struggle. King was actually in Memphis, where he was assassinated, at the behest of Lawson, who was working with the mainly Black sanitation workers in the city. When Lawson rose to speak at the memorial service for his student and friend John Lewis, he uttered a single word, *satyagraha*, then paused. How many in attendance that day understood the meaning and the gravity of what Lawson had just said? Though Lawson went on to give Lewis a beautiful eulogy, he could have stepped down from the pulpit after just that one word. For those who understood *satyagraha* and Lawson's role in bringing that Gandhian precept to the forefront of the Black Freedom Struggle, that one word would have been enough.

Lawson, like many other leading figures in the Black Freedom Struggle, was also an alumnus of the Fellowship of Reconciliation. In 1956, having just returned from India, where he studied *satyagraha* with Gandhi's followers, Lawson entered Oberlin College. A professor there introduced Lawson to Martin Luther King Jr., who promptly pleaded with him to come south. "Come now," King said. "We don't have anyone like you down there." That same year, Lawson moved to Nashville, enrolled in the Divinity School at Vanderbilt University, and was the Southern director of James Farmer's CORE. In 1958, Lawson began training members of various groups involved in the Black Freedom Struggle, including King's followers, in *satyagraha* and the use of nonviolent methods using a classroom in a church basement. John Lewis studied *satyagraha* with Lawson during this time.

On April 12, 2022, on the campus of Howard University, US

Secretary of State Antony Blinken welcomed Indian Minister of External Affairs Dr. Subrahmanyam Jaishankar to the United States for discussions on exchanges between the two countries in higher education. Blinken noted the long history of Howard University's connection, and therefore America's connection, with India through institutions of higher education. He cited Howard Thurman as being one of the first representatives responsible for that connection and observed that what Thurman took away from India and his meeting with Gandhi changed the course of civil rights history forever through Thurman's relationship with Martin Luther King Jr. There was, however, one glaring omission in Blinken's address regarding Howard Thurman. Blinken never addressed the issue of whether the US State Department in 1935 supported the British Home Office's active resistance to Thurman's trip or whether the State Department supported Thurman.

There were a handful of precepts of Gandhian nonviolence taught by men like Thurman, Lawson, and Lewis to protesters during the civil rights era. They are still as relevant today as they were in the 1940s, 1950s, and 1960s. Martin Luther King Jr. often referred to six principles of nonviolence he learned from his mentors, who studied with Gandhi. They are paraphrased here:

1. First, nonviolent resistance is not a method for cowards; it is a form of resistance. If one uses this method because one

is afraid or merely because one lacks the instruments of violence, one is not truly nonviolent. This is why Gandhi often said that if cowardice is the only alternative to violence, it is better to fight. He made this statement conscious of the fact that there is always another alternative: No individual or group need submit to any wrong, nor need they use violence to right the wrong. There is always the way of nonviolent resistance. This ultimately is the way of the strong person. It is not a method of stagnant passivity. The phrase "passive resistance" often gives the false impression that this is a sort of "do-nothing" method, in which the resister quietly and passively accepts evil. But nothing is further from the truth. For while the nonviolent resister is passive in the sense that she is not physically aggressive toward the opponent, her mind and emotions are always active, constantly seeking to persuade the opponent that he is wrong. The method is passive physically but strongly active spiritually. It is not passive nonresistance to evil; it is active nonviolent resistance to evil.

2. A second basic fact that characterizes nonviolence is that it does not seek to defeat or humiliate the opponent, but to win his friendship and understanding. The nonviolent resister must often express protest through noncooperation and boycotts, but the resister realizes that these are not ends in themselves; they are merely a means to awaken a sense of moral shame in the opponent. The end is redemption and reconciliation. The aftermath of nonviolence is the creation of the beloved community, while the aftermath of violence is tragic bitterness.

3. A third characteristic of this method is that the attack is directed against forces of evil rather than against persons who happen to be doing the evil. It is evil that the nonviolent resister seeks to defeat, not the persons victimized by evil. If she is opposing racial injustice, the nonviolent resister has the vision to see that the basic tension is not between races.

4. A fourth point that characterizes nonviolent resistance is a willingness to accept suffering without retaliation, to accept blows from the opponent without striking back. "Rivers of blood may have to flow before we gain our freedom, but it must be our blood," Gandhi said to his countrymen. "The nonviolent resister is willing to accept violence if necessary, but never to inflict it. He does not seek to dodge jail. If going to jail is necessary, he enters it 'as a bridegroom enters the bride's chamber.'"

   One may well ask: "What is the nonviolent resister's justification for this ordeal to which he invites others, for this mass political application of the ancient doctrine of turning the other cheek?" The answer is found in the realization that unearned suffering is redemptive. Suffering, the nonviolent resister realizes, has tremendous educational and transforming possibilities. "Things of fundamental importance to people are not secured by reason alone, but have to be purchased with their suffering," said Gandhi. He continued, "Suffering is infinitely more powerful than the law of the jungle for converting the opponent and opening his ears, which are otherwise shut to the voice of reason."

5. A fifth point concerning nonviolent resistance is that it avoids not only external physical violence but also internal violence of spirit. The nonviolent resister not only refuses to shoot his opponent, but he also refuses to hate him. At the center of nonviolence stands the principle of love. The nonviolent resister would contend that in the struggle for human dignity, the oppressed people of the world must not succumb to the temptation of becoming bitter or indulging in hate campaigns. To retaliate in kind would do nothing but intensify the existence of hate in the universe. Along the way of life, someone must have sense enough and morality enough to cut off the chain of hate. This can only be done by projecting the ethic of love to the center of our lives.

6. A sixth basic fact about nonviolent resistance is that it is based on the conviction that the universe is on the side of justice. Consequently, the believer in nonviolence has deep faith in the future. This faith is another reason why the nonviolent resister can accept suffering without retaliation. For the resister knows that in the struggle for justice, there is cosmic companionship. It is true that there are devout believers in nonviolence who find it difficult to believe in a personal God. But even these persons believe in the existence of some creative force that works for universal wholeness. Whether we call it an unconscious process, an impersonal Brahman, or a Personal Being of matchless power and infinite love, there is a creative force in this universe that works to bring the disconnected aspects of reality into a harmonious whole.

CHAPTER 10

BLACK TROOPS ONLY

IN JUNE 1943, WHITE UNITED STATES AIR FORCE MILITARY Police members ordered pubs in the town of Bamber Bridge, England, to post segregated drinking hours for Black and white GIs. Pub owners agreed. But when the MPs returned the next day, historian Anthony Burgess reports, they found signs in the windows reading "Black Troops Only."

Black soldiers stationed in Bamber Bridge belonged to the 1511th Quartermaster Truck Regiment, which provided logistical support for the US Eighth Air Force Division out of Air Force Station 569 (also known as "Adams Hall"). The 234th US Military Police Company, also stationed in Bamber Bridge, apparently wanted to impose a Jim Crow–style color ban on local pubs due to fears that Black troops, supposedly incensed with the recent racial uprising back home in Detroit, might take out their frustrations on white troops if they intermingled while drinking.

On the evening of June 24, 1943, Private Eugene Nunn stopped at Ye Olde Hob Inn in Bamber Bridge for a drink. Having just finished a supply run to Manchester in his truck, Nunn was in his field jacket rather than his Class A dress uniform. Nunn and other patrons were apparently trying to extend drinking hours at the pub beyond "last call." Three white officers who may have been inside the pub hailed military police patrolling the area to report trouble at the inn. White MPs Corporal Roy A. Windsor and Private First Class Ralph Ridgeway arrived to reprimand, if not arrest, Nunn for being out of uniform. An argument ensued, and locals, including a British soldier and women members of the British Auxiliary Territorial Service, jumped to Nunn's defense and that of the other Black soldiers who gathered around Nunn.

"Why do you want to arrest them?" the British soldier challenged the MPs. "They're not doing anything or bothering anybody."

The situation escalated when Black Private Lynn M. Adams brandished a beer bottle at the MPs, causing Roy A. Windsor to draw his gun. A Black staff sergeant, William Byrd, stepped between Nunn and Windsor, calming Windsor and coaxing him to holster his weapon. But as the MPs drove away, Adams hurled a beer bottle at their jeep, which shattered, spraying them with beer. The MPs vowed to return. While the MPs gathered reinforcements, the Black soldiers headed back to their barracks from the pub in the company of the white women from the British Auxiliary Territorial Service. Exactly the kind of behavior that got Black men lynched in the Jim Crow South.

MPs intercepted the group, and a violent fight broke out. Private Nunn punched an MP. Another MP fired his handgun, hitting Private Adams in the neck. MPs fired again on the Black soldiers, injuring several more. Then the two sides dispersed—the Black soldiers carrying their wounded comrades back to their barracks at Adams Hall, along with reports that white MPs were gunning to kill Black men. Black troops inside the camp raided the armory and armed themselves as a result.

Unable to calm the anxious Black troops, white Major George C. Heris called upon the only Black officer at Adams Hall, Lieutenant Edwin C. Jones, for help.

"I am one of you, boys," Jones told the Black soldiers. "You put up your arms. I know Colonel Pitcher [the absent unit commander] and Major Heris have been with us 100 percent. We cannot take these things into our own hands. We'll go back to our barracks, and the guilty ones will suffer, and he will see that justice is done."

That seemed to calm the situation.

But around midnight, a dozen or so MPs roared into the Black soldiers' camp in two jeeps and an armored vehicle with a machine gun mounted on top, which only confirmed the Black soldiers' worst fears. They scrambled for arms, and a series of gun battles took place between them and the white MPs, spreading out of the camp and into Bamber Bridge itself. Black soldiers even warned local residents to stay inside and seek cover.

"I would rather die fighting for my race," one Black soldier was overheard saying, "than I would against our enemies."

By 4:00 a.m. on June 25, 1943, the "Battle of Bamber Bridge" was over, and one Black solider, Private William Crossland, lay dead, shot in the back by an MP. Several soldiers and a few MPs were wounded.

The commanding general of the Eighth Air Force Service Command, Major General Henry Miller, reported on the incident soon after. While acknowledging the poor treatment of Blacks by white officers and MPs, Miller blamed the Battle of Bamber Bridge on the importation into England of racist attitudes from America, the liberal views of the English on race, the tendency of Black soldiers to want to stand up to discrimination and take the law into their own hands, and the Black-owned American newspaper *The People's Voice*, which aggressively reported on injustices done to Black Americans.

Only the Black men of the 1511th stood trial. Of the thirty-five Black soldiers court-martialed, twenty-eight were convicted of mutiny and given prison sentences ranging from three months to fifteen years, some with hard labor. Reading reports of the trial, one comes away with a military version of the courtroom drama in *To Kill a Mockingbird*.

The trial was plagued with contradictory testimony and the inability of white witnesses to positively identify Black defendants. Higher-ranking white officers who should have interceded to stop the bloodshed were reported to have hid, run, or simply cried. Still, the military and the prosecution, of course, contended it was a fair trial. Even the defense attorney, a Southern white lawyer, claimed the trial was fair. Edwin C. Jones, the only Black officer at Adams Hall, was never allowed to testify or even to speak with the defense.

"It was not a fair trial," Jones said, "and was nothing other than a kangaroo court."

Reviews by senior military officers, pressure by local residents in support of the Black troops, and the military's need for personnel as the war ground on resulted in some sentences being vacated and the return to active duty of some of the Black troops convicted.

Still, the Black soldiers were never exonerated. The white officers and MPs never stood trial. The US military made only nominal changes to the structure of segregated Black units.

But in June 2022, eighty years after the incident, local residents erected a memorial garden to the Battle of Bamber Bridge, commemorating the death of Private William Crossland and honoring the Black troops they had supported.

In choosing to impose Jim Crow rules on Bamber Bridge, white officers and military policemen had brought their racist views in front of the wrong group of people. Lancashire had a long history of supporting the rights of Black Americans, going back at least to the Civil War era.

In the late 1850s, scandal-ridden former South Carolina Governor James H. Hammond declared, "I firmly believe that American slavery is not only not a sin, but especially commanded by God through Moses, and approved by Christ through his apostles . . . Slavery is the corner-stone of our republican edifice," he said. "I repudiate, as ridiculously absurd, that much lauded but nowhere accredited dogma of Mr. Jefferson that 'all men are born equal.'"

As a senator in March 1858, Hammond verbally tussled with New York Senator William Seward:

> Without firing a gun, without drawing a sword, should they make war on us we could bring the whole world to our feet . . . What would happen if no cotton was furnished for three years? I will not stop to depict what everyone can imagine, but this is certain: England would topple headlong and carry the whole civilized world with her, save the South. No, you dare not make war on cotton. No power on earth dares to make war upon it. Cotton is king.

Hammond, through his hubris, coined the phrase "Cotton is king." When the South seceded and America descended into civil war, Southern international diplomacy coalesced around this notion that the world could not survive without cotton, and hence without slavery. Using this "King Cotton Diplomacy," the Confederacy attempted to coerce England and France into alliances by withholding cotton. The effort failed, but the disruption in raw cotton shipped to England did, however, help plunge the Lancashire textile industry into what has been called the Cotton Famine.

Still, British textile workers stood with enslaved Black Americans, as residents of Bamber Bridge stood with Black troops, often against their industrial masters. Writing to Abraham Lincoln on New Year's Eve in 1862, the day before the Emancipation Proclamation was to go into effect, Mayor Abel Heywood of

Manchester, then within the ancient county boundaries of Lancashire, expressed the views of several thousand working-class men, who unanimously approved his correspondence. The long letter reads, in part:

> As citizens of Manchester, assembled at the Free-trade Hall, we beg to express our fraternal sentiments towards you and your country . . . One thing alone has, in the past, lessened our sympathy with your country and our confidence in it—we mean the ascendancy of politicians who not merely maintained negro slavery, but desired to extend and root it more firmly. Since we have discerned, however, that the victory of the free North, in the war which has so sorely distressed us as well as afflicted you, will strike off the fetters of the slave, you have attracted our warm and earnest sympathy.

Over Rooley Moor, outside the town of Rochdale in Lancashire, there's a plaque erected by the BBC History Project, spurred by the work of historian David Olusoga, that reads:

> In memory of the
> ROCHDALE
> MILLWORKERS
> who supported the struggle
> against slavery during the
> American Civil War
> 1861–65

The plaque commemorates the mill workers who would not process cotton delivered to them from the American South, but it also marks and memorializes the all-brick, handlaid "Cotton Famine Road" that they built as a public works project during those hard times. The four-mile Cotton Famine Road, still standing today, runs through Rooley Moor, connecting the village of Catley Lane Head in the south to Ding Quarry in the north. It is an enduring reminder of the connection between the people of this Lancashire region and the struggle for freedom by Black men and women in America.

General Miller also laid blame for the Battle of Bamber Bridge at the feet of *The People's Voice*, a Black-owned newspaper that he felt agitated Black troops at Bamber Bridge by reporting on the wrongs done to Blacks. What he left unsaid was how displeased the US military was with the Double V Campaign spearheaded by *The People's Voice.*

The People's Voice, also known simply as the *Voice*, was a Harlem-based newspaper that was started in 1942 by legendary Harlem congressman Adam Clayton Powell Jr. The *Voice* reported and investigated extensively on the news of Harlem and the treatment of Blacks in American institutions, including the military. *The Pittsburgh Courier*, one of the most widely circulated Black-owned newspapers at the time, responded to a request from President Franklin D. Roosevelt that such newspapers tone down their reporting of the mistreatment of Blacks in America and increase their support of the war effort. One result was the Double V Campaign.

The double V sign featured the index and middle fingers of each hand forming a *V*. The campaign originated in a letter written by twenty-six-year-old James Thompson to *The Pittsburgh Courier* entitled "Should I Sacrifice to Live 'Half-American'?" in which Thompson suggested the double V sign:

> The V for victory sign is being displayed prominently in all so-called democratic countries which are fighting for victory over aggression, slavery, and tyranny. If this V sign means that to those now engaged in this great conflict, then let we colored Americans adopt the double VV for a double victory. The first V for victory over our enemies from without, the second V for victory over our enemies from within. For surely those who perpetrate these ugly prejudices here are seeking to destroy our democratic form of government just as surely as the Axis forces.

The *Voice* joined the *Courier*, *The Chicago Defender*, and the *Amsterdam Star-News*, all Black-owned newspapers, in promoting the campaign, which received wide support in the Black community and featured slogans, posters, and pictures. That Black soldier at Bamber Bridge who said he would rather die for his race than his country expressed the sentiment embodied by the Double V Campaign, which many white Americans and many US military leaders viewed as subversive.

"The world's greatest democracy fought the world's greatest racist with a segregated army," historian Stephen Ambrose wrote.

Langston Hughes captured this tragic dilemma in his poem "Beaumont to Detroit: 1943" in these lines, "You tell me that hitler / Is a mighty bad man. / I guess he took lessons / from the ku klux klan."

The *Voice* also covered the 1943 racial unrest in Detroit, which was intimately connected to the war. With the US entering World War II, Detroit's automotive industry was converted to military production. High wages attracted large numbers of Black Southern workers hoping to escape withering sharecropping and Jim Crow conditions. Even though President Franklin D. Roosevelt issued Executive Order 8802 on June 25, 1941, prohibiting racial discrimination in the nation's defense industry, the order was unevenly applied. Black Americans were excluded from many national defense jobs, particularly the skilled and managerial positions. This, combined with Detroit's lack of housing and police brutality against Black residents, set the conditions for racial conflagration.

Not only Blacks migrated north to Detroit. Whites did, too, bringing with them their ugly racial stereotypes and white supremacist beliefs. By 1943, the Ku Klux Klan had established a substantial presence in Detroit, and in the later 1930s, members of its offshoot group, the Black Legion, had been arrested and convicted of murder and attempted murder. In 1942, when Detroit attempted to construct more housing, the effort was met with resistance and slogans reading "We Want White Tenants In Our White Community."

Lasting three days, from June 20 to 22, 1943, the unrest was centered in the Black neighborhood of Paradise Valley, the poorest area in Detroit. Armed white mobs from outside of Paradise Valley descended on the Black neighborhood, destroying property and killing and injuring residents while the Detroit police watched without intervening. But armed Black residents of Detroit fought back, also looting businesses owned by whites.

The Detroit racial unrest followed similar uprisings that summer in New York City; Los Angeles; Beaumont, Texas; and Mobile, Alabama. On June 22, 1943, six thousand federal troops were ordered into Detroit to quell the uprising and restore the peace. In all, thirty-four people were killed, twenty-five of them Black, killed mostly by Detroit's white police force. Four hundred thirty-three people were wounded (75 percent of them Black), and property valued at two million dollars (worth thirty-four million dollars in 2023) was destroyed.

Racial uprisings rarely happen in a vacuum. Eighty years earlier, in 1863, during the Civil War, Detroit also exploded over race. In 1863, as in 1943, Detroit was a city with Black and white residents born in the South. Detroit was a stop on the Underground Railroad, but many escaping enslaved people simply chose to stay there rather than cross over the river into Canada.

While in 1863 no automobile industry existed for conversion to national defense, the Union Army had an active draft that many white Detroit residents resented. Why fight for the freedom of Black people? Especially when they might take your job?

The uprising began with the trial of Thomas Faulkner, a

mixed-race man accused of molesting two young white girls. Guards escorting Faulkner into court were ordered to fire blank rounds into an imposing white mob to keep them at bay. A live round was fired, and Charles Langer, a German onlooker in the crowd, was killed. Incensed white residents turned their wrath on local Blacks. Black civilians were attacked, Black businesses were looted and destroyed, and Black homes were burned down.

Joshua Boyd, a formerly enslaved man saving money to purchase the freedom of his wife and family, escaped from a burning building only to be caught and beaten to death by the crazed white mob. Black residents fled the area, north to Canada or west to the nearby independent city of Corktown. By eleven that night, the violence subsided after Detroit had ordered in federal troops from Ypsilanti and Fort Wayne. Records show two civilian deaths, one white and one Black, but many more residents, mainly Black men, women, and children, were badly beaten and injured. Over two hundred Blacks and a few whites lost their homes in the uprising, which wrought an estimated fifteen thousand dollars to twenty thousand dollars (five hundred thousand dollars in 2023) in property damage, principally for Blacks.

Thomas Faulkner was convicted and received a life sentence. Then, several years later, the two girls at the center of his conviction completely recanted their testimony—Faulkner never molested them, as he'd always contended—and his conviction was vacated. No one was ever arrested for murdering Joshua Boyd.

History almost always has a backstory. The racial epithets, insults, unfairness, and bullets leveled at Black troops in Bamber

Bridge surely carried the weight of this history, even if it did not carry the names of Thomas Faulkner and Joshua Boyd; it carried the depth of the 1863 racial uprising in Detroit, even if the *Voice* only mentioned what took place in 1943.

⁘ ⁘ ⁘ ⁘

As early as the American Revolution, military service for Black Americans meant their hopes clashed with white fears. Blacks serving in the military felt that if they offered exemplary service, they would be granted equal treatment in return. Whites feared that heroic service by Blacks would demand equal treatment at home, disrupting white supremacy.

In Dunmore's Proclamation of 1775 issued by the royal governor of Virginia, John Murray, the Fourth Earl of Dunmore, freedom was offered to any enslaved person who left their master and joined British forces against them. An enraged slave owner, Thomas Jefferson, wrote in the Declaration of Independence that King George was "now exciting those very people to rise in arms against us," although the passage did not make it into the final version.

An outraged Virginia Assembly responded a month later with a proclamation of its own, which read, in part, "It is enacted, that all negro or other slaves, conspiring to rebel or make insurrection, shall suffer death."

Estimates place the number as high as one hundred thousand enslaved people who crossed over to the British lines during the American Revolution. They were known as "Black Loyalists" and after their service to the British, some of them were resettled in England. Most were shipped to Nova Scotia, where they faced harsh winters with little support from the British government. Some of those in Nova Scotia were then transported to Sierra Leone and left to their own devices to set up a colony.

Enslaved and free Black soldiers fought with the Continental Army in every major battle of the American Revolution. But at the beginning of the American Revolution, few white leaders thought it advisable to admit Black soldiers into the ranks of the Continental Army. When George Washington took command of the fledgling army in July 1775, he issued orders to recruiters prohibiting them from recruiting Blacks. A war council with his generals on October 8, 1775, unanimously supported the idea that no Blacks should serve in the army. The question of Black soldiers in the army again came up on October 18, 1775, before Benjamin Franklin and the Committee of Conference. Again, they voted in favor of excluding Blacks from military service.

War, however, dictates its own logic.

Dwindling Continental Army numbers, stories of valor on the part of Blacks fighting against the British, and British tactics like Dunmore's Proclamation had an effect on changing attitudes toward Black soldiers. Alexander Hamilton captured this transformation in a letter to John Jay regarding a plan to enlist three to four battalions of Black soldiers from the South:

> The contempt we have been taught to entertain for the blacks, makes us fancy many things that are founded neither in reason nor experience; and an unwillingness to part

> with property of so valuable a kind, will furnish a thousand arguments to show the impracticability, or pernicious tendency, of a scheme which requires such sacrifices. But it should be considered, that if we do not make use of them in this way, the enemy probably will; and that the best way to counteract the temptations they will hold out, will be to offer them ourselves. An essential part of the plan is, to give them their freedom with their swords. This will secure their fidelity, animate their courage, and, I believe, will have a good influence upon those who remain, by opening a door to their emancipation.

Thus, toward the end of the American Revolutionary War, Blacks were recruited into the Continental Army, where just shy of ten thousand troops served in all-Black units and integrated units as well: the first integrated armed forces in America and the last until the end of the Second World War. When the Revolutionary War ended, some whites kept their promises and granted formerly enslaved Black soldiers their freedom; other Black men were forced back to being enslaved. Black troops emerged from the war with some measure of hope.

By the Civil War, much of that hope had faded in the face of rising racism and white supremacy. In September 1862, around the time he released a draft of the coming Emancipation Proclamation, Abraham Lincoln also issued this warning about Black soldiers: "If we were to arm them, I fear that in a few weeks the arms would be in the hands of the rebels." An Ohio congressman expressed a widespread view that Black men might distinguish themselves in combat, an even worse fate than Lincoln feared: "If you make him the instrument by which your battles are fought, the means by which your victories are won, you must treat him as a victor is entitled to be treated, with all decent and becoming respect." How awful it would be for white Americans to treat Black Americans with "all decent and becoming respect."

By the summer of 1862, Baton Rouge had fallen to Union forces—so, too, had New Orleans. What now kept Major General Benjamin Franklin Butler sweating through the sweltering Louisiana nights was protecting the gains made by his Union troops. He ordered a wide swath of forest to be cut down, clearing the area from the Mississippi River to Lake Pontchartrain around New Orleans in order to make it more defensible against the forces of cunning Confederate General Meriwether Jeff "Swamp Fox" Thompson, which threatened from the north. Butler gave that order to General John W. Phelps, reasoning that Phelps could enlist the large number of runaway enslaved men ("contraband," they were called) at the camp. But Phelps refused.

A Vermont native and graduate of West Point, Phelps had been training freemen and the formerly enslaved as fighting forces. Instead of axes, Phelps requested arms. President Lincoln forbade using Black troops, Butler reasoned with Phelps, even ordering the disbanding of the 1st South Carolina Infantry Regiment (African Descent) organized by General David "Black David" Hunter. Butler also ordered runaways returned to their masters. Besides, Butler told Phelps, the arms and equipment sent to him were specifically reserved for white men—or, as General William T. Sherman would say a year later, "I would prefer to have this a white man's war."

Phelps stood his ground.

"While I am willing to prepare African regiments for the defense of the Government against its assailants I am not willing to become the mere slave-driver you propose."

With that, Phelps resigned. Butler denied it. Phelps then mailed his commission back to Lincoln. "Mad as a March Hare on the 'nigger question,'" Butler said to his wife.

While Lincoln brooded over Phelps's resignation, Butler's need for troops grew. Out of desperation, Butler impressed former Confederate soldiers into the Union's ranks. He requested reinforcements from the US War Department. When the department refused, he threatened "to call on Africa for assistance."

Ultimately, Butler made that call.

Established in 1861 in New Orleans, the 1st Louisiana Native Guard of the Confederate States of America was organized as a militia of free Blacks fighting on the side of the Confederacy. But the Louisiana legislature passed a law in early 1862 that militias were to be composed of only "free white males capable of bearing arms," and the all-Black Native Guard disbanded. Then Union troops, and the Union Navy under Admiral David G. Farragut, laid siege to New Orleans, and the Confederacy briefly reinstated the Native Guard as a last-ditch effort to stave off the assault. The unit was finally disbanded when the city fell in the spring of 1862.

In the fall of 1862, Butler ordered officers from the Native Guard rounded up. To his surprise, mostly light-skinned men stood before him, yet they had chosen a man he described "as dark as the ace of spades" to be their spokesman.

"My officers, most of them, believe that Negroes won't fight," Butler said.

"Oh, but we will," said the group.

"Then tell me why some Negroes have not in this war struck a good blow somewhere for their freedom?" Butler asked the spokesman. "All over the South, the men have been conscripted and driven away to the armies, leaving ten Negroes in some districts to one white man, and the colored men have simply gone on raising crops and taking care of their women and children."

The spokesman hesitated.

"Whatever the answer may be, it shall harm no one of you," said Butler.

"General, will you permit a question?"

"Yes," answered Butler.

"If we colored men had risen to make war on our masters, would not it have been our duty to ourselves, they being our enemies, to kill the enemy wherever we could find them, and all the white men would have been our enemies to be killed?"

"I don't know but what you are right," Butler said. "I think that would be a logical necessity of insurrection."

"If the colored men had begun such a war as that, General, which general of the United States Army should we have called on to help us fight our battles?"

Butler stammered. That question, he admitted, had no answer.

"Well, why do you think your men will fight?" Butler asked.

"General, we come of a fighting race. Our fathers were

brought here as slaves because they were captured in war, and in hand-to-hand fights, too. We are willing to fight. Pardon me, General, but the only cowardly blood we have got in our veins is the white blood."

The 1st Louisiana Native Guard of the United States of America "became soldiers of the United States on the 22d day of August, 1862. In a very short time three regiments of infantry and two batteries of artillery were equipped, drilled, and ready for service. Better soldiers never shouldered a musket," Butler said.

Many Black soldiers and sailors followed. About 179,000 Black soldiers served in the Union Army, another 19,000 in the Union Navy. Roughly 40,000 Black members of the military died during the years of conflict, 75 percent of those from disease and from the refusal of field hospitals to treat soldiers of color. Early in the conflict, Black soldiers received seven dollars per month serving in the US military, while white soldiers received thirteen dollars per month. After a nationwide outcry, which included a number of white soldiers, Congress passed an act in 1864 that granted equal pay. While that may have brought pay equity to Blacks and whites serving in the armed forces, problems of unequal promotion and prejudice plagued Black people in the military during the Civil War and still plague Black people in the military today.

Still, Black Union soldiers pursued the Confederacy to the end.

In the battles of his Overland Campaign, Ulysses S. Grant crossed the Rapidan River with eight thousand Black troops to engage Robert E. Lee's forces. Simultaneously attacking Richmond, Benjamin F. Butler, who had returned from lessons learned in Louisiana, had with him five thousand Black infantrymen and eighteen hundred Black cavalries.

After a long ten-month siege of Petersburg, Virginia, in which Black troops sustained heavy losses, Lee abandoned both Petersburg and Richmond, fleeing west toward Appomattox with the US Colored Troops 2nd Regiment in hot pursuit. It ended there, with Black troops "moving forward at double quick" and Confederate soldiers "retreating in confusion."

On land and sea, Black troops were involved in every theater of the Civil War. They served with distinction and died with honor. Yet their bravery and courage rarely received official recognition. The Medal of Honor, created by the US Congress during the Civil War, was bestowed upon fourteen hundred Union troops. Only twenty-five Black soldiers received the medal. At his own expense, General Benjamin Butler created a medal officially known as the Army of the James Medal but popularly known as the Butler Medal or the Colored Troops Medal, which he issued to two hundred Black Union soldiers for their bravery and heroism in the Richmond and Petersburg campaigns. After Butler's removal from command, Black troops were forbidden to pin his "unofficial" medal on their uniforms.

The Civil War brought an end to slavery in the United States, but it was only a temporary end to the oppression of the formerly enslaved. During Reconstruction, for approximately a decade after the Civil War, Blacks held political office from local sheriffs to US senators, Blacks voted, and Black communities thrived. It seemed as though the sunlight of American democracy was breaking through the dark cloud of American slavery. But white resentment, hatred, and supremacy festered just below the surface.

By the middle of the 1870s, the Ku Klux Klan and other violent groups, such as the Red Shirts and White League, had become well-established; massacres and lynchings of Black people by white mobs grew steadily; the Union withdrew its troops from the South; Northern attention, as expressed in newspapers, fatigued from reports of the plight of the formerly enslaved; often at gunpoint, whites took back office and power from Blacks; and the institution of white supremacy and discrimination known as Jim Crow became firmly entrenched in the South.

"It is impossible to create a dual personality," wrote professors Philip Klinker and Rogers Smith in *The Unsteady March*, "which will be on the one hand a fighting man toward the enemy, and on the other, a craven who will accept treatment as less than a man at home."

Kentucky in 1868 exemplified the threats Black veterans faced. When delivering his annual report to Congress in November of that year, Secretary of War John McAllister Schofield wrote of attempts by the department to deliver money owed to Black Civil War veterans by the Department of War:

> More than 1,100 colored soldiers have received their bounty from the bureau during the year. In many cases, delay in payment has been unavoidable. It has been difficult to reach claimants in remote and mountainous districts. Having

> served in the Union Army, they have been the especial objects of persecution, and in hundreds of incidents have been driven from their homes. The outrages perpetrated by the Ku-klux Klan have caused a great exodus into other states.

Schofield was, of course, understating the problem. Black veterans were frequent targets of white hate. From the end of Reconstruction to the beginning of the Black Freedom Struggle (the Civil Rights Movement), tens of thousands of Black veterans were hounded, harassed, and harangued; some were hanged, lynched while still proudly wearing the uniforms in which they fought for the freedoms of their tormentors. Often, Black veterans were killed by mobs or persons acting under official authority—like state and local police or city and state leaders. Besides those actually murdered, others barely escaped death, while untold others were injured physically, emotionally, or psychologically.

"The people where the outrages occur warn, conceal and protect the evil-doers," Schofield also said.

The Equal Justice Initiative in its report "Lynching in America: Targeting Black Veterans" chronicled many of the Black veterans lynched, murdered, or nearly killed by whites between the end of the Civil War and the end of World War II:

- In 1880, Johnson Whittaker, one of the first Black cadets at West Point, was badly beaten by three white men. Academy officials accused him of staging the attack and expelled him.
- In the 1880s, Robert Robinson, a Black soldier stationed at Fort Shaw in Montana, was accused of murder, but before

he could stand trial, a white mob entered the jail, asked the sheriff for the keys to Robinson's cell, dragged him out, and lynched him.

- In 1918, Sergeant Edgar Caldwell, a decorated World War I soldier with the 24th Infantry, was kicked and beaten by the conductor and the motorman of an Anniston, Alabama, streetcar for refusing to leave the "white section" of the car. When his assailants refused to stop, Caldwell drew his service revolver and fired on them, killing one. Caldwell was handed over to local police by the US Army. He was convicted of murder and sentenced to death in a trial that lasted five days. His appeal reached the Supreme Court, which refused to overturn his conviction. On July 30, 1920, Edgar Caldwell was hanged before a crowd of several thousand.
- A few months after returning from World War I, Black veteran Ely Green was driving in downtown Waxahachie, Texas, when he was told by a white policeman that the man was going to beat the army uniform off of him. Several officers dragged Green from his car and beat him mercilessly in front of a large crowd.
- When Black veteran Daniel Mack brushed up against a white man in Sylvester, Georgia, an altercation ensued, and Mack was arrested. "I fought for you in France to make the world safe for democracy," Mack said at his arraignment. "I don't think you've treated me right in putting me in jail and keeping me there, because I've got as much right as anyone to walk on the sidewalk." To which the presiding judge replied, "This is a white man's country, and you don't want to forget it," then sentenced Mack

to thirty days on a chain gang. While serving out his sentence, Mack was dragged from his cell, beaten, and left for dead.

- On July 25, 1946, George W. Dorsey, his wife, Mae Murray Dorsey, and Roger Malcolm and his wife, Dorothy, who was seven months pregnant, were lynched near Moore's Ford Bridge in Walton County, Georgia. George Dorsey had been home for only nine months after serving five years in the Pacific Theater during World War II. Though the lynchings drew national attention and an investigation by the FBI and President Harry S. Truman offered $12,500 for information leading to a conviction, no one was ever brought to trial for the murders.
- On February 12, 1946, Isaac Woodard, a Black veteran who'd served in the Pacific during World War II, asked a Greyhound bus driver if he had time to use the restroom. The driver cursed at Woodard, then threw him off the bus at the next stop, where Chief of Police Linwood Shull and several other officers awaited. The officers beat Woodard so badly, they permanently blinded him. But a judge fined him fifty dollars and denied his release for medical attention. A blind Woodard would later say, "Negro veterans that fought in this war . . . don't realize that the real battle has just begun in America. They went overseas and did their duty and now they're home and have to fight another struggle, that I think outweighs the war."
- Veteran of World War II and civil rights leader Hosea Williams said, "I had fought in World War II, and I once was captured by the German army, and I want to tell you the Germans never were as inhumane as the state troopers of Alabama."

These are just a handful of the many instances of white men and women attacking Black men who'd served on their behalf in the US military. US Senator James Vardaman of Mississippi may have summed up best the hatred he and other whites felt for Black veterans when he warned on the Senate floor in 1917, "Impress the Negro with the fact that he is defending the flag, inflate his untutored soul with military airs, teach him that it is his duty to keep the emblem of the Nation flying triumphantly in the air—it is but a short step to the conclusion that his political rights must be respected."

It did not matter if any Black soldier in the 1511th at Bamber Bridge, England, knew the name of even one Black soldier who had been beaten or lynched in America after having served their country in a war. What mattered is that they felt the centuries-old anger and rage of the white MPs and white officers toward them, inexplicable yet palpable all the same, and they knew, as did those Black veterans who had fallen to white mobs before them, that if they didn't stand up to fight for themselves, no one else would, and in all likelihood, they would end up dead. Though Private William Crossland of Pittsylvania County, Virginia, is listed by the US Army Air Forces as a casualty of war, he really is a casualty of hatred, racism, and white supremacy.

CHAPTER 11

THE MARCH THAT NEVER HAPPENED, THE MAN WHO WAS NEVER THERE

"WHY SHOULD WE MARCH?" THE ORGANIZERS ASKED. THEN they answered, "Millions of Negro Americans all over this great land claim the right to be free. Free from want! Free from fear! Free from Jim Crow!" No, this was not the March on Washington that took place on a hot summer's day in late August 1963. This was not the March on Washington where Martin Luther King Jr. spoke of his "dream" to the hundreds of thousands assembled before him and to millions around the world. This was not the March on Washington that followed the Birmingham campaign and presaged the Selma-to-Montgomery marches.

The year was 1941. Pearl Harbor had not yet been bombed; still, signs of America's impending entrance into a world war abounded. "Winning democracy for the Negro," said A. Philip Randolph, one of the march organizers, "is winning the war for democracy."

This was the first march on Washington, scheduled for July 1, 1941—the one that never took place. The march made for strange bedfellows. On one side were march organizers A. Philip Randolph and Bayard Rustin. Pitted against the march were President Franklin Delano Roosevelt and, early on, some prominent Black organizations such as the NAACP. While so much attention has been placed on Martin Luther King Jr. and the second March on Washington, the critical importance of the first march on Washington has been lost, even though it was the culmination of events taking place decades before 1941, with an impact reverberating for decades to come.

As America geared up for war, more national defense jobs became available, and more Black Americans sought them. But a war overseas has never given rise to a lessening of racial discrimination and hatred at home. James Howard "Dutch" Kindelberger, CEO of North American Aviation, a subsidiary of General Motors, said, "While we are in complete sympathy with the Negro, it is against company policy to employ them as aircraft workers or mechanics . . . regardless of their training . . . There will be some jobs as janitors for Negroes."

Through a series of mergers and acquisitions, North American Aviation later became part of Boeing.

In response to this sentiment in America, A. Philip Randolph issued a call for:

> An "all-out" thundering march on Washington, ending in a monster and huge demonstration at Lincoln's Monument, will shake up white America . . . The Negroes' stake

in national defense is big. It consists of jobs, thousands of jobs. It may represent millions, yes, hundreds of millions of dollars in wages. It consists of new industrial opportunities and hope. This is worth fighting for . . .

Most important and vital to all, Negroes by the mobilization and coordination of their mass power, can cause PRESIDENT ROOSEVELT TO ISSUE AN EXECUTIVE ORDER ABOLISHING DISCRIMATION IN ALL GOVERNMENT DEPARTMENTS, ARMY, NAVY, AIR CORPS, AND NATIONAL DEFENSE JOBS. [Emphasis in the original.]

But Roosevelt would have none of it, and he let Randolph know that in an Oval Office meeting in late June 1941.

But who was A. Philip Randolph?

Most mentions of Asa Philip Randolph describe him as a labor union organizer and head of the Brotherhood of Sleeping Car Porters (BSCP), both of which are true. Few mention that Randolph founded one of the first successful Black unions, and fewer still say anything about the important place that sleeping car porters occupy in the history of Black America.

Sleeping car porters, or Pullman porters, referred specifically to how George Mortimer Pullman, from his headquarters in Chicago, hired newly freed, formerly enslaved men en masse around the end of the Civil War to fulfill his dream of creating a luxury railroad experience for white Americans, whom he believed would feel most comfortable being attended to by subservient Black men in uniform. Many whites called any Pullman porter George, a derisive name harkening back to slavery, when enslaved males were simply called by the first names of their masters.

Along the tracks, porters faced many challenges—racial insults and indignations from white passengers and railway crew, exceptionally long hours away from their families, and low wages. George Pullman expected them to get by on tips. My grandfather, John B. Ford, was a Pullman porter who for many years worked the Winsted Express, which ran between New York City and Winsted, Connecticut. Robert L. Duffus reported on him in *The New York Times*:

> Every night Ford sleeps on his car at Winsted. At 6:45 in the morning he starts for New York, where he arrives at 10:23. If he is lucky he gets home by 11:30. Four hours with his family and he leaves again, to take his car back to Winsted on the 4:25. Such is his life—a pretty useful one, according to those who have occasion to travel between New York and stations on the New Haven line.

Many porters held advanced degrees. They were respected and admired within their communities. My grandfather told *The New York Times* in 1924, "I was studying to be a minister, though I'm past that now . . . I know a couple of doctors—brothers—who stayed ten years in the service [as Pullman porters] after they'd taken their degrees. They were saving money all the time. When they'd got enough they set up in practice."

Pullman porters were the eyes and ears of Black America, my grandfather told *Collier's: The National Weekly* in 1924:

> I have carried many of the big men of this country. They are just like other people. Mr. John D. Rockefeller, senior, was just a nice old man. Mr. J. Pierpont Morgan just a quiet gentleman. Former [New York State] Governor Whitman, the same. If someone hadn't told me President Coolidge was in my car, I would never have known it.

The Chicago Defender, *The Pittsburgh Courier*, and *The New York Age*—several of the major Black newspapers of the early twentieth century—built a brisk business around Pullman porters providing daily information and occasional scoops, writing columns, and even tossing newspaper bundles off trains at designated spots in Black communities. Presidents, politicians, tycoons, sports stars, and celebrities all road the train, and Pullman porters listened in on their stories.

Beyond the subservience of Black men desired by white Americans, Pullman porters also represented a "New Negro," a term popularized by Harlem Renaissance intellectual Alain Locke. Having fought and died to save democracy in World War I, Black American soldiers returned to a still rampantly racist country. They'd bled on the battlefields of France only to be lynched in the cotton fields of the South. The opportunities afforded white Americans—educational, political, economic, and social—were dangled just beyond Black Americans' reach.

In 1919, white American mobs attacked more than two dozen Black communities across the United States. Only this time, Black Americans fought back.

When a white lynch mob attacked the Black community in North Platte, Nebraska, a Pullman porter broke the story of hundreds of Black men, women, and children driven from their homes. When that porter contacted a local branch of the NAACP, the organization contacted the governor, the mob's advance was stopped, and the Black community returned home safely, unlike many Black families in other communities around the country during the summer of 1919, which was known as Red Summer.

Enter A. Philip Randolph, who was tapped by Pullman porters to lead them in forming the BSCP. The union fought for higher wages and better working conditions for the porters. Though the Pullman Company planted moles inside of organizing meetings, in 1925 Randolph successfully formed the BSCP, the first predominantly Black labor union. A majority of Pullman porters never enrolled in the union, and it never received full recognition by the American Federation of Labor (AFL). Still, Randolph and the BSCP won their first labor contract with the Pullman Company in 1937.

Being a Pullman porter also served as a platform for training and launching future Black leaders. E. D. Nixon masterminded and helped bankroll the 1955–1956 Montgomery bus boycott while working as a Pullman porter. In his autobiography, Malcolm X, a Pullman dinner car waiter, wrote about relationships between Pullman porters and customers on trains. Gordon Parks, also a Pullman porter, found a magazine on a train with Dust Bowl images of poor white women and children. The images inspired his legendary career in photography and filmmaking. Parks also went on to become the first Black photojournalist for *Life* magazine.

Traveling widely, spreading news that knit together a disparate national Black community, providing a training ground for future Black leaders. As important as Pullman porters were, they were not the first group of Black Americans to take on these roles. Peeling back yet another layer of the importance of A. Philip Randolph and the Brotherhood of Sleeping Car Porters requires traveling back in time some two hundred years before the date of the first march on Washington. Here, a group of Black Americans collectively known as Black Jacks occupied positions that Pullman porters eventually held. Black Jacks were Black seamen in the Age of Sail.

By the early 1800s, when the US census recorded Blacks—enslaved and free—at just over 18 percent of the total US population, Black men worked at an astounding 18 percent of all US seafaring jobs. They toiled as carpenters and caulkers, cooks and deckhands, first mates, and, in some cases, even captains. Black sailors faced the privations, hardships, and fears all sailors face, on top of the racism and brutality singled out for them by ship owners, captains, and crew. But they also enjoyed the adventure, the relative freedom, and the autonomy of being sailors.

Black Jacks instilled pride in many Black Americans and fear in many whites.

Field slaves or house slaves. That's the popular view of the only two types of enslaved men and women on Southern plantations. Field slaves worked hard lives outside. House slaves worked easier lives inside. This historical view, despite lacking evidence, evolved into many stereotypical images of enslavement. Malcolm X's distinction between the "house Negro" and the "field Negro" is one of the more famous:

> You have to read the history of slavery to understand this. There were two kinds of Negroes. There was that old house Negro and the field Negro. And the house Negro always looked out for his master. When the field Negroes got too much out of line, he held them back in check. He put 'em back on the plantation. The house Negro could afford to do that because he lived better than the field Negro. He ate better, he dressed better, and he lived in a better house. He lived right up next to his master—in the attic or the basement. He ate the same food his master ate and wore his same clothes. And he could talk just like his master—good diction. And he loved his master more than his master loved himself. That's why he didn't want his master hurt. If the master got sick, he'd say, "What's the matter, boss, we sick?" When the master's house caught afire, he'd try and put the fire out. That was the house Negro.
>
> But then you had some field Negroes, who lived in huts, had nothing to lose. They wore the worst kind of clothes. They ate the worst food. And they caught hell.

> They felt the sting of the lash. They hated their master. Oh yes, they did. If the master got sick, they'd pray that the master died. If the master's house caught afire, they'd pray for a strong wind to come along. This was the difference between the two. And today you still have house Negroes and field Negroes. I'm a field Negro.

As a charismatic orator, Malcolm, with this two-minute riff, brought audiences to their feet, laughing and shouting encouragement. After he first debuted this sketch in 1963, it became a staple of many of his talks until his assassination in 1965. Unfortunately, he failed at the very homework he urged of others. Malcolm had not read the history of slavery well enough to know that not only was his a false and often baseless dichotomy, but also that he'd left out at least one important category of slave. Had Malcolm done his homework, perhaps the "boat Negro" would have been incorporated into his routine. Plantation owners feared boat Negroes more than they feared either house Negroes or field Negroes.

"Dont let the Boat Negroes go amongst the Plantation Slaves," South Carolina plantation owner Henry Laurens cautioned his overseers in 1764.

In the eighteenth and nineteenth centuries, boat Negroes were called patroons by Southern whites, a strange name, given its seventeenth-century Dutch usage to describe the massive manors enslaving Black men and women in New York City and upstate, along the shores of the Hudson River.

"Load the boat as well as you can & take care to prevent

any intercourse between Boat and Plantation Negroes and let me know how Abram the Patroon of the Boat behaves," Laurens told his overseers in a 1765 letter.

Periaguas, petty-augers, pereaugers, periaugers, petiaugers, pettiaugers, peteaugers, petteaugers, *piraguas* (Spanish), *pirogues* (French). The small workboats run by patroons went by many similar names and spellings, all tracing their origin to a Galibi (a Carib language) word of first contact, *piraua*, meaning "canoe."

Periaguas were inexpensive boats, built on plantation grounds rather than in shipyards, from age-old techniques first developed by Native Americans. Irish medical doctor and naturalist John Brickell, who traveled through Virginia and North Carolina in the early eighteenth century, wrote about periaguas. Brickell notes that they were "generally made out of one peice of large Timber, and that moft commonly of the Cyprefs kind, which they make hollow and fhaped like a Boat, with Mafts, Oars, and Padles, according to their fize and bignefs."

Working the rivers was dangerous and exciting, said Richard "Look-Up" Jones, an ex-slave from South Carolina and a patroon. Jones had earned the nickname Look-Up from his constant skyward gaze. He said, "I run on Broad River fer over 24 years as boatman, carrying Marse Jim's cotton to Columbia fer him. Us had de excitement on dem trips. Lots times water was deeper dan a tree is high. Sometimes I was throwed and fell in de water. I rise up every time, though, and float and swim back to de boat and git on again."

Plantations prospered thanks to patroons and periaguas.

Boats were the lifeblood of early America. Colonists arrived here because of boats. Colonists survived and thrived here because of boats. Over the riverine networks of the Virginia Tidewater, the South Carolina Lowcountry, and the North Carolina lowlands, Native Americans had for millennia traded, traveled, and made war. Europeans forcibly took over the lands, evicting Native residents, using the river systems to explore deeper into Native-held territory to conduct war against them and then to claim their lands.

Tobacco, sugar, rice, and cotton were shipped to larger ports on periaguas manned by enslaved patroons and their enslaved crews. From Charleston and Norfolk and Wilmington, these goods became part of an international trade heading north along the coast or east across the Atlantic, creating power and wealth for men who lived remotely, far upstream from the ports. On the return legs of this trade, European or Caribbean finished products came via large ships only so far as these larger ports, where patroons and periaguas transported them the final miles upriver to their consumers.

Henry Laurens of South Carolina presided over the Continental Congress meeting in Philadelphia, helping to wage war on Britain and forge the United States. To transport their tobacco to market, Thomas Jefferson and George Washington relied on periaguas and their enslaved crews. Families like the Laurenses, Jeffersons, Washingtons, and the generations of their descendants reaped the financial and political rewards that Look-Up Jones and families like his never did.

With Black Jacks delivering such benefits to their enslavers, what did white enslavers have to fear? What was the important historical truth that Malcolm X so spectacularly missed?

Very simply, it has to do with the nature of boats. Anyone who's ever helmed boats knows how unpredictably they steer and how boats are subject to the vagaries of wind, weather, and water, not the whims and whimsies of men. The elements are the masters of boats. Enslaved people knew this. Enslavers did, too, and they feared the freedom experienced by Black Jacks even as the enslavers profited from their enslavement.

When a revolution in Haiti placed a formerly enslaved man, Toussaint L'Ouverture, in charge of the country, Thomas Jefferson openly expressed his concerns. "We may expect therefore black crews, supercargoes & missionaries thence into the Southern states," he said. "If this combustion can be introduced among us under any veil whatever, we have to fear it."

Black Jacks trafficked in goods, but they also trafficked in ideas. "Worldly and often multilingual slave sailors regularly subverted plantation discipline," wrote nautical historian W. Jeffrey Bolster. Paul Cuffee, a Black Jack and ship captain, helped foment the largest slave rebellion in South Carolina history, led by Denmark Vesey. Using his skills as an enslaved ship's caulker and a vast amount of nautical knowledge, Frederick Douglass donned the traditional garb of a sailor and borrowed a Seamen's Protection Certificate from a free Black Jack. He slipped away from Baltimore to Philadelphia by train on September 3, 1838, blending in unnoticed among other free Black Jacks.

One held on to a Seamen's Protection Certificate tightly. Issued by the United States starting in 1796, the certificate identified its holder as a protected citizen, both abroad and at home, regardless of race. This strange and anomalous certificate was one of the first official documents declaring free Blacks to be citizens of this country. Black Jacks returned from sea with good documents, good news, and good hope. Black Jacks, enslaved and free, witnessed a world of promise beyond enslavement, and much like the Pullman porters following them, they returned to disparate Black communities throughout the United States with just such news, helping to agitate and organize for change.

Sometimes Black Jacks were paid. Sometimes they ran black markets beyond the clutches of their enslavers. When Black Jacks were paid, they made relatively good money for their travails, from which they provided for their families on land. Black Jacks also helped to build institutions like Black churches, which became the foundation of Black communities across the nation. More than one Black Jack slipped effortlessly from the cockpit of a ship to the pulpit of a church, preaching and teaching from real-world experience.

We return now to the Oval Office in late June 1941, when President Franklin Delano Roosevelt sat with A. Philip Randolph, a man knowingly or unknowingly carrying a tremendous weight of Black history that had gone before him. In attendance with Randolph were Walter White, head of the NAACP, and Fiorello La Guardia, mayor of New York City.

"Mr. President," A. Philip Randolph said, "time is running on. You are quite busy, I know. But what we want to talk with you about is the problem of jobs for Negroes in defense industries. Our people are being turned away at factory gates because they are colored. They can't live with this thing. Now, what are you going to do about it?"

"Well, Phil, what do you want me to do?"

"Mr. President, we want you to do something that will enable Negro workers to get work in these plants."

"Why, I surely want them to work, too," Roosevelt replied. "I'll call up the heads of the various defense plants and have them see to it that Negroes are given the same opportunity to work in defense plants as any other citizen in the country."

"We want you to do more than that. We want something concrete, something tangible, definite, positive, and affirmative."

"What do you mean?" asked Roosevelt.

"Mr. President, we want you to issue an executive order making it mandatory that Negroes be permitted to work in these plants."

"Well, Phil, you know I can't do that. If I issue an executive order for you, then there'll be no end to other groups coming in here and asking me to issue executive orders for them, too. In any event, I couldn't do anything unless you called off this march of yours. Questions like this can't be settled with a sledgehammer."

"I'm sorry, Mr. President," said Randolph, "the march cannot be called off."

"How many people do you plan to bring?" Roosevelt asked.

"One hundred thousand, Mr. President."

A disbelieving Roosevelt turned to Walter White. "Walter, how many people will really march?"

"One hundred thousand, Mr. President," White answered.

"Gentleman, it is clear that Mr. Randolph is not going to

call off the march," La Guardia interjected, "and I suggest we all begin to seek a formula."

The formula found was simple. Roosevelt issued Executive Order 8802, the first presidential directive on race since Reconstruction. "There shall be no discrimination in the employment of workers in defense industries and in Government, because of race, creed, color, or national origin," it read. He also established the Fair Employment Practices Committee (FEPC) with a mission to enforce that executive order. In response, A. Philip Randolph called off the march. Many felt Randolph gave in too hastily; they felt he sold out.

A. Philip Randolph was not the only organizer of the first march on Washington; the other person, whose name is too frequently omitted, was Bayard Rustin. Randolph asked Rustin to join him in organizing the march.

Bayard Rustin, you may recall from a previous chapter, was a dedicated member of the Fellowship of Reconciliation (FOR) who lived nearby the Harlem Ashram and studied nonviolent methods there with Muriel Lester, Gandhi's close friend and representative. Rustin would later make a pilgrimage to India, not long after Gandhi's assassination, to study directly with Gandhi's followers, then return to lead a major nonviolent action in America against the wishes of mainline Black leaders—the Freedom Ride of 1947. But in 1940, Randolph asked Rustin, known even then as a brilliant organizer, to organize the youth division of the first march on Washington. While Rustin's age may have kept him out of the Oval Office meeting, the other aspect of his life that distanced him from many Black leaders throughout his life, perpetually consigning him to the shadows of the Black Freedom Struggle, was that he was gay and open about his homosexuality.

Rustin's pacifist and nonviolent roots ran deep. He was born in 1912 in West Chester, Pennsylvania, and raised by his grandmother, who was active in the Society of Friends (Quakers) and in the nascent Black Freedom Struggle. She was a member of the NAACP, and as such, Black leaders like W. E. B. Du Bois and Mary McLeod Bethune frequented Rustin's home. While at City College of New York in 1938, Rustin joined the Young Communist League (YCL) because of the Communist Party's willingness to take a stand on race relations in America. In particular, the Communist Party aligned itself with Black Americans who were, at that time, being lynched and under the violent hand of racial segregation. Rustin became a youth organizer for the YCL. But with the onset of World War II, the Communist Party declared it was more important to fight fascism than racism, and Rustin resigned from the YCL.

Rustin's anger at Randolph's quid pro quo with Roosevelt caused a temporary rift between the two. During that breach, Rustin threw himself into working with FOR, whose renowned pacifist leader, A. J. Muste, hired Rustin in the late summer of 1941 to be the race relations secretary of the organization. Muste was one of the first leaders to introduce Rustin to Gandhian nonviolent methods of protest. Apart from FOR, Rustin also organized the Quaker American Friends Service Committee (AFSC) and the War Resisters League (WRL). He crisscrossed the country, speaking and giving workshops on nonviolence to integrated groups. In 1942, when a barber refused to cut Rustin's hair because he was Black, Rustin organized a group of students from a local college to boycott the business. Refused service at a Midwestern restaurant in a college town, Rustin organized students to protest the restaurant's practices. When he declined to move to the back of a bus on a ride from Louisville, Kentucky, to Nashville, Tennessee, in 1942, he was forcibly removed from the bus by police, beaten, and then arrested. After white passengers spoke on his behalf, the local Nashville District Attorney refused to press charges, and Rustin was released.

Rustin would later speak of this incident with the *Washington Blade*, a long-time LGBTQ+ newspaper. In an interview, only recently discovered, he said that while going to sit in the rear of a bus, a young child reached out to touch the necktie he was wearing when the child's mother said, "Don't touch the nigger." Rustin said he then realized that if he acquiesced and went quietly to the back, that child would grow up believing that Black people liked sitting there, so he declined. "I owe it to that child," he said, "not only to my own dignity, I owe it to that child, that it should be educated to know that blacks do not want to sit in the back . . ."

In that same interview, Rustin said about "coming out" as gay, "[I]f I didn't, I was a part of the prejudice. I was aiding and abetting the prejudice that was a part of the effort to destroy me."

Word got around that Rustin was a brilliant orator and organizer, and he was being called the Fellowship's "one-man nonviolent army." Rustin's actions preceded and presaged similar actions central to the Black Freedom Struggle of the 1950s and 1960s.

Muste encouraged Rustin to join with other activists to form the Congress on Racial Equality (CORE) in 1942, which provided Rustin with yet another opportunity to travel the country promoting nonviolence and racial equity. Rustin traveled to California in support of Gordon Hirabayashi, a Japanese American citizen and University of Washington student, who refused to turn himself in for internment. Hirabayashi's case was one of a handful the US Supreme Court rejected in favor of internment. Not long after Rustin's return, A. J. Muste, impressed with Rustin's organizing talents, appointed him FOR's secretary for student and general affairs.

Then, in 1943, A. Philip Randolph, fresh from his compromise with Roosevelt, called on Black Americans to "harness the flow of rising resentment and indignation on the part of Negro Americans that has become intensified due to the war." Randolph proposed a Chicago conference entitled "We Are Americans Too," and A. J. Muste offered Rustin's services to organize the event. Randolph and Rustin were working together again. Rustin spoke at the conference and taught workshops on Gandhian nonviolence, using examples from his own life as teaching moments. Rustin was a huge success, which led to his speaking and organizing in Black communities around the country. Soon after, Randolph asked Muste for more of Rustin's time for a new action he was planning: to protest segregation in the armed forces.

That same year, Rustin had his own run-in with the armed

forces. As a lifelong Quaker, pacifist, and conscientious objector (CO), Rustin could have opted for work in one of the many CO camps spread across the United States instead of reporting for induction into the military upon notification from the Selective Service System. Rustin, however, refused any and all cooperation with the war, especially based on his staunchly pacifist views and his strong opposition to the segregation of and discrimination against Blacks in the armed services. In his defense, he submitted to the federal government a pamphlet he had written, *Interracial Primer*, and an article that appeared in *Fellowship Magazine*, "The Negro and Non-Violence." Rustin was charged with violating the Selective Service Act in January 1944, and a federal judge sentenced him to three years in prison.

He was booked into the Ashland, Kentucky, federal penitentiary, with this advisory issued by prison officials:

> It is believed that this inmate will continue to bring up racial problems in this institution, as has been his practice before being committed here, and it is further indicated by his actions that he is already engaged in practices of agitating other inmates on the race problem. His adjustment in this institution is doubtful.

Rustin lived up to the prison officials' expectations. He refused to sit at segregated dining tables, taking a seat next to other conscientious objectors, who were white. He would not take a seat in the "colored" section at the prison's movie showings. He reprimanded the prison's medical doctor for calling him "boy."

Protesting over these conditions and others, such as segregated living arrangements, mail policies, and medical care, earned Rustin a number of disciplinary write-ups, quarantine, and even time in solitary confinement. A trained vocalist, Rustin, from his quarantined cell, would belt out Billie Holiday's "Strange Fruit," about the lynching of Blacks in the South, to the delight and applause of the Black inmates. It did not take Rustin long to be branded "an extremely capable agitator" by prisoner head Robert Hagerman, who ultimately sought advice from the director of the Federal Bureau of Prisons, James Bennett, on how to handle Rustin.

While Rustin, deeply rooted in pacifist and Gandhian beliefs, agitated, he also negotiated with prison officials like Hagerman. Because of Rustin's agitation and negotiations, a number of prison reforms at Ashland were initiated, including integrated dining tables, a course on US history taught to the entire prison population by Rustin, integrated seating at church, and the prison's first-ever integrated choir, which Rustin led.

A shift came when Rustin attempted to move beyond personal protest and organize the prison population as a whole. Ashland prison officials intervened, letting it be known that Rustin was an "admitted homosexual," which diminished his standing among those inmates and correctional officers who'd begun to follow him, and got him placed in solitary confinement.

Still, Rustin would not back down. Back among the general population after solitary, Rustin continued organizing sympathetic prisoners to protest racist prison policies. When Ashland officials would not agree to demands for change, Rustin organized a hunger strike.

"He continues to be an institutional problem," said a January 1945 special report on Rustin. "Subject is described as a homosexual, an obstructionist, and a rabble-rouser," the report continued.

Finally, Hagerman had enough. He recommended Rustin's transfer for early release to the farm camp at the federal penitentiary in Lewisburg, Pennsylvania, from where he was released in June 1946.

World War II was over. Franklin Roosevelt was dead. Harry S. Truman was president. Free to pursue his national organizing and activism again, Rustin rejoined with Randolph in a push to desegregate the US military. Rustin and his mentor established a nonviolent action committee called the Committee to End "Jim Crow" in the Armed Services, with the purpose of using Gandhian nonviolence to end segregation and discrimination in the military.

Rustin was also back organizing with FOR. It was 1947 when he organized and participated in the first-ever Freedom Rides. During these postwar years, Rustin's scope of effort began to enlarge from the United States to the struggle of oppressed and marginalized people of color throughout the world. In 1945, while still in prison, Rustin had organized FOR's Free India Committee. After his release, he was arrested numerous times for nonviolent protests he'd organized in support of ending British colonial rule in India and Africa. He traveled to India in 1948 to study with Gandhi's followers. In 1951, Rustin led the creation of the Committee to Support South African Resistance, which has now become Africa Action. In 1952, he met with Kwame Nkrumah of Ghana and Nnamdi Azikiwe of Nigeria, leaders of independence movements who would go on to become the first presidents of their independent countries.

There seem to be little in terms of modern-day efforts or tactics for social justice and social change that do not bear Rustin's imprint. But his work with A. Philip Randolph and the Committee to End "Jim Crow" in the Armed Services might seem most surprising. Why would a devout pacifist and devoted conscientious objector work so hard on behalf of desegregating the US military? Bayard Rustin was a master strategist who knew the military was a microcosm of American society. "If the millions of Negroes and white people in the Army are in mixed units," he wrote, "they will eat, travel, and sleep together. They will have recreation together, work together, and travel on boats about the world together. In the South they will live, sleep, and work together in and beyond army camps. What could be a more revolutionary blow to the caste system? How under these circumstances could Jim Crow survive?"

A 1947 House Armed Services Committee bill mandated the segregation of the US armed forces. Though the bill never passed, it prompted Rustin and Randolph to create, support, and link together a number of organizations focused on desegregating the military, including the Committee Against Jim Crow in Military Service and Training, the Committee to End Segregation in the Armed Forces, the League for Nonviolent Civil Disobedience

Against Military Segregation, and the Commission of Inquiry into the Effect of Segregation and Discrimination on the Morale and Development of the Negro Soldier.

Rustin made clear in a 1948 New York City speech to activists entitled "Jim Crow Army" how much of what he'd done until this point was focused on desegregating the military:

> The Journey of Reconciliation (the Freedom Bus Rides of 1947) was organized not only to devise techniques for eliminating Jim Crow in travel, but also as a training ground for similar peaceful projects against discrimination in such major areas as employment and in the armed services. The use of these methods against Jim Crow military service is a regrettable necessity. Today no single injustice more bitterly stands out in the hearts and minds of colored people the world over, or continues more successfully to frustrate the United States' efforts abroad, than the continuation of discrimination and segregation in our military forces.

He also intended that nonviolent resistance remain a key principle of this effort.

> As a follower of the principles of Mahatma Gandhi, I am an opponent of war and of war preparations and an opponent of universal military training and conscription; but entirely apart from that issue, I hold that segregation in any part of the body politic is an act of slavery and an

> act of war. Democrats will agree that such acts are to be resisted, and more and more leaders of the oppressed are responsibly proposing nonviolent civil disobedience and non-cooperation as the means.

At a meeting in March 1948, Randolph told President Harry S. Truman, "Negroes are in no mood to shoulder a gun for democracy abroad so long as they are denied democracy here at home." A few days later, before the Senate Armed Services Committee, Randolph said he would advise acts of nonviolent resistance rather than induction into a Jim Crow military. "This time Negroes will not take the Jim Crow laws lying down," he testified. "The conscience of the world will be shaken as by nothing else when thousands and thousands of us second-class Americans choose imprisonment in preference to permanent military slavery."

While Randolph worked the corridors of power, Rustin organized the power of the streets, crisscrossing the country once again. He won the consent and cooperation of Black veterans and Black members of the armed forces. He encouraged local groups across the nation to use Gandhian nonviolent means to spread the message through such methods as person-to-person contact, letters to newspaper editors and politicians, and nonviolent protest. At a protest in front of the White House with Randolph and other activists, Rustin carried a sign that read "If we must die for our country, let us die as free men—not as Jim Crow slaves." He led protests outside of the party headquarters of Republicans and Democrats in Washington, DC, and took part in similar nonviolent protests at the party conventions in the summer of 1948.

After all, 1948 was an election year, and Truman, much like modern-day Democratic candidates, needed the overwhelming support of Black voters to win a second term. This escalating campaign led by Rustin and Randolph finally pushed Truman to issue Executive Order 9980 and 9981 in July 1948. The first order reestablished the Fair Employment Practices Committee, first established by Roosevelt in 1941 but since gutted by congressional conservatives. Executive Order 9980 ordered the federal government to put in place "a policy of fair employment throughout the Federal establishment, without discrimination because of race, color, religion, or national origin." Order 9981 was the order Rustin and Randolph had worked so hard for. "It is hereby declared," Executive Order 9981 stated, "there shall be equality of treatment and opportunity for all persons in the armed services without regard to race, color, religion, or national origin. This policy shall be put into effect as rapidly as possible."

The executive orders were tepid at best, and real desegregation of the armed forces was still several years away. But with the issuance of those two executive orders, A. Philip Randolph shut down the League for Nonviolent Civil Disobedience Against Military Segregation. One can only imagine that for Rustin, a man for whom concession was not a final step but only a first step, Randolph's action cut deeply.

Rustin recalled his response: "A number of 'Young Turks' and I decided to outflank Mr. Randolph." They took to the Black press, calling Randolph "an Uncle Tom, a sellout, a reactionary, and an old fogey out of touch with the times." Rustin had broken with his mentor, and he avoided Randolph for two years, afraid he would not be forgiven. But in 1950, Rustin sought to make amends by paying his old friend and mentor a visit at his office. "As I was ushered in," Rustin recalled, "there he was, distinguished and dapper as ever, with arms outstretched, waiting to greet me, the way he had done a decade ago. Motioning me to sit down with that same sweep of his arm, he looked at me and, in a calm, even voice, said: 'Bayard, where have you been? You know that I have needed you.'"

They never broke ranks again. Instead, one might argue, Rustin and Randolph became the principal architects of the Black Freedom Struggle of the 1950s and 1960s, even as the more well-known leaders of that struggle wrestled to contend with Rustin's sexuality.

After a speech in Pasadena, California, on the night of January 21, 1953, local police officers spotted Rustin having sex with one of two men in a parked car. Rustin was arrested on a "morals charge," sentenced to sixty days in jail (he served fifty), and required to register as a sex offender. It began a "dark period" in his life. A. J. Muste dropped him from his Fellowship of Reconciliation post. All of his subsequent speeches were canceled. He struggled to find work, at one point taking a job as a furniture mover. "I know now," he wrote three months after his arrest, "that for me sex must be sublimated if I am to live with myself and in this world longer."

Ultimately, on September 25, 1953, Rustin was offered the position of executive secretary of the War Resisters League. He was back in the struggle for civil rights with the unwavering support of A. Philip Randolph. "If the fact is, he is homosexual," Randolph said of Rustin, "maybe we need more of them; he's so talented."

Rustin and Randolph, along with Ella Baker and Stanley Levison, formed a group called In Friendship in 1956, which provided economic aid to the victims of racial violence in the South, especially to those affected by the Montgomery bus boycotts. Randolph encouraged Rustin to go down to Montgomery to meet a young preacher named Martin Luther King Jr. According to Michael G. Long, one of Rustin's biographers, Rustin arrived to a King household filled with guns. King had read Gandhi, but at that point, he saw nonviolence as a tactic, not a lifestyle. That was soon to change, with Rustin firmly establishing in King's mind that nonviolence had to be the cornerstone of this new movement for civil rights.

Randolph and Rustin soon recognized the power of this new Southern Black Freedom Struggle. They both lent their considerable experience, power, and prestige to King's emerging leadership. "From the Montgomery bus boycott in 1955, for the next two years following to May 1957 [the three-year anniversary of the *Brown v. Board of Education* decision], the center of gravity and the center of activity for the whole civil rights movement was the church people and ministers of the south," Rustin would later write.

Rustin was referring, of course, to ordained men and women, many of whose names we know, and to ordinary church folk like Rosa Parks, John Earl Reese, Willie Edwards Jr., the four school-age girls killed in Birmingham (Addie Mae Collins, Denise McNair, Carole Robertson, and Cynthia Wesley), Mack Charles Parker, Corporal Roman Ducksworth Jr., Herbert Lee, Lamar Smith, Virgil Ware, and many others whose names we do not know.

Rustin, though he preferred working in the background of the Southern Black Freedom Struggle, was still controversial. He labored to establish the Southern Christian Leadership Conference (SCLC). But he was forced to resign from SCLC when other Black leaders pressured King to distance himself from Rustin. When Rustin organized a nonviolent protest at the 1960 Democratic Convention, Representative Adam Clayton Powell Jr., sent by politicians to stop the protest, threatened to expose a fabricated story that King had had an affair with Rustin. That was only thwarted when one of King's advisors threatened Powell with exposing the many women Powell had, in fact, slept with.

From 1960 to 1963, Rustin was essentially persona non grata in the Southern Black Freedom Struggle. Those were also the years when King and others felt the movement was flagging, losing steam at just the wrong time. Rustin was tentatively integrated back into the Birmingham campaign.

Then, in 1962, Randolph proposed to King and SCLC an event that would potentially turn things around in a very powerful way—a march on Washington in the summer of 1963. Black leaders at the time knew there was only one person capable of organizing such a large event in such a short period of time, but they never spoke his name.

Roy Wilkins, head of the powerful NAACP, said to Rustin, "I don't want you leading that march on Washington, because you know I don't give a damn about what they say, but publicly I don't want to have to defend the draft dodging. I know you're a Quaker," Wilkins went on, "but that's not what I'll have to defend. I'll have to defend draft dodging. I'll have to defend promiscuity. The question is never going to be homosexuality; it's going to be promiscuity, and I can't defend that. And the fact is that you were a member of the Young Communist League. And I don't care what you say, I can't defend that."

A plan was hatched, reportedly by King and John Lewis, to appoint A. Philip Randolph to lead the March on Washington in 1963, knowing full well that Randolph, now coming to the end of a long, distinguished career in labor unions and civil rights, would, in turn, name Rustin to actually do the work. Randolph was appointed to lead the march. He did, in fact, name Rustin as his deputy to organize and arrange all of the details.

Refusing to move to the back of a bus, lunch counter sit-ins, freedom bus rides, beatings and arrests for peaceful protest, mass marches, negotiation with power, integration over segregation, community organizing, nonviolent actions. Name a signature method of the Southern Black Freedom Struggle, and there's one man who'd done that a decade or two before; one man, often on his own, who had endured the violence and brutality directed against him for the chance to stand up for the nonviolent beliefs he held so dearly; one man who had shared with so many others how to wage a nonviolent battle for freedom and equality.

As he grew older, with his mop of unruly salt-and-pepper hair,

Bayard Rustin became reminiscent of another great Black leader who had also sported a salt-and-pepper mane: Frederick Douglass. Both were great orators. Both were legendary organizers. Both fought hard for the rights of Black Americans. But where Frederick Douglass's voice was well-known and well-respected, Bayard Rustin's voice was perpetually hidden in the shadows of a movement to which he gave life.

Now, decades after his death, that's slowly beginning to change, as Bayard Rustin receives the recognition he so fully deserved during his life. In 2013, Rustin was posthumously awarded the Presidential Medal of Freedom by President Barack Obama. In 2020, Governor Gavin Newsom of California posthumously pardoned Rustin for his 1953 sexual offense. And in 2023, a major biopic called simply *Rustin* brought the life and work of this hidden voice to the awareness of millions.

CHAPTER 12

A HIGH PRICE FOR FREEDOM, PART I

AS JIMMIE LEE JACKSON LAY DYING, HE LOOKED UP FROM his hospital bed into the eyes of Barbara Lum, a nun and a nurse at the Good Samaritan Hospital in Selma, Alabama, the only hospital in a nine-county region that would accept Black patients in 1965. "Sister, don't you think this is a high price to pay for freedom?" he whispered. Several days later, Jimmie Lee Jackson was dead.

Why Jimmie Lee Jackson lay dying in a Selma hospital, shot by Alabama state trooper James Bonard Fowler, is not a simple question to answer, though many simple answers have been given. The simple answer that Jimmie Lee wanted and deserved the right to vote and that he was barred from that right by Alabama's racist laws and the violent enforcement of them by law enforcement officials and the white public is true, but it's not enough. The simple answer that Jimmie Lee Jackson was a casualty in a struggle for freedom waged by Martin Luther King

Jr. and the Southern Christian Leadership Conference (SCLC) is true, in part, but it's not enough. King, it turns out, was actually late to the voting rights movement in Selma and surrounding areas—more than forty years late, by some reckoning. And the simple answer that Jimmie Lee Jackson was a victim of hatred, bigotry, and the police's overuse of lethal force against Black men and women is true, but it, too, is not enough.

To better understand why Jimmie Lee Jackson lay dying in that Selma hospital and the high cost of freedom he paid, one must understand the forces bearing down on Selma in the days and decades before Jimmie Lee's death and the forces unleashed when he died.

Prior to Jimmie Lee's death, Selma teetered on the verge of erupting.

Voting rights were the cause. In 1961, Black residents of Dallas County, home to the city of Selma, outnumbered white residents 57 percent to 43 percent, yet less than 1 percent of the estimated fifteen thousand Black residents eligible to vote were actually allowed to register. Keeping Black men and women away from the polls was a cornerstone of the South's Jim Crow laws, created in the decades following the Civil War and memorializing racism by denying Blacks basic civil rights and freedoms.

Restricting registration hours, criminalizing the provision of water to those waiting in line to register, public threats and intimidation, outright violence—the tactics used by white elected officials against Black voter registration throughout the twentieth century are eerily similar to those put forth against Blacks registering to vote, as well as those voting, today. Added to this were even more onerous measures such as poll taxes, literacy tests, and proofs of comprehension by verbatim recitation of the US Constitution.

Long before the Student Nonviolent Coordinating Committee's Freedom Summer of 1964, which registered Blacks to vote across the South; long before Martin Luther King Jr.'s arrival in Selma in the early 1960s; long before the Voting Rights Act of 1965, Black Americans began fighting back.

In an 1895 speech in Atlanta, Georgia, Booker T. Washington framed the Atlanta Compromise, in which he stated a belief that Black Americans, particularly those in the South, should relinquish their struggle for political rights (such as voting or equal treatment under the law) in return for being provided with economic opportunity and due process. Washington believed the path forward for Black Americans lay in education and hard work.

Many Black Americans did not agree, among them W. E. B. Du Bois, who, in 1905, along with other prominent Black leaders, formed the Niagara Movement as a "mighty current" for change in all aspects of Black American life, including the political sphere that Washington and his supporters eschewed. Scheduled to meet in Buffalo, New York, near Niagara Falls, the first gathering of the Niagara Movement fled to Erie, Ontario, in Canada to avoid confrontation with Booker T. Washington's ardent supporters. The Niagara Movement lasted a mere five years, but from its demise arose one of the nation's most powerful and long-lasting civil rights organizations, the National Association for the Advancement of Colored People (NAACP), founded in 1909. Du Bois, who cofounded the NAACP along with Mary White Ovington, Moorfield Storey, and Ida B. Wells, was appointed the director of publications for the organization. He invited members of the Niagara Movement to join, which most did.

In 1918, not even ten years after the founding of the NAACP, Charles J. Adams founded an NAACP chapter in Selma, Alabama. Adams risked continual threats of violence and retaliation from the Ku Klux Klan and other local white groups but continued to advocate for the civil rights of Black Americans. J. L. Chestnut, a prominent Black lawyer, activist, and author from Selma, remembered Adams, as many also did, as "the NAACP in Selma." In the mid-1920s, Adams founded the Dallas County Voters League (DCVL) to help Black Americans register to vote. Like Adams himself, the DCVL met and worked for many years under oppressive racism and bigotry. Adams was harassed by law enforcement in and around Selma, jailed several times, and ultimately left Selma for Detroit in 1948.

With Adams's departure, Selma resident Sam Boynton stepped in to lead the DCVL and Selma's NAACP. Boynton's wife, Amelia, joined his advocacy for voting rights. It is Amelia Boynton, known as the "mother of the voting rights movement," who received international recognition for photographs of her beaten unconscious by Alabama state troopers and left for dead on the Edmund Pettus Bridge, then cradled in the arms of another marcher on Bloody Sunday, March 7, 1965.

The DCVL, composed of the Boynton family and a handful of members willing to risk the violence and retaliation of the Ku Klux Klan, the White Citizens' Council, and state and local authorities, labored for years in the 1950s trying to help Black residents of the Selma area register to vote. They were joined in this effort in November 1962 by Student Nonviolent Coordinating Committee organizers Bernard and Colia Lafayette, who'd arrived in Selma to initiate a voter registration project. Working with the DCVL, the Lafayettes had little success. At every turn, their efforts at voter registration were met with stiff resistance from local white authorities. Bernard and Colia were threatened, arrested, and beaten. On the night of June 12, 1963, the same night that Medgar Evers was assassinated, Bernard barely survived a beating from the local Ku Klux Klan.

Bernard Lafayette had attended the American Baptist Theological Seminary in Nashville, Tennessee, in 1958, where, as a freshman, he participated in weekly meetings on nonviolence with fellow students John Lewis, James Bevel, and Diane Nash, taught by the Reverend James Lawson, then a representative of the Fellowship of Reconciliation, who himself had studied nonviolence under the tutelage of Bayard Rustin.

Colia Lafayette was born in rural Hinds County, Mississippi. She'd joined the NAACP while at Tougaloo College, became the special assistant to Medgar Evers, and founded the North Jackson NAACP Youth Council. When she moved to Selma with her husband, she served as the SNCC field secretary while he served as the director of the SNCC Black Belt Alabama Voter Project. Later, Colia would move on to Birmingham, Alabama, where, under the leadership of Martin Luther King Jr., she sustained a severe beating by local law enforcement on May 8, 1963.

To counteract the literacy test requirements of local Jim Crow voting laws, the Lafayettes, along with the Boyntons and other members of the DCVL, established what were known then as Citizenship Schools. While first organized by Esau Jenkins and Septima Clark on Johns Island, South Carolina, in 1954, with a loan from the Highlander Center, Citizenship Schools began as places to teach Blacks to read. But these impromptu schools, held in church basements and homes, quickly evolved into centers for civic education on democracy, justice, economic and political power, civil rights, and, always, the right to vote. In the 1960s, Citizenship Schools expanded to include credit unions, nursing homes, kindergartens, and low-income housing projects.

While the Highlander Center may seem like a footnote in the story of Citizenship Schools, Highlander was actually central to the Black Freedom Struggle in America in the 1950s and 1960s. Established as the Highlander Folk School in 1932 during the Great Depression by social activist Myles Horton, educator Don West, and Methodist minister James A. Dombrowksi, Highlander originally served as an educational and training center for leaders in the labor movement, especially throughout the American South. In the 1950s, Highlander refocused on the issues of civil rights and desegregation, becoming a center for the training of leaders in the Black American struggle for civil rights. It was a retreat from the fray of the struggle, a quiet mountain place to contemplate and to plan, a vibrant center to learn from new ways of thinking and discover new ways of acting. Many figures central to the Black Freedom Struggle, especially in the South, passed through Highlander—some more than once. Martin Luther

King Jr. was there, but so, too, were James Bevel, Rosa Parks, John Lewis, Vincent and Rosemarie Harding, Julian Bond, and Bernard Lafayette.

Not only an educational and political center, Highlander was also a cultural center of the Black Freedom Struggle. "We Shall Overcome" came, in part, from Highlander. It was adapted from a gospel song by Zilphia Horton, wife of Myles Horton, and originally sung by tobacco factory workers during the 1945–1946 Charleston Cigar Factory strike. The song was soon published by legendary folk singer Pete Seeger in his *People's Songs Bulletin* and taught by Guy Carawan, who succeeded Zilphia Horton as Highlander's music director, to a group of SNCC members on a visit to the HBCU Shaw University. No song of the struggle for freedom, no song advocating democracy and nonviolence, is more recognizable than "We Shall Overcome," which has since become a central piece of democracy movements around the world—from Tiananmen Square to the Middle East.

Those in the Black Freedom Struggle revered Highlander; many in Tennessee, birthplace of the Ku Klux Klan, reviled it. Because of its long-standing support of workers' and civil rights, the school was closed by the state in 1961. But the staff moved it to Knoxville, Tennessee, where it was reorganized under the name Highlander Research and Education Center to continue its work. Today the Highlander Research and Education Center is located in New Market, Tennessee, where it's been since 1971.

But back in 1963, Bernard and Colia Lafayette of SNCC, working with the Boyntons of the DCVL, were largely unsuccessful in registering Blacks to vote in Selma. Shortly after the Lafayettes left in the summer of 1963 to return to college, Prathia Hall and Worth Long of SNCC took over the voter registration campaign in Selma. They, too, faced frequent arrests, brutal attacks, and continual threats on their lives. Soon after the Lafayettes left Selma, on September 15, 1963, the 16th Street Baptist Church was bombed less than a hundred miles away in Birmingham, Alabama, and four young Black girls were killed by the Ku Klux Klan, which had planted nineteen sticks of dynamite connected to a timing device under the church's steps.

The Birmingham bombing reverberated in Selma's Black community, especially among high school and college students, who mounted a relentless campaign of sit-ins at local eateries to protest segregation, police violence, and restrictions on voting. Many were beaten, and many were arrested, among them John Lewis, then the chairman of SNCC. "Freedom Day" protests became commonplace. With only two days during the month when Black residents could register to vote, these Freedom Days were supported by many national figures. Dick Gregory and his wife, as well as writer James Baldwin and his brother, vocally supported Freedom Day. Many local leaders and law enforcement officers viewed these days as an opportunity to show overwhelming violence and force to suppress any attempt by Black citizens to register.

A year later, President Lyndon B. Johnson signed the Civil Rights Act of 1964 into law. Some hoped that the law, with its provisions for enforcement, would lead to a dismantling of Jim Crow across the South. But it did not. Jim Crow remained, and

Southern whites pursued it with greater vengeance and even greater impunity. Then, on July 6, 1964, John Lewis led a group of fifty Black citizens to the Dallas County Courthouse to register to vote, where the vehemently racist sheriff Jim Clark arrested every one of them before they had the opportunity to exercise their rights. Three days later, Alabama circuit court judge James Hare issued an injunction that forbade the gathering of three or more people in the name of civil rights or voter registration. Effectively quelling any further efforts by SNCC and the DCVL.

Something had to give. Frederick Douglas Reese, then the president of the DCVL, invited the Southern Christian Leadership Conference (SCLC) to come to Selma to assist with the voting rights campaign there. The DCVL was opposed to SCLC's presence, so Reese, along with seven others, known as the Courageous Eight (Ulysses S. Blackmon Sr., Amelia Boynton, Ernest Doyle, Marie Foster, James Gildersleeve, J. D. Hunter Sr., Henry Shannon Sr., and Reese), actually put forth the invitation. SCLC accepted.

SCLC, it should be remembered, though founded by Martin Luther King Jr. in 1957 after the successful Montgomery, Alabama, bus boycott, was actually the brainchild of Bayard Rustin, with help from Ella Baker, who foresaw an organization bringing together nonviolent leaders of a broad movement for desegregation and equal rights across the South. But when SCLC dispatched James Bevel, Diane Nash, James Orange, and others to organize for voting rights in Selma, they brought to light a simmering conflict between their organization and the SNCC.

Those in the movement often referred to the two organizations as Slick (SCLC) and Snick (SNCC). The conflict between them has been frequently painted as generational—the restless youth of SNCC versus the cautious old guard of SCLC. Or religious—Christian SCLC versus secular SNCC. Or even tactical—militant SNCC versus moderate SCLC. There's a more nuanced way to understanding the tension between the two groups.

SNCC saw change coming from the bottom up, while SCLC saw change coming from the top down. SNCC sought decentralized grassroots leadership rather than the hierarchical charismatic leadership of King and SCLC. SNCC had seen its members killed, and grassroots leadership, the organization believed, guaranteed SNCC's survival in the event of any particular leader's death. The roots of present-day activist organizations such as Black Lives Matter can be found in this approach.

Many SNCC members also saw SCLC mass protests as generating media attention for national SCLC goals, such as the passage of a voting rights or civil rights bill, while SNCC was focused on grassroots democracy—the inability of individual Blacks to vote or the desegregation of a given lunch counter. Of course, the two goals were not necessarily at odds with each other. National legislation made the realization of local goals possible, and publicizing the plight of local Black Americans demonstrated the need for enforceable national legislation. But members of SCLC and SNCC did not always see it that way, and the tensions came to a head in August 1964 at the Democratic National Convention in Atlantic City, New Jersey.

To better understand what happened in Atlantic City that August, step back two months to June, when SNCC, under the leadership of Bob Moses, rolled out a long-planned volunteer voting registration campaign in Mississippi, the state next door to Alabama, known as Freedom Summer. They sought to register as many Black voters as possible. The campaign brought together four mainline organizations—SNCC, CORE, the NAACP, and SCLC—under an umbrella group called the Council of Federated Organizations (COFO) to counteract the heinous and violent ways that white Mississippians suppressed and supported keeping Black Mississippians from voting. Just as in Alabama, poll taxes, literacy tests, and arbitrary approvals were put in place to prevent Blacks from registering. And also as in Alabama, arrests, beatings, evictions, arson, murder, and other forms of demeaning and intimidating actions were carried out by local officials, local law enforcement, and local citizens against Blacks.

Most Freedom Summer volunteers were young white college students from the North. Many were Jewish. None were welcomed by white Mississippians, who met their arrival with hatred and violence. Drive-by shootings took place; Molotov cocktails were thrown. The homes where students stayed were bombed. On June 21, 1964, not long after Freedom Summer began, James Chaney, Andrew Goodman, and Michael Schwerner were arrested, then ambushed and killed by the local Ku Klux Klan, who boasted Cecil Price, the arresting Neshoba County deputy sheriff, as one of their members. While many remember the murders of these three young men, few recall hearing about the bodies of seven Black men and one Black boy discovered in the swamps and backwaters of Mississippi while searching for the bodies of Chaney, Goodman, and Schwerner.

Unrelenting murderous violence and hatred stymied the young people of Freedom Summer from registering voters in the South. But this did not render them helpless. Charles Cobb, a leading member of SNCC, established a series of "Freedom Schools" across Mississippi that summer. Modeled, in part, after the Highlander-supported Citizenship Schools, Freedom Schools, with college students as teachers, promoted voter literacy and civic education but also taught Black Americans about Black history, for the very first time, from living rooms, church basements, and gatherings under trees. "Freedom Libraries" also spread across Mississippi during Freedom Summer, providing Blacks with access to books and literary guidance they had never had before. "Freedom Houses" were communal living spaces where volunteers were housed when no other accommodations were available. In these Freedom Houses, many volunteers had their first experiences of interracial living, and some their first experiences of interracial sex. It was, after all, the 1960s, when, beyond the Black Freedom Struggle, a sexual revolution was unfolding.

But talking about racial equity and actually living it are not the same. Some SNCC members grew resentful of the Northern white college students whom they perceived as being condescending and paternalistic toward Black Mississippians. When added to this the brutal violence Freedom Summer volunteers met, a strong sense of the necessity for Black autonomy and self-determination grew, particularly among younger SNCC members, ultimately flowering in a call for "Black Power." SNCC found itself at the heart of this call, with members such as Stokely Carmichael, H. Rap Brown, and Charles Cobb advocating for a break with the moderate and nonviolent beliefs of mainstream organizations such as SCLC and the NAACP. The modern-era Black Power Movement can trace its origins, in part, to Freedom Summer.

Freedom Summer also gave birth to the Mississippi Freedom Democratic Party (MFDP), established by COFO as an integrated alternative to Mississippi's regular Democratic Party, which opposed the Black Freedom Struggle and allowed only whites to participate. With participation in Mississippi's Democratic Party blocked by arbitrary rules, physical intimidation, and outright violence, COFO simply decided to establish a party fashioned in its own beliefs, and it hoped to seat the party at the Democratic National Convention later that summer in Atlantic City, New Jersey.

At its peak, prior to the August 24, 1964, Democratic National Convention, the MFDP had eighty thousand members. But President Lyndon B. Johnson, in office after John F. Kennedy's assassination and up for election to a full term, feared losing the votes of Southern whites. Johnson, along with Hubert Humphrey, Walter Mondale, and much of the white liberal political establishment, engineered a compromise when the MFDP sought to unseat the regular Mississippi Democratic Party. In exchange for being given two at-large, nonvoting seats, the MFDP would back down from its intraparty challenge.

That's when Fannie Lou Hamer, whom Johnson sought to block from speaking, rose in defense of the MFDP and its fight to represent Mississippi at the convention. Addressing the credentials committee, she spoke eloquently of the repression and intimidation she and other Black Mississippians faced when attempting to exercise their constitutional rights to register to vote and to cast a ballot. "We didn't come all this way for no two seats," she said, "'cause all of us is tired."

King and SCLC initially supported the MFDP's right to be seated at the convention. With a compromise put forth, which was rejected by the MFDP, SNCC criticized the Democratic Party, but SCLC took a neutral stance, refusing to criticize white liberal Democrats out of fear of losing influence and support in Washington, DC. That drove the wedge between SCLC and SNCC even deeper.

An active movement in pursuit of voting rights in Selma had been underway since at least the mid-1920s. So in the fall of 1964, after Freedom Summer and the Democratic National Convention, when SCLC accepted the invitation of the Courageous Eight to undertake a voting rights campaign in the counties around Selma, the organization and their leader, Martin Luther King Jr., not only arrived late to the effort but stepped into a growing breach with SNCC. James Bevel, Diane Nash, and James Orange, SCLC field organizers who had been unofficially working on voting rights in the Selma area since late 1963, were placed in charge of the new Selma voting rights campaign.

King kicked off the campaign on January 2, 1965, with a speech given at a mass meeting in the city's Brown Chapel AME Church, in defiance of Judge Hare's injunction that no more than two people gather to discuss voting or civil rights. The SCLC leader had just returned from Oslo, Norway, where he'd accepted the 1964 Nobel Peace Prize. After his speech in Selma, SNCC and SCLC entered a period of détente, working together to expand Black voter registration.

Three days after his thirty-sixth birthday and back in Selma from a meeting with President Lyndon B. Johnson on the passage of a voting rights bill, King was assaulted in the lobby of the Hotel Albert by James George Robinson. King was punched several times and kicked in the groin before members of his entourage intervened. King had attempted to register as the first Black guest of this formerly segregated establishment. Robinson's attack on King was all the more poignant in a hotel built by enslaved men and women, which featured horseshoe impressions on an inside staircase, reportedly from Union soldiers who had stormed the hotel during the Civil War. Robinson was a member of the National States Rights Party, an organization cofounded by white extremist J. B. Stoner, who opined that Black men and women came from apes and that being Jewish was a crime that should be punishable by death. King refused to press charges against Robinson.

King was not alone in experiencing the violence of those dead set against Blacks having the right to vote. Sworn law enforcement officers and a local posse under the command and control of Sheriff Jim Clark assaulted and arrested Black voter registrants attempting to enter the Dallas County Courthouse. Even teachers seeking to register to vote were beaten back by Clark's forces. After US District Court Judge Daniel Thomas issued a ruling that at least a hundred people must be permitted to wait in line to register without fear of arrest, Clark's officers systemically counted Blacks lining up to register, then beat and arrested any beyond that first hundred.

On January 25, 1965, the day of Judge Thomas's order, Clark twisted the arm of fifty-four-year-old local Black activist Annie Lee Cooper, who was waiting to register on the steps of the Dallas County Courthouse. Cooper spun around and punched Clark in the face. He fell to the ground. She pounced on him, pinning him down until she was pulled away by four of Clark's officers, whereupon Clark beat her mercilessly with his billy club. A waiting crowd of Black residents, also in line to register to vote, sought to intervene in support of Cooper but then heeded Martin Luther King Jr.'s orders to pull back and avert certain bloodshed.

Here, also, the backstory of this encounter between Cooper and Clark is significant, though rarely reported. When Annie Lee Cooper and a coworker had attempted to register to vote in October 1963, they were summarily fired from their jobs as practical nurses at Dunn's Rest Home in Selma, suffering humiliation, insults, and assault by Dunn's management. Thirty-eight Black women and fellow workers walked off their jobs in protest and support. They, too, were fired, and photos of these forty women who stood up for their rights were circulated among potential white employers. Firing Black workers who were attempting to register or who were supporting voting registration campaigns was a common tactic employed by management of white institutions in Selma. Fifteen months later, when Clark assaulted Cooper on the steps of the Dallas County Courthouse, Cooper was still unemployed. Sometime later, she recalled her encounter with Clark:

> I saw Jim Clark fling Mrs. Boynton [Amelia Boynton, mentioned earlier in this chapter] around like a leaf a day or two before. Clark was larger than I on the outside, but I was larger than he on the inside. The altercation started . . . Jim Clark could not take me down alone. The town sheriff and I were going at it blow for blow, punch for punch, and lick for lick, with our fists. It was a plain old street brawl. Suddenly he cried out to his deputies: "Don't y'all see this nigger woman beatin' me? Do some'um." At the urging of the sheriff the others came to his aid. All four of them closed in on me.
>
> Clark took his nightstick and prepared to land a blow. Before he knew it, I had his arm and held it back with a tight grip. Clark brought his billy club over my face. He managed to put enough power in his swing to graze me across the upper part of my eye with the nightstick. The blow stung and was hard enough to draw blood. It struck me over my eye. I was fiercely holding his hand so he could not strike me again. I heard Dr. King urging the marchers to stay calm. He was afraid the marchers were going to turn violent while watching the Policemen attack me. It was four against one. It took everything each of the four had to manhandle me.

The deputies wrestled me down onto the pavement, as the crowd looked on. Clark planted his knee in my stomach, as the deputies had me on my back. That was the only way he could have gotten his knee in my stomach. He stood no chance of wrestling me to the ground alone. The deputies rolled me over on my stomach and handcuffed my hands behind my back. They lifted me to my feet and took me to the paddy-wagon. I was taken through an alley in town. While walking through the alley, Clark took his billy club and landed a blow on my head. It was a fierce lick. The blow cracked my skull . . .

I remained locked up in the town jail the rest of the day. About 11 pm one of the deputies came to my cell. Jim Clark was nearby sleeping off his drunk. He was a heavy drinker. The deputy said: "I'm going to let you go before Sheriff Clark wakes up in a drunken stupor and decides to kill you."

Although she had violated a key tenet of nonviolence, the local Black community rallied around Annie Lee Cooper, even if SCLC leadership did not. SCLC's position, as articulated by James Bevel in a mass meeting the night of Annie Lee Cooper's arrest, was that, by resorting to violence in the face of violence, Annie Lee Cooper had shifted her eyes away from the prize—voter registration—and onto the contestants. Bevel, nicknamed the Prophet for the skullcap he wore, was right. The contest between the burly sheriff and the outraged Black woman became an instant media sensation. She later told *Jet* magazine, "I try to be nonviolent, but I just can't say I wouldn't do the same thing all over again if they treat me brutish like they did this time."

One cannot help hearing in Annie Lee Cooper's words a paraphrase of those spoken by Fannie Lou Hamer: "We didn't come all this way to be brutalized, 'cause all of us is tired."

Jim Clark's rough handling of Amelia Boynton had impacted not only Annie Lee Cooper but others as well. A group of Selma teachers incensed by Boynton's treatment descended on the courthouse to register. Repelled by Clark after three attempts, the group retreated to the Brown Chapel AME Church. But this opened the way for others in Selma's small but influential Black middle class to step into the voting rights campaign. From undertakers to beauticians, a wide swath of Black Selma stood firmly behind the effort.

A week after Annie Lee Cooper's run-in with Jim Clark, on February 1, 1965, Martin Luther King Jr. and his chief SCLC lieutenant, Reverend Ralph Abernathy, were in jail with more than seven hundred voting rights protesters. The group, led by King, had intentionally violated a Selma police traffic order on their way to the Dallas County Courthouse, hoping for arrests on the Selma side of the Edmund Pettus Bridge, where they would find themselves in Chief Wilson Baker's jail rather than that of Dallas County Sheriff Jim Clark. Refusing to post bail, King and Abernathy also hoped to heighten international awareness of the plight of Black Americans and the need for national voting rights legislation. The pair remained in jail for four days, from where King issued "A Letter from a Selma, Alabama, Jail," part of a preplanned publicity and fundraising campaign undertaken by SCLC.

The same day that King and Abernathy were arrested, SNCC and SCLC expanded the Selma campaign beyond Dallas County into nearby Perry County, where more than seven hundred Black students and adults, including SCLC's main organizer, James Orange, were arrested.

On behalf of the Selma voting rights campaign, King and Abernathy got what they sought. Building pressure for change had escaped from Selma. The same day of their arrest, students from the nearby Tuskegee Institute, in conjunction with SNCC, mounted acts of civil disobedience in support of the Selma voting rights campaign. Many were arrested. New York, Chicago, Detroit, Los Angeles, and many other cities saw sit-ins at federal buildings and protests in solidarity with the Selma campaign. Pickets appeared in front of the White House.

Even Malcolm X stepped into the fray. After the assault on King at the Hotel Albert and the arrest of white supremacist George Lincoln Rockwell during King's appearance at a Freedom Day event on the steps of the Dallas County Courthouse, Malcolm X, who had since been dismissed from the Nation of Islam by Elijah Muhammad, sent a telegram to Rockwell that read, "I am no longer held in check from fighting white supremacists by Elijah Muhammad's separatist Black Muslim movement." And he further warned Rockwell, "If your present racist agitation against our people there in Alabama causes physical harm to Reverend King or any other Black American . . . you and your Ku Klux Klan friends will be met with maximum physical retaliation from those of us who . . . believe in asserting our right of self-defense—by any means necessary."

On February 3, 1965, while King and Abernathy sat in jail, Malcolm X spoke to an audience of more than three thousand at the Tuskegee Institute, mostly students. In attendance were SNCC organizers Silas Norman and Fay Bellamy, who invited him to speak to a gathering of students the following day in Selma. Over the objections of SCLC, in particular from its executive director, Andrew Young, Malcolm X addressed three hundred students at the Brown Chapel AME Church, the headquarters of the Selma voting rights campaign.

Martin and Malcolm personified the rift between SCLC and SNCC. When asked at a press conference if he was going over to the Dallas County Courthouse in solidarity with those seeking to register to vote, Malcolm X replied:

> I'd rather not say right now what I'm going to do. But I'm going to do, while I'm here, whatever will produce some positive and constructive results.
>
> I might point out that I am 100 percent for any effort put forth by Black people in this country to have access to the ballot. And I frankly believe that since the ballot is our right, that we are within our right to use whatever means is necessary to secure those rights. And I think that the people in this part of the world would do well to listen to Dr. Martin Luther King and give him what he's asking for, and give it to him fast, before some other factions

> come along and try to do it another way. What he's asking for is right. That's the ballot. And if he can't get it the way he's trying to get it, then it's going to be gotten, one way or the other.

When speaking to students at the Brown Chapel AME Church, from whom he received an uproarious round of approval, Malcolm included a familiar riff about docile "house Negroes" versus determined "field Negroes." While historically the comparison was inaccurate, Malcolm always delivered the lines to the delight of those in attendance. King thought the reference to "house Negroes" was a dig at him. But Malcolm X reassured Coretta King in a private meeting he had with her that he was in Selma to help, not to hurt, the work of her husband. He was in Selma to remind recalcitrant, racist whites what the alternative was if they didn't give Black residents the voting rights they sought.

Less than three weeks after Malcolm X was in Selma, members of the Nation of Islam assassinated him at the Audubon Ballroom in Manhattan. In his "A Letter from a Selma, Alabama, Jail," King lamented, in all caps, "THIS IS SELMA, ALABAMA. THERE ARE MORE NEGROES IN JAIL WITH ME THAN THERE ARE ON THE VOTING ROLLS."

Events moved rapidly. The day of Malcolm's speech at the Brown Chapel AME Church, President Lyndon B. Johnson made a public statement in support of voting rights and SCLC's Selma campaign. At the White House's urging, District Court

Judge Daniel Thomas ratcheted up the pressure by issuing an injunction that suspended Alabama's literacy test, ordering Selma to take a hundred applications each registration day (beyond just allowing a hundred people to stand in line without fear of arrest) and to guarantee that all voter registration requests received by the beginning of June 1965 would be processed before the end of July.

But the morning Malcolm X arrived in Selma with their two main leaders in jail, SCLC Executive Director Andrew Young and other SCLC leaders decided to suspend the protests and attempts to register to vote that had become a staple and rallying point of the Selma voting rights campaign. They sought to mull over President Johnson's address to the nation and Judge Thomas's latest favorable injunction. James Bevel dissented, calling for the protests to continue, and was backed up by King, who, from his jail cell, called Young and told him the same.

On February 5, King bailed himself and Abernathy out of jail. On February 9, he left Selma for Washington, DC, where he met with Attorney General Nicholas Katzenbach, with Vice President Hubert Humphrey, and briefly with President Johnson. King's message was clear and direct: Voting rights legislation was needed sooner rather than later to avert a catastrophe. When King returned to Selma on February 10, he sounded much like Fannie Lou Hamer when he said to his staff that "to get the bill passed, we need to make a dramatic appeal through Lowndes and other counties because the people of Selma are tired."

With escalating violence keeping away those attempting to register to vote and few having actually succeeded in getting onto the voter rolls, the Alabama voting rights campaign pivoted to a new strategy to keep local folks engaged in the struggle. Grade school and high school students were pragmatically enlisted in the protests. Mothers and fathers had to work during the day, which meant nighttime protests that few favored because it gave police and the Ku Klux Klan too many opportunities to attack under the cover of darkness. Unlike their parents, young people could be free during the day to protest. And there was no better way to engage parents than to engage their children first.

Weighing more than three hundred pounds and standing over six feet tall, the imposing SCLC organizer James Orange went by the nickname of Shack Daddy. In a later interview with *Southern Exposure* magazine, Orange recalled how he came by that name:

> That's when Dr. King started calling me Shack Daddy. He made a speech, saying that we were shacking with the community, we wasn't there to live, we weren't gonna marry the community. Our job was to get stuff started and then move on and get stuff started in other areas. I guess more people know me, man, as Shack Daddy than they do as James Orange.

Born in Birmingham, Orange worked alongside James Bevel to mobilize young people in SCLC's Birmingham Children's Crusade in 1963. The strategy proved extremely effective. In many of the iconic yet tragic images from Birmingham, like snarling dogs set on protesters and fire cannons turned on them, children were on the other end of the dogs' teeth and the jet sprays. Those pictures of Southern white racism and violence directed at innocent children worked their way into the living rooms of America through the nightly news. Sadly, it took that level of Southern white depravity for concerned white Americans to realize and demand that something must be done.

CHAPTER 13

A HIGH PRICE FOR FREEDOM, PART II

CRITICAL MOMENTS OF THE BLACK FREEDOM STRUGGLE IN Alabama took place beyond Selma. With that city as a hub, the DCVL and SNCC had for years focused their voting rights efforts on the surrounding counties of Perry, Wilcox, Marengo, Greene, Hale, and Lowndes. When King and SCLC accepted the invitation from the Courageous Eight to come to Selma, they, too, welcomed the opportunity to push for voting rights and civil rights in these neighboring counties. James Orange brought his skills as a youth organizer in Birmingham to bear in the city of Marion, Alabama, the seat of Perry County.

Marion is located just twenty-two miles northwest of Selma. And so what happened in Marion greatly affected what happened in Selma, and vice versa. On February 2, 1965, in Marion, sixteen Black men and women were arrested for a sit-in at a segregated eatery. The following day, James Orange led a group of more than seven hundred students to the Perry County jailhouse in Marion, where these sixteen were being held, to protest their arrest. The students sung freedom songs, and when ordered to stop by a state trooper, Orange turned to them and said, "Sing another song." State troopers then loaded the students into school buses, arresting them for unlawful assembly and disobeying an officer, ultimately hauling them off to a work camp sixty miles away and imposing a one-hundred-dollar bond on each student.

That got the attention of adults, who poured into Zion United Methodist Church that night looking for their kids. When told by organizers what had happened, these parents chose to return to Marion the following day, and they chose to march. They were also arrested.

Appalling conditions met Black freedom activists in Alabama's segregated jails. Although SCLC and SNCC tried to assist those arrested with bail, the growing numbers of arrestees quickly depleted their funds. Most arrested were not as fortunate as King or Abernathy. Lacking the resources to bail themselves out, they languished in jail cells for days and months. Cells built for ten housed nearly ten times that amount. Jails served unfit food, sometimes forcing arrestees to drink from toilets. Holding cells possessed inadequate sanitation. Rats and roaches ran rampant. Trials and lawyers were in short supply. And, perhaps most important, inmates lived under the continual threat of beatings and assaults and even lynchings by their jailers.

Several days in jail finally led to the release of adults and students, but not to the cessation of protests. On February 15, 1965, the last day of the month to register to vote, Orange organized a protest of some four hundred students, who gathered outside the Perry County Courthouse in support of nearly three hundred adults attempting to register inside. King arrived from Selma later in the day in support of the effort, but despite it all, most of those adults were not allowed to register.

Orange would not relent. Three days later, on the morning of February 18, he stood in front of the Perry County Courthouse in Marion, across the street from Zion United Methodist Church, at the head of about 125 students, who were demanding their parents be given the right to register to vote. Police Chief T. O. Harris ordered the protesters to disperse. When they disobeyed his command, James Orange was arrested for contributing to the delinquency of minors. Orange's arrest brought about legitimate concerns for his safety. Many feared he would be lynched.

News of Orange's arrest spread fast, as did worry over his safety while in jail. SCLC planned a night march on February 18, 1965, from Zion United across the street to the Perry County Courthouse in support of Orange. Nighttime marches, as mentioned earlier, were dicey affairs, and this one even more so because local officials had received orders from state officials to target the organizers of the march, especially C. T. Vivian.

Black Marion residents who'd come to Zion United in support of Orange did not like what they'd been seeing outside all day. One of the attendees, Willie Nell Avery, recalled how, from her window at work in downtown Marion, she saw state troopers arrive regularly throughout the day. City and state police pulled into the city, many with lines of extra uniforms hung on rods stretched across the backs of their cruisers. To Avery, that suggested they were planning to deputize local whites, give them uniforms, and turn them loose, unrestrained, on the marchers, a common tactic employed throughout the South against those fighting for their freedom.

Dressed in street clothes, infamous Dallas Country Sheriff Jim Clark also stood outside Zion United, where inside local residents gathered ahead of the protest. Rumor had it that Clark sought to beat or even kill C. T. Vivian over a protest that took place several days earlier during a registration attempt at the Dallas County Courthouse. Clark ordered a group of about sixty to disperse. When Vivian refused, Clark punched him in the face, smashing his jaw and fracturing several teeth. Even though Vivian needed medical and dental care, he exhorted demonstrators to chant "Don't beat us; if we're wrong, arrest us." Such a calm demeanor enraged Clark. Still, Vivian later made it to Marion from Selma, sneaking in and out of a rear door at Zion United, speaking to the assembled crowd, without ever confronting the sheriff.

Shortly after 9:00 p.m., after the singing and speeches inside Zion United, attendees arose from the pews to line up for the march to the jail. On the steps outside, march leaders sat discussing strategy: Albert ("Big Al") Turner, head of the Perry County Civic League, a local organization focused on voting rights; SCLC organizer Willie M. Bolden; and a local pastor, Reverend James Dobynes. Not fifty feet from the church's door, Marion Chief of Police T. O. Harris ordered the marchers to return to their homes or to the church. Warned that there might be trouble, the march leaders were prepared to head back. Dobynes requested a moment of prayer. As he knelt, streetlights around him went out. While he was still in prayer, a police billy club came down on him, cracking his skull open. Dobynes, in a later statement made under oath, said,

> While I was praying a trooper struck me across the head with his stick, opening a bloody wound. They drug me off and carried me to jail, beating me all the way. I was charged with unlawful assembly. I kept praying all the way to jail. They kept telling me to shut up, but I kept praying. When I got to jail, blood was streaming down my face like water. Someone at the jail said, "You black [expletive deleted], you ought to bleed to death."

Bolden recalled having the barrel of a pistol shoved into his mouth and being told by an officer, "If you breathe, nigger, I'll blow your fuckin' brains out."

Self, don't breathe, Bolden repeated over and again to himself.

"Are you an outsider?" a state trooper asked Big Al Turner. Turner's answer really didn't matter to the trooper. Turner was clubbed while reaching for his driver's license.

A massive, coordinated police attack had begun in earnest.

Not all the marchers had even left Zion United when the police outside began beating protesters and shoving them. Many were pushed and beaten back into the church. Those unable to make it inside against the tide of those flooding out broke off from the group and began running for safety to their cars or to Mack's Café, passing through a gauntlet of swinging billy clubs on their way.

Inside the church, Big Al Turner took charge, and the confrontation quickly became a standoff. "We weren't going to have anybody come into the church and beat folks about the head." Years later, Turner recalled what he told the officers that night. "If you get by one, the next one will get you." He then reflected on the fighting mood inside the church. "After we busted a couple of heads, they stopped attempting to get through the door." The troopers then settled for a siege of Zion United, surrounding the church to keep protesters pinned inside.

Outside the church, the local white community jumped into the fray, especially against the national press. With black spray paint in hand, white townsfolk ran up to cameramen, blackening their camera lenses so the police rampage could not be filmed. Richard Valeriani of NBC was struck so hard with an ax handle, he thought he was going to die. Pete Fisher of UPI received a beating by white Marion residents while the police and FBI stood by. The beatings were not confined to marchers. On his way home from work, John C. Lewis (unrelated to SNCC's John R. Lewis) was pulled over and dragged out of his car by two state troopers. Even when one trooper vouched for Lewis, the other casually said, "Let's beat him anyway." Lewis was left on the side of the road for dead.

But the worst attack by local police and state troopers came against protesters who'd first split off from the main group. Barred entrance back into the church, they fled for safety, many to nearby Mack's Café, where waiting state troopers clubbed them as they entered.

Twenty-six-year-old Jimmie Lee Jackson had driven his family to the mass meeting at Zion United that evening. He did not go inside with them, nor did he participate in the attempted march; instead, he left, returning later in the midst of the carnage to pick up his grandfather and his mother and drive them home. Upon his return, Jimmie Lee ran into his grandfather, eighty-two-year-old Cager Lee, badly injured yet behind Zion, directing people to go home while looking for his fifty-year-old daughter, Viola Jackson, Jimmie Lee's mother.

Cager Lee, interviewed by *The New York Times*, said, "I was at the back of the church. The men with clubs come around saying, 'Nigger, go home.' They hauled me off and hit me and knocked me to the street and kicked me. It was hard to take for an old man whose bones are dry like cane." He continued, "One of them knew me. He say, 'Why, that's Cager. What are you doing here, Cager?' and they let me up."

Jimmie Lee joined Cager in search of Viola, and together they made their way to Mack's Café, located behind the church. Many marchers locked out of Zion United had made their way to Mack's. Jimmie Lee and Cager found Viola and her sixteen-year-old daughter, Emma Jean, in the café. But Alabama state troopers were in hot pursuit of marchers fleeing to Mack's. They burst into the café, trapping Jimmie Lee and his family inside. Only Cager Lee managed to slip out before the troopers arrived. Jimmie Lee, his mother, and his sister did not.

Although the exact timing and sequence of events vary from witness to witness and nearly all Black witnesses inside the café offer a different report than that delivered by the state police or the FBI, it appears that state troopers started beating Jimmie Lee badly. Viola, drink bottle in hand, interceded, trying to pry the troopers off her son. But the troopers then turned on her. She later reported, "Two of them hit me on the head. They knocked me down and started beating me on the floor."

Jimmie Lee then leapt to his mother's aid, trying to protect her from the berserk officers when one trooper pinned him against a cigarette machine, and another, James Bonard Fowler, fired two shots at point-blank range into his stomach.

Emma Jean would later report, "I kept talking to Jimmie to calm him down. He did not appear as if he were going to cause trouble." She said that she picked up a bottle and flung it at the troopers attacking her mother and brother.

Charles Pryor, a Black man inside Mack's, said that Jimmie Lee picked up a bottle to hurl at the troopers beating his mother, but Emma Jean had taken it from him. Pryor then said:

> I left the café and went about 50 feet and stopped. I looked back and saw several state troopers chasing Jimmie Lee Jackson towards me. Jackson fell to the ground near the corner of the church. Several state troopers kicked Jackson and hit him while he was on the ground. There were many troopers standing around him. Jackson got up and ran around the corner of the church to the post office. State troopers caught him again and the last I saw he was on the ground.

Willie Lee Smith, who witnessed the shooting, later reported that a state trooper clubbed Jimmie Lee over the head, then drew his revolver and fired at Jimmie Lee. Mack's customer Jeff Moore corroborated Smith's testimony, adding he heard one trooper ask, "Who got him?" And the trooper who shot Jimmie Lee replied, "I got him!"

As Jackson stumbled wounded from Mack's, state troopers continued to beat him until he lay unconscious. Only then did they transport him to the Perry County Hospital. He did not immediately succumb to Fowler's gunshots.

Norma Reen Shaw, the on-duty manager of Mack's Café, reported that, after the shooting, state police evacuated all patrons and took the keys to the establishment from her with assurances that they would lock up. The next morning, she found the door of the café open and a section of the wall behind where Jimmie Lee had been standing when he had been shot had been cut out and removed.

When the FBI interviewed Jackson from his hospital bed, he recalled going to Mack's Café to transport his grandfather to the hospital. He also recalled drinking a Coke after being pushed back inside, when he saw state troopers beating his mother. He stated that his sister held him back. Then he reported that he was close to a door leading to the dance hall inside of Mack's when a state trooper shot him in the stomach. According to Jackson, he ran out of Mack's, where he was hit with clubs and kicked repeatedly until he dropped to the ground in front of the nearby bus station.

Perry County Sheriff William Loftis wasted little time in issuing a warrant that same evening for Jimmie Lee Jackson's arrest for "assault with intent to murder."

Deputy Sheriff William Perkins reportedly transferred Jimmie

Lee Jackson to the Perry County Hospital, where Reverend James Dobynes, already there for his wounds at the hands of state troopers, reported that hospital staff left Jackson on a gurney, covered in blood, crying out in pain. Dobynes overheard nurses saying that "they weren't going to put their hands on that nigger; he could just lay up there and die before they give a shit."

Perry County Hospital staff later insisted they had not delayed Jackson's treatment. He was transferred to Good Samaritan Hospital in Selma for an operation to remove bullet fragments from his body. Good Samaritan Hospital had opened the year prior to tend to Black residents of Selma. Founded by the Fathers of St. Edmund, the hospital was staffed by the Sisters of St. Joseph.

While Jackson fought for his life, the finger-pointing and deflection of blame began. Perry County Sheriff William Loftis blamed outside agitators for the melee and for Jackson being shot. "[O]utside integration leaders from Selma" provoked the conflict in Marion, Loftis said.

"We're sorry that someone was struck," Marion Mayor R. L. Pegues said. "Actually, very little went on. It all happened in a very short time."

Marion Police Chief T. O. Harris insisted that many of the injuries sustained by marchers were self-inflicted. "Some of them were hurt by themselves and others," he said, "in the effort to cause them to go back to the church."

Governor George C. Wallace and other top Alabama officials blamed the carnage in Marion on "communist agitators" like Martin Luther King Jr.

In an editorial the day after Jackson was shot, the *Montgomery Advertiser*, long antagonistic to the Black Freedom Struggle, even dissented from officials in Marion. Dubbing the event "the Marion Massacre," the editorial went on to say, "What happened in Marion last night was a nightmare of state police stupidity and brutality."

News of the "massacre" and of Jimmie Lee Jackson's shooting traveled quickly to Selma. King wired US Attorney General Nicholas Katzenbach, requesting federal intervention and protection of those seeking to register to vote in Marion. "Chaos and savagery in the name of law enforcement" must be dealt with swiftly, King said.

Katzenbach replied that he'd dispatched the FBI to investigate the previous night's events and would prosecute any violation of voting rights. Even before King's telegram arrived on Katzenbach's desk, J. Edgar Hoover, director of the FBI, who deplored King, told the attorney general that FBI agents "observed no police brutality" in Marion but did see "an unruly mob" attack state and local police. Katzenbach requested additional FBI resources in Marion, and Hoover dispatched four additional agents to interview witnesses—arrestees, police, and others. But Hoover reported that Alabama Director of Public Safety Al Lingo shut down the bureau's ability to interview state troopers.

Big Al Turner had his hands full. On February 19, the night after the Marion Massacre, protesters arrived at Zion United, ready to live out the words not of the nonviolent teacher Mahatma Gandhi but of the Harlem Renaissance poet Claude McKay, who'd penned the short poem "If We Must Die" nearly a half century earlier:

> If we must die, let it not be like hogs
> Hunted and penned in an inglorious spot,
> While round us bark the mad and hungry dogs,
> Making their mock at our accursèd lot.
> If we must die, O let us nobly die,
> So that our precious blood may not be shed
> In vain; then even the monsters we defy
> Shall be constrained to honor us though dead!
> O kinsmen! we must meet the common foe!
> Though far outnumbered let us show us brave,
> And for their thousand blows deal one death-blow!
> What though before us lies the open grave?
> Like men we'll face the murderous, cowardly pack,
> Pressed to the wall, dying, but fighting back!

Car trunks brimmed with shotguns, long rifles, and rounds of ammunition. Fortunately, Governor George C. Wallace, Mayor R. L. Pegues, Sheriff William Loftis, and Chief T. O. Harris seemingly called off their dogs. A one-block march from Zion United to the county courthouse, then back, took place without incident.

Three days after the Marion Massacre, Jimmie Lee Jackson, a farmer and pulpwood chopper who earned six dollars a day, lay in critical condition. Many accounts have described him as an army veteran who served in Vietnam. But there is no evidence from his family or records from any branches of the military that he ever served. Still, too many Black veterans met a similar fate upon returning to America.

Jimmie Lee Jackson graduated from Lincoln High School in Marion, becoming the youngest deacon ever in the city's St. James Baptist Church. He lived in a "shotgun house" and briefly left Marion, looking for work in Indiana. After his father died in a car accident, Jimmie Lee returned as the primary caretaker for Viola, Cager Lee, and Emma Jean. He and his girlfriend, Addie Heard, had a child named Cordelia.

Dr. William Dinkins, a Black physician, attended to Jimmie Lee Jackson when he arrived at Good Samaritan Hospital in Selma, opening his abdomen to remove bullet fragments. A week after surgery, Jackson was sitting up in bed, having given interviews to the FBI and praying with Martin Luther King Jr. He seemed to be recovering well when Good Samaritan called in a white surgeon, who insisted Jackson needed a second surgery. Dr. Dinkins vehemently disagreed but was ultimately overruled. During surgery, Jackson showed signs of hypoxia. Dinkins then asked the anesthesiologist to administer pure oxygen to Jackson, but again he was overruled by the white surgeon, who called for more anesthesia. Jimmie Lee Jackson died on the operating table. Dinkins believed it was due to an overdose of anesthesia. Good Samaritan reported that Jackson died of massive sepsis, though there were no signs of systemic infection in the days leading up to his second surgery. The surgeon was not interviewed by the FBI.

Big Al Turner remembered Jimmie Lee as "a real quiet, orderly, mannerly, clean guy that did what most of us did at the time, and that was work."

Jackson was not a voting rights activist or a member of SNCC, SCLC, or the Perry County Civic League (PCCL). He simply wanted to vote and had unsuccessfully attempted to register several times. He occasionally attended mass meetings at Zion United after SCLC launched its voting rights campaign. Said Marion resident Florence Lauderdale, "He went to register, but *everyone* went. We did that when we should have been voting."

Malcolm X's assassination came three days after Jimmie Lee Jackson's shooting. Five days after that, on February 26, 1965, Jimmie Lee Jackson died. At one of two funeral services held for Jackson, Martin Luther King Jr. eulogized the young man:

> Jimmie Lee Jackson's death says to us that we must work passionately and unrelentingly to make the American dream a reality. His death must prove that unmerited suffering does not go unredeemed. We must not be bitter and we must not harbor ideas of retaliating with violence. We must not lose faith in our white brothers.

The bomb set off in Marion sent shock waves around the world. From Marion, King said, "We have now reached the point of no return." He continued, "We must let [Governor] George Wallace know that violence of state troopers will not stop us." In Selma he suggested a motorcade to Montgomery, with carloads of people from all over the state. That evening, as King's aides and local

SCLC and SNCC activists gathered to plan for the motorcade, James "The Prophet" Bevel, who supported James Orange's efforts in Marion that had led to Orange's arrest and the subsequent police attack, rose to take personal responsibility for the Marion Massacre and Jimmie Lee Jackson's death. An older SCLC activist, Lucy Foster, countered Bevel, proposing that Jimmie Lee's casket be brought to Montgomery, laying the blame and his body where it really belonged: at the doorstep of Governor George Wallace. Bevel and the other SCLC aides seized on Foster's idea, thus giving birth to a Selma-to-Montgomery march.

But SNCC opposed it.

John Lewis recalled, "The SNCC people, especially [James] Forman, were dead set against it. They felt that such a march would do more for King than it would for Selma. I disagreed. I knew the feelings that were out there on the streets. The people of Selma were hurting. They were angry. They needed to march. It didn't matter to me who led it. They *needed* to march."

The people of Marion were also hurting. They *needed* to march as well. SNCC also felt that a march led by King would rile up further hatred from local whites, leaving them to handle the messy aftermath when SCLC left town. The march, after all, had protesters walking through the infamous Lowndes County, well-known for the violence and hatred of its local Ku Klux Klan.

On Wednesday, March 3, after King eulogized Jimmie Lee Jackson in Marion, Bevel announced that the Nobel laureate would return from meetings in New York to lead a massive fifty-four-mile march from Selma to Montgomery that Sunday, March 7.

King, however, had other plans. While he'd given the march his blessing, he did not return to Selma to lead it. Instead, he went to Atlanta, where he said he'd neglected his congregation at Ebenezer Baptist Church for far too long and needed to deliver that Sunday's sermon. That forced SNCC's hand. King's absence would further raise the stakes for those marching, putting them in even greater danger. SNCC Executive Secretary James Forman sent King a letter, signed by Lewis, SNCC's chairman, stating, "We strongly believe the objectives of the march do not justify its dangers . . . consequently, the Student Nonviolent Coordinating Committee will only live up to those minimal commitments . . . to provide radios and cars, doctors and nurses, and nothing beyond that."

But at an Atlanta meeting the night before the march, the leadership team of SNCC agreed to allow its members to participate in the march as long as they did not represent the organization. "I'm a native Alabamian," Lewis told his friends that evening in Atlanta. "I grew up in Alabama. I feel a deep kinship with the people there on a lot of levels. You know I've been to Selma many, many times. I've been arrested there. I've been jailed there. If these people want to march, I'm going to march with them. You decide what you want to do, but I'm going to march."

Lewis rushed the four hours by car back to Selma to participate in the march, but his principled stance cost him friends, and the leadership of SNCC passed from Lewis to Stokely Carmichael the following year. When Lewis arrived at Brown Chapel AME Church at 12:30 p.m. the day of the march, nearly five hundred people had already gathered. Some SCLC members were busy with nonviolent training classes. But off to one side, SCLC march leaders Hosea Williams and James Bevel were in a heated discussion with SCLC Executive Director Andrew Young, there to deliver the message that King, still in Atlanta, wanted the march delayed until Monday. SNCC labeled King's absence a cop-out, but rumors later circulated that SCLC had become aware of a credible threat to King's life and had persuaded him to wait a day longer.

Bevel and Williams were furious. Lewis agreed with them that the people of Selma and Marion had spoken by their presence. They were ready, and to turn them back home would be a great injustice and an insult to Jimmie Lee Jackson's sacrifice.

Young, realizing the march was unstoppable, called King in Atlanta, then returned with the news that King had said one of them—Williams, Bevel, or Young—should be selected to colead the march with Lewis. After a coin toss, Hosea Williams was selected.

Doctors and nurses from the Medical Committee for Human Rights had arrived on Saturday to set up a field clinic in the Brown Chapel AME Church's parsonage. Few expected they would reach Montgomery. Most anticipated a confrontation. Alabama Governor George Wallace declared, "I'm not going to have a bunch of niggers walking along a highway in this state as long as I'm governor."

Alabama Director of Public Safety Al Lingo, Dallas County Sheriff Jim Clark, Selma Police Chief Wilson Baker, and Selma

Mayor Joseph Smitherman heard George Wallace loud and clear. They were only too glad to enforce his edict. The Edmund Pettus Bridge crosses the Alabama River out of Selma on the way to Montgomery, and later, Wallace would say he had not wanted marchers to proceed beyond the end of the bridge on the Montgomery side. Clark made certain that did not happen.

Sheriff Jim Clark commanded his own private militia. He'd deputized about two hundred white men over the age of twenty-one, many of them also members of the Ku Klux Klan, National States Rights Party, or other white supremacist groups. Clark outfitted them with cheap badges, unofficial khaki uniforms, and plastic safety helmets. Some possessed electric cattle prods and hardwood clubs. Others, mounted on horseback, carried long leather whips to lash people on foot.

American policing bears witness to a long history of deputizing local white citizens to hunt down and brutalize Blacks, stretching as far back as colonial times. Sheriffs routinely deputized white men as "slave patrols" to capture or kill runaways. Laws on the books of several colonies made it a felony for Blacks to carry guns or weapons and enforced the enlistment of white men to maintain the social order dictated by white enslavers. So Jim Clark acted out of an ancient playbook when creating his own vigilante police squad in Selma.

Marchers left Brown Chapel AME Church at about 4:00 p.m. on March 7, walking two by two. When Williams and Lewis, at the head of the march, crested the Edmund Pettus Bridge, what they saw stopped them in their tracks. "There, facing us at the bottom of the other side," Lewis wrote, "stood a sea of blue-helmeted, blue-uniformed Alabama state troopers, line after line of them, dozens of battle-ready lawmen stretched from one side of [the bridge] to the other." Lewis continued:

> Behind them were several dozen more armed men—Sheriff Clark's posse—some on horseback, all wearing khaki clothing, many carrying clubs the size of baseball bats. On one side of the road I could see a crowd of about a hundred whites, laughing and hollering, waving Confederate flags. Beyond them, at a safe distance, stood a small, silent group of Black people. I could see a crowd of newsmen and reporters gathered in the parking lot of a Pontiac dealership.

Lewis recalled several state troopers donning gas masks as Alabama state trooper Major John Cloud stepped forward and announced through a bullhorn, "This is an unlawful assembly. Your march is not conducive to public safety. You are ordered to disperse and go back to your church or to your homes."

Williams and Lewis chose to bring the marchers to a halt and kneel in prayer instead. As they did, Major Cloud barked, "Troopers, advance!"

And then yet another police massacre began.

"Get 'em! Get the niggers!" a white woman shouted. Alabama state troopers went forward to "get 'em."

In the March 8, 1965, edition of *The New York Times*, reporter Roy Reed described the state troopers marching forward:

> The first 10 or 20 Negroes were swept to the ground screaming, arms and legs flying, and packs and bags went skittering across the grassy divider strip and on to the pavement on both sides.
>
> Those still on their feet retreated.
>
> The troopers continued pushing, using both the force of their bodies and the prodding of their nightsticks.
>
> A cheer went up from the white spectators lining the south side of the [bridge].

Newsweek magazine's William Crook wrote about how troopers marched in a "flying wedge" formation, bulldozing their way into Williams and Lewis, shoving them backward into the marchers behind them. They were toppled, "like dominoes," Crook wrote, before troopers rushed into the marchers, swinging their billy clubs wildly against Black bodies and skulls. "We're being killed," Crooks reported one marcher yelling.

Billy clubs flailed. Bodies fell. Horses trampled human bodies. Marchers ran. But after the troopers came Jim Clark and his deputized thugs, smashing through the marchers, knocking down and beating anyone still standing. This lawless gang of law enforcement officers, possemen, and plain thugs tracked and beat protesters back over the Edmund Pettus Bridge and throughout the streets of Selma. Doctors and nurses from the Medical Committee for Human Rights raced through the streets, lifting the crippled, injured, and unconscious into ambulances, shuttling frenziedly between this war zone and the makeshift hospital inside Zion United.

Some marchers sought refuge in the Carver Projects, but Clark and his posse swarmed in after them. Clark fired tear gas into homes to drive people outside, where he and his mob could attack them. Selma Police Chief Wilson Baker tried to stop him, but Clark shouted in his face, "I've already waited a month too damn long!"

When smoke from the tear gas settled as the bloodlust of the state troopers and Sheriff Jim Clark had been sated, John Lewis stumbled toward Brown Chapel AME Church. He had been knocked unconscious and had a fractured skull, a concussion, and scars he would bear for life. Amelia Boynton lay on the ground, beaten unconscious; a photograph of her lying on the roadway of the Edmund Pettus Bridge circulated internationally. Lynda Blackmon Lowery, fourteen years old, had been savagely attacked by a policeman and required thirty-five stitches over her face and head. In this uniquely American carnage, a hundred of the marchers required medical intervention, and hundreds more bore psychological and physical scars for the rest of their lives.

By the late evening of Bloody Sunday, a crowd of nearly eight hundred gathered in Brown Chapel AME Church. Sheyann Webb, nine years old at the time, remembered everyone singing "Ain't Gonna Let Nobody Turn Me 'Round" with new lyrics: "Ain't gonna let George Wallace turn me 'round . . . Ain't gonna let Jim Clark turn me 'round . . . Ain't gonna let no state trooper turn me 'round . . . Ain't gonna let no horses . . . Ain't gonna let no tear gas . . . Ain't gonna let nobody turn me 'round. Nobody!"

"We was singing and telling the world that we hadn't been whipped," Sheyann Webb said.

At this meeting, march leader Hosea Williams told the crowd at Zion United about being better treated by his German captors in World War II than by the state troopers of Alabama.

Coleader John Lewis, blood splattered over his clothes and caking on his head, refused to seek treatment before addressing those assembled. "I don't know how President Johnson can send troops to Vietnam. I don't see how he can send troops to the Congo. I don't see how he can send troops to Africa, and he can't send troops to Selma, Alabama. Next time we march, we may have to keep going when we get to Montgomery. We have to go to Washington."

Lyndon B. Johnson, and much of the world, may have heard Lewis's call. Johnson issued a statement in which he deplored "the brutality with which a number of Negro citizens of Alabama were treated." SNCC temporarily put aside all differences with SCLC and immediately joined the Alabama campaign, holding a sit-in occupation of Attorney General Nicholas Katzenbach's office on March 8. That same day, the executive board of the NAACP unanimously passed a strong resolution:

> If Federal troops are not made available to protect the rights of Negroes, then the American people are faced with terrible alternatives. Like the citizens of Nazi-occupied France, Negroes must either submit to the heels of their oppressors or they must organize underground

to protect themselves from the oppression of Governor Wallace and his storm troopers.

"Mr. President," wrote labor leader Walter Reuther, "I join in urging you to take immediate and appropriate steps including the use of Federal marshal and troops if necessary, so that the exercise of constitutional rights including free assembly and free speech be fully protected."

Meanwhile, frantic calls flew back and forth between Selma and King and his top aides in Atlanta. SCLC knew something needed to be done. King, Bevel, Nash, and others began plans for a second march on Tuesday, March 9, 1965. King issued a telegram with a national plea for help:

> In the vicious maltreatment of defenseless citizens of Selma, where old women and young children were gassed and clubbed at random, we have witnessed an eruption of the disease of racism which seeks to destroy all of America. No American is without responsibility. All are involved in the sorrow that rises from Selma to contaminate every crevice of our national life. The people of Selma will struggle on for the soul of the nation, but it is fitting that all America help to bear the burden. I call therefore, on clergy of all faiths representative of every part of the country, to join me for a ministers' march to Montgomery on Tuesday morning, March 9th. In this way all America will testify to the fact that the struggle

in Selma is for the survival of democracy everywhere in our land.

Men and women of all faiths responded.

SCLC also mounted a legal effort to injunct state troopers and Jim Clark from brutalizing marchers on this second march. The request fell on the desk of US District Judge Frank Johnson, who had a history of supporting the pleas of Black Alabamians. But Johnson would not rule until the matter could be argued before him, and in return, he issued a temporary restraining order against SCLC holding the march, placing King in a bind: He'd promised a march, but now that meant violating a federal judge's order, something he'd sworn never to do.

On Monday night, March 8, King announced there would be no march on Tuesday. But a few hours later, in the emotionally charged atmosphere of those gathered at Brown Chapel AME Church, King changed his mind, stunning those in attendance by announcing that a march to Montgomery would be held the next day.

The remainder of Monday night and well into the early hours of Tuesday morning, King huddled with federal officials on the ground in Selma and over the phone with Attorney General Katzenbach in Washington. The results of those discussions were known only to a few close aides.

But later Tuesday afternoon, King departed with a group of two thousand over the same route that Lewis and Williams had taken two days earlier. As the column of marchers approached the

Edmund Pettus Bridge, a US marshal read aloud Judge Johnson's injunction against the march, but marchers pushed on. And just as on Sunday, when they crested the bridge, Lingo and Clark, state troopers and possemen, massed on the other side, waiting. Marchers readied for their attack.

Only this time, the troopers and possemen stood by as King brought the marchers to a halt. He led the group in prayer and then in the singing of "We Shall Overcome," after which, to the surprise of most, the state troopers stepped aside, allowing the marchers to pass. But instead, King turned the column around and headed back toward Selma and Brown Chapel AME Church. Many who had come expecting a confrontation in support of civil rights were disappointed. Some felt betrayed. Others expressed open hostility. Word spread that King had made a secret agreement with federal officials to hold only a symbolic march to the bridge and then back to Selma, where he would await Judge Johnson's order. With Sunday known as Bloody Sunday, many referred to that day as Turnaround Tuesday.

With a long history of their church supporting abolition and civil rights, many Unitarian Universalist ministers had responded to King's national call to come to Selma. Later in the evening of March 9, Unitarian Universalist minister James Reeb and two fellow ministers decided on dinner at Walker's Café, a Black-owned establishment in Selma. By all accounts, Sam Cooke's "A Change Is Gonna Come" played on the jukebox as the trio finished their meal. They headed from Walker's to Brown Chapel AME Church, where King was expected to speak.

"Hey, you niggers!" a voice called out.

A heavy club swung at Reeb. With a thud, he went down. The ministers were punched and kicked and brutalized. Their attacker yelled, "You want to know what it's like to be a nigger around here?" After being struck, Reeb lapsed into unconsciousness. Two days later, on March 11, Reverend James Reeb died when his wife made the excruciating decision to remove him from life support.

King eulogized Reeb at Brown Chapel AME Church on Monday, March 15. That evening, Lyndon B. Johnson addressed a joint session of Congress, delivering a speech that some observers claimed was the most brilliant of his presidency. He introduced the Voting Rights Act with these words:

> At times history and fate meet at a single time in a single place to shape a turning point in man's unending search for freedom. So it was at Lexington and Concord. So it was a century ago at Appomattox. So it was last week in Selma, Alabama. There, long suffering men and women peacefully protested the denial of their rights as Americans. Many were brutally assaulted. One good man, a man of God, was killed, was clubbed by a mob of white supremacists as he walked from a Selma restaurant with two others.

King and Lewis, though invited by Johnson to be present in Washington, were crammed in the living room of a Montgomery dentist, listening to Johnson's speech, when the president's oration reached a crescendo:

> But even if we pass this bill, the battle will not be over. What happened in Selma is part of a far larger movement which reaches into every section and state of America. It is the effort of American Negroes to secure for themselves the full blessings of American life.
>
> Their cause must be our cause too. Because it is not just Negroes, but really it is all of us, who must overcome the crippling legacy of bigotry and injustice.
>
> And we shall overcome.

King, Lewis would later write, shed a tear at those words. In the summer of 1965, Johnson's voting rights bill was passed.

Others were less enthralled. Stokely Carmichael lamented that it took the death of a white man, rather than the many deaths of Black men and women, to cause Washington's political establishment, and the nation, to act. Jim Forman of SNCC told a reporter that, by using the anthem of the Black Freedom Struggle in the speech, "Johnson spoiled a good song that day."

On the day following Johnson's speech to Congress, at a mass meeting held by SCLC, Forman whipped up the crowd with a fiery speech, demanding that Johnson put an end to the violence and murder of Black people in Alabama who were simply desiring to exercise their rights. "If we can't sit at the table of democracy," Forman warned, "we'll knock the fucking legs off."

King, who spoke after Forman, tried to quiet and calm the crowd. He was met with little success until some aides rushed up to the podium, then whispered in his ears. Those gathered seemed to instinctively know that something big had just happened. King nodded, tamping down the air, thus bringing the assembly to silence. Judge Frank Johnson's ruling was in.

Frank Minis Johnson was a man of the law. As a US district court judge in Alabama, he'd ruled in Rosa Parks's favor in Montgomery in 1956, striking down the "Blacks to the back of the bus" rule in public transportation. Now, the decision that King communicated from the podium, the decision Johnson issued in this case, allowed the Black Freedom Struggle to advance one step farther. Johnson lifted his judicial restraint against the march, imposing one on police and state troopers from attacking the marchers. He did so having heard from President Lyndon B. Johnson (no relationship) that the order for the march to proceed would be enforced by federal troops if necessary.

Governor George C. Wallace reacted vehemently to his college classmate's ruling, calling Frank Johnson an "integrating, carpetbagging, scalawagging, race-mixing, bald-faced liar."

But Johnson's ruling allowed King to lead the third Selma-to-Montgomery march, planned for March 21–24, 1965. On Sunday, March 21, almost eight thousand people from around the world departed the Brown Chapel AME Church in Selma to begin the fifty-four-mile march to Montgomery, escorted by members of the Alabama National Guard, since federalized by President Johnson. From this march came the iconic photograph of Martin Luther King Jr. hand in hand with his wife, Coretta, and arm in arm with Ralph Abernathy and his wife, Juanita, and with Fred Shuttlesworth, Ralph Bunche, Rabbi Abraham

Joshua Heschel, and many others. But it is little reported that on March 23, hundreds of Black marchers donned kippots, Jewish skullcaps, in support of and admiration for Rabbi Heschel and Rabbi Maurice Davis at the head of the march. The kippots became known as freedom caps.

A star-studded list of entertainers performed for the marchers on the evening of March 24 as they camped on the outskirts of Montgomery. Harry Belafonte; Sammy Davis Jr.; Nina Simone; Joan Baez; Tony Bennett; and Peter, Paul and Mary were among them. The next day, twenty-five thousand people marched from the encampment to the steps of the Alabama State Capitol building, where King delivered his "Our God Is Marching On" speech.

Like the Edmund Pettus Bridge that marchers crossed over to get to the state capitol in Montgomery, "Our God Is Marching On" was itself a bridge. A bridge inviting white Americans, particularly poor white Americans, to understand how racism had historically manipulated them.

King was certainly aware of many in the Black community disaffected by nonviolence, perhaps prescient of the growing unrest that would erupt the following summer in New York City, Detroit, Los Angeles, and other cities and communities across the nation. So this speech offered Black Americans fearful of nonviolence in the face of the recalcitrant violence of whites a bridge to leave behind those fears.

But King's words were also a bridge to an unseen future he didn't live long enough to witness. Paraphrasing the nineteenth-century abolitionist Theodore Parker, King said in this speech,

"The arc of the moral universe is long, but it bends toward justice." Who cannot hear future Black President Barack Obama's elocution of that same sentence in his own orations?

How long until we as a society, as a nation, as a world, cross that bridge to reach the end of that arc? King asked the crowd. "Not long!" he replied, and the audience echoed him many times. Here in this marvelously framed short speech of just a little over three minutes, often called the "How Long? Not Long!" speech, King built a bridge for us all. King's speech was not merely a historical reference to a time gone by, but as a call to action as well.

The very issues protesters marched for in Alabama in February and March 1965 are still with us today. Police violence plagues this nation. Too many young Black men and women, like Jimmie Lee Jackson and George Floyd and Breonna Taylor, have had their lives cut short unnecessarily by the police. Voting rights are under attack. Even though the third Selma march resulted in the passage of the Voting Rights Act of 1965, now the Supreme Court and legislatures around the country are working tirelessly to send the country back to a Jim Crow era before March 1965, when Black Americans and other communities of color were denied access to the ballot. And angry white men, self-deputized by the oration of an angry white president, march in violence. They are afraid of those not like them, afraid that the half-realized democracy that afforded them status just above being Black is now crumbling. We saw them marching and killing and spewing hate in Charlottesville for their Unite the Right rally in August 2017, and we saw them again marching on this nation's capitol during the January 6 insurrection.

Yet of all the things King did say in this brilliant oration, there is one thing he omitted that was omitted also by Lyndon B. Johnson in his speech to the joint session of Congress—one thing far too many of us do not know or fail to recall. If only the president had mentioned that two good men, two men of God, had been killed by the evils of racism and white supremacy in Alabama. For the Selma-to-Montgomery march did not begin in Selma. It really began in Marion on February 18, 1965, when Alabama state trooper James Bonard Fowler fatally shot Jimmie Lee Jackson in Mack's Café behind the Zion United Methodist Church.

Without Jimmie Lee Jackson's murder, there would have been no Bloody Sunday, nor Turnaround Tuesday, nor Harry Belafonte's mellifluous voice rising above the crowd outside the Alabama State Capitol. Without Jimmie Lee Jackson's murder, John Lewis would not have suffered a fractured skull on March 7, the Rev. James Reeb would likely not have been murdered, Lyndon B. Johnson would not have pushed through voting rights legislation when he did, and Martin Luther King Jr. would not have led one of the largest marches in the history of the Black Freedom Struggle.

Jimmie Lee Jackson's horrific murder can also be understood as the subtle, gentle flap of a butterfly's wings setting off an unseen, unanticipated, and unplanned-for chain of events. Some argue that the final Selma-to-Montgomery march, rather than King's assassination, really marked the end of the traditional civil rights era, the culmination of this phase of the Black Freedom Struggle.

After the march, SNCC and SCLC grew further and further apart. The struggle shifted from the rural South to the urban North. Even King directed his attention to the broader struggle for freedom and democracy waged by people of color around the world.

While there are many historical, political, social, and strategic lessons that can be derived from the Selma and Montgomery campaigns of the Southern Black Freedom Struggle, there is also a personal lesson that comes from this effort as well. What Edmund Pettus Bridge is each of us called on to cross in order to bring about fundamental changes within ourselves and within society? Is it the bridge from nonvoting to voting? Is it the bridge from supporting authoritarian rule in America to advancing and expanding democracy? Is it the bridge from castigating the strangers among us to welcoming them as brothers and sisters? Is it the bridge from violent retribution in the face of differences to nonviolent resolution of those differences? How we answer these questions, and how we act on our answers, will measure how well we have understood the high price for freedom that Jimmie Lee Jackson paid.

ACKNOWLEDGMENTS

IT'S HARD TO IMAGINE WRITING THIS BOOK WITHOUT thinking of two of my mentors, teachers, and friends: the late Dr. Lerone Bennett Jr. and Dr. Vincent Gordon Harding. Every time I contemplate the African American past, I feel the presence of these two lions of Black history speaking to me. I only hope that I can do justice to what I hear their voices saying.

Amistad, an imprint of HarperCollins Publishers, has made a wonderful home for me. Working with Amistad's head, Abby West, and editor Makayla Tabron offered me a unique opportunity. I asked Abby and Makayla to help shape this book so its message reached as wide an audience as possible. I believe they did just that, for which I am very grateful.

An author needs a great agent, and I have one of the best in Leslie Meredith of Dystel, Goderich & Bourret. Leslie offered her insights as a former editor and helped to successfully guide this book through the publishing process.

BIBLIOGRAPHY

The bibliography, notes, and references for the essays included in this book can be found online at www.ahighpriceforfreedom.com/references.